RAISING OUR VOICES

League of Women Voters Metro St. Louis 1960–2022

NICOLE EVELINA

Raising Our Voices
League of Women Voters Metro St. Louis 1960-2022
All Rights Reserved.
Copyright © 2023 League of Women Voters of Metro St. Louis
v5.0

The opinions expressed in this manuscript are solely the opinions of the author and do not represent the opinions or thoughts of the publisher. The author has represented and warranted full ownership and/or legal right to publish all the materials in this book.

This book may not be reproduced, transmitted, or stored in whole or in part by any means, including graphic, electronic, or mechanical without the express written consent of the publisher except in the case of brief quotations embodied in critical articles and reviews.

Outskirts Press, Inc.
http://www.outskirtspress.com

ISBN: 978-1-9772-5510-5

Cover illustration © 2023 www.gettyimages.com. All rights reserved - used with permission.

Outskirts Press and the "OP" logo are trademarks belonging to Outskirts Press, Inc.

PRINTED IN THE UNITED STATES OF AMERICA

Dedication

To the thousands of League members and leaders who made the League's education and advocacy efforts possible the last 60+ years, empowering voters and defending democracy.

Epigraph

"For more than a century, women and the League have been on the front lines of democracy, and today's commitment is the next step in fulfilling our mission to empower voters and defend democracy."

– Dr. Deborah Turner, President of the League of Women Voters of the United States, announcing the League's "Making Democracy Work" initiative in July 2021.

"The LWV is still an anomaly in American politics. It is non-partisan and political. It educates and advocates. Its members are feminist, but the LWV describes itself as a citizens' organization, not as a feminist organization. It trains women leaders, but it cannot support them if they run for public office…Throughout its history, the LWV has brought women's voices to major public policy issues, work that has advanced the status of women in American society."

– Nancy M. Neuman, *The League of Women Voters: In Perspective 1920-1995*, p. 5. Note that men have been full voting members since 1974.

Table of Contents

Foreword i
Introduction vii

Chapter 1: The 1960s 1
    Voter Services 3
    Education 7
    Environmental Concerns 15
    The Borough Plan 18
    Merit System 23
    Charter Amendment 25
    Redistricting 28
    City Redevelopment 31
    League Activities 37
    Women Who Made an Impact in the 1960s 42
        Ida Perkins Johnson West 42
        Teresa Fischer 44
        Virginia Deutch 47
    Main Sources Chapter 1 – 1960s 49

Chapter 2: The 1970s 53
    Equal Rights Amendment (ERA) 62
    City Redevelopment 74
    Transit 79
    Welfare 81
    Charter Efforts 82
    Non-Partisan Court Plan 84

Education 85
Environment 90
League Activities 100
Women Who Made an Impact in the 1970s 102
    Janet Rosenwald Becker 102
    Janet Helen Atlee Shipton 104
    Pat Rich 106
Main Sources Chapter 2 – The 1970s 108

Chapter 3: The 1980s 115
Voter Services 116
Redistricting 123
Freeholders Plan 127
Education 129
Pay Equity 131
Riverport Dome 134
Environment 137
Transit 142
Zoo-Musuem District 144
League Activities 145
    Sue Shear 146
Women Who Made an Impact in the 1980s 153
    Harriett Woods 153
    Sydell Shayer 155
    Agnes Garino 157
    Deborah Waite Howard 160
    Barbara Bair Shull 162
Main Sources Chapter 3 – The 1980s 164

Chapter 4: The 1990s **171**
   Voter Services 172
   "Motor Voter" Law 175
   Redistricting 177
   Campaign Finance Reform 178
   Term Limits 181
   Blue Cross Blue Shield Lawsuit 182
   Education 185
   Housing 188
   Environment 191
   Transit 195
   Health Care 196
   Gun Control 199
   League Activities 203
   Women Who Made an Impact in the 1990s 206
      K Wentzien 206
      Linda Claire McDaniel 208
      Nancy Bowser 210
   Main Sources Chapter 4 – The 1990s 212

Chapter 5: The 2000s **217**
   Voter Services 218
   Election Reform 223
   Missouri Voter ID Laws 227
   National Popular Vote 229
   Charter Revision 230
   Death Penalty 232
   Education 234
   Environment 239
   Equal Rights Amendment Ratification 244

League Activities 248
Women Who Made an Impact in the 2000s 251
   Lois Bliss 251
   Carol Portman 253
   Mickey Croyle 255
Main Sources Chapter 5 – The 2000s 257

Chapter 6: The 2010s 263

Voter Services 264
Voter ID Laws 268
Voting Rights Act..269
"Motor Voter" Violations 271
Redistricting...272
Missouri Primary Changes......................................276
Education...277
Health Care..280
Death Penalty...283
Environment...285
Gun Safety 289
Minimum Wage 290
League Activities 291
Women Who Made an Impact in the 2010s 298
   Kathleen Farrell 298
   Louise Wilkerson...299
   Nancy J. Miller 301
   Catherine Stenger 304
Main Sources Chapter 6 – The 2010s 306

2020 and Beyond **319**
   Protecting Voters and Their Rights During
      the Covid-19 Pandemic 319
   Voter Services 320
   Voting Legislation..322
   Redistricting 329
   National Popular Vote 333
   Health Care...334
   Environment..335
   Equal Rights Amendment Ratification............................337
   League Activities 338
   Looking Forward 343
   Main Sources – 2020 and Beyond 344

Lifetime Members..349
League of Women Voters Past Presidents.............................351
Acknowledgements 360
Index 362
About the Author 373

Foreword

LITTLE DID I know in 1957 when I became a member of the League of Women Voters (LWV) that I was embarking on a six-decade journey with an organization that would influence my life in unforeseen ways. At age 27, I was a young mother looking for a stimulating, friendly and broadening experience. I was not disappointed. I am grateful for the opportunity to write this foreword because it enables me to relive the wonderful years of my life in the League. The League has always been recognized for its story. It is recognized for the issues it undertakes, the voters that it has educated and the public policies that it has influenced. This all comes alive in this book. It is the sequel to the St. Louis League's previous book, *The League of Women Voters in St. Louis: The First 40 Years* by Avis Carlson.

The League's main objective at its beginning in 1919 was to provide an education for women so they would become informed voters. After all, voting was new. It didn't take long for the women to realize that this need was also applicable to men. That's why the League provided its services to both men and women.

The League is a non-partisan political organization. Members are volunteers who provide services to voters, including voter registration, Voters Guides, candidate forums and Speakers Bureau presentations. The League studies and takes positions on governmental issues, but we never endorse candidates.

This book chronicles many of the significant public policies of the last 60+ years and does it by decades, beginning with the 1960s.

The League has a formal process for adopting positions on issues that starts with members voting at an annual meeting or convention to approve a study group on an issue deemed both timely and important. The study process was not always simple. Some of the issues were controversial. How the League handled them could affect the League's public perception as well as its ability to successfully accomplish its desired end. Our local and state studies were professional, complete, accurate and ended with a recommendation to remedy problems that were identified.

For example, in the '60s, we held a conference on whether the United States should recognize mainland China. We invited an avowed Communist speaker despite questions about whether or not it was a smart decision for the League to make. The League is confronted with similar situations today. It could be reproductive choice, charter schools or climate change. We are not afraid of the challenge.

Why do people join the League? Many want to educate themselves and the community. They want to educate and register voters. They want to study an issue, learn how government works, meet their legislators, advocate for the League and for themselves on issues they care about. They want to make a difference.

The League has long been recognized for registering voters. That is frequently the first task new members want to do. It is a defined accomplishment with thousands of youth, new citizens and others registered every year.

The basic foundation of the League has remained the same since its inception in 1919. But it has changed in both frivolous and significant ways. By choice and technology. The way women dress is very different. Members are no longer listed with their marital status. We are now a coed organization. Men became full voting members as have non-citizens and individuals sixteen or older. And they are all as active in the organization as they choose.

We no longer have to suffer with an offset press. We have the latest technology to operate our office. It makes it so much easier to communicate with the community and each other.

By the 1960s, the League had already involved itself in water conservation and protection. I was a relatively new member and was not aware of all the subjects on the League's agenda. What caught my attention was an article in a national magazine on the environment. It rated national organizations that concentrated on water problems, and it listed the League of Women Voters as the most effective of all.

There are a variety of methods to promote change. After the Watergate scandal in the early 1970s, the League joined a coalition for campaign finance reform and gathered signatures to place a reform bill on the statewide ballot.

In 1976, LWV of the United States expanded its voter service work to include sponsoring presidential debates.[1] The League sponsored and moderated the debates in 1976, 1980 and 1984. The debate between Ronald Reagan and Walter Mondale took place in Kansas City, Missouri, on Oct. 21, 1984.

The political parties formed a Presidential Debates Commission before the 1988 debates that set a format that did not meet League standards for fairness or nonpartisanship. Since the Commission would not budge, the League withdrew its participation. At a televised news conference, LWVUS President Nancy Neuman said, "The League has no intention of becoming an accessory to the hoodwinking of the American public."

The list of issues on the League's agenda in the 1980s was lengthy, including pay equity and the ERA, election laws, the Zoo-Museum District, and more. At the 1992 and 1994 national conventions, gun violence became a front and center issue. Rather than go through a two-year study as was usual, the delegates voted to concur with the Illinois League's position that called the proliferation of handguns and semiautomatic assault weapons a major health and safety threat.

When I look back at the last 60 years, I realize that the League is still working on most of the same issues. We have been successful in making progress in these areas, but change is slow and incremental.

And I realize that the League will be working on some issues for many more years. It is the story of our lives: health, education, environment, good government, and our democracy. The new century did add a new dimension to our lives. There was a coalescing of the people. The reinvigorated Women's Movement and Black Lives Matter both call for action.

The national League was founded in February 1920 and the St. Louis League began months earlier, in fall 1919. The St. Louis League held celebrations for its big 50th, 60th, 65th, 70th, 75th and 90th birthdays, but Metro's Centennial celebration lasted two years, 1919-2000.

Our Centennial offered an opportunity to highlight that the St. Louis League had a Colored Division and an integrated board in 1920. The Colored Division became a standing committee in 1922 and remained that way until the mid-1940s when the membership was fully integrated.

The first president of the League of Women Voters of Missouri (LWVMO), Edna Gellhorn, refused to meet in buildings that excluded women of color and also ended affiliation with Federated Clubs, which prohibited Negro membership. She served as president of the St. Louis League in 1925 and again from 1943-1944. I had the privilege of meeting her soon after moving to St. Louis.

At a centennial gala at the Sheldon Concert Hall on Nov. 13, 2019, the actual 100th anniversary, all past St. Louis area League presidents were honored. See the complete list of past presidents starting on Page 351. A special guest was Gay Gellhorn, Edna's granddaughter.

This book summarizes the time I have spent as a League member. I think of it as my story. I want to leave you with my favorite quote from the *St. Louis Post-Dispatch*. "The League has made itself into a mighty vital institution. If it didn't exist, somebody would have to invent it."

– Sydell Shayer, Lifetime League Member,
  Creve Coeur, Missouri

***Sydell Shayer has been active
in the League since 1957.***

Introduction

THE BOOK YOU hold in your hands or on your e-reader is a labor of love. Everyone involved—from the benefactor who made it possible, to the researchers, writers, interview subjects and editors—is a League member, eager to see our history captured for posterity.

We are fortunate that in 1959, our League had the foresight to chronicle its first 40 years of work in a book by League member Avis Carlson appropriately titled *The First 40 Years: 1919-1959*. This new history is a hefty second volume to that seminal work, picking up right where it left off in 1960. It attempts to capture the work of the League in the St. Louis area over the next six decades, culminating in 2022.

It is impossible to cover every activity of the League of Women Voters from 1960-2022 and still result in a readable book, so there may be committees or issues members recall being a part of that are not covered here. We have chosen to focus primarily on items of significance at the City-County level, foregoing most hyper-local activities except for when they are historic, such as the Kirkwood charter, or affect the entire St. Louis area. Likewise, we have omitted many items taken up exclusively at the state and national levels unless our local League played a significant role in them.

We have tried to retain some of the local flavor by including profiles of outstanding members and the voices of local League members through the nearly 30 oral histories conducted for this book. We could have profiled hundreds of League leaders but selected members based on their variety of involvement, their impact on League issues and their strong commitment to the League.

You will notice that even long before the individual Leagues merged, we refer to the St. Louis League. This is for ease of reading and is often used as a catch-all for all of the Leagues in St. Louis County and the City League. No disrespect is meant to any local League nor is this meant to minimize the contributions they made to their communities; if we had unlimited space, we would include a detailed history of each League. But for brevity's sake we have sometimes combined them into a single term.

A Quick Primer

For those not familiar with the League of Women Voters (LWV), here is a quick overview to help you better understand our organization and this book.

Like many other groups, we function at the national, state, and local levels. Every local League member automatically becomes a member at all three levels.

LWV of the United States (LWVUS) is our national organization. You'll often see it called the National League or LWVUS for short. Its job is to lobby Congress on programs (issues) adopted by delegate vote at the bi-annual national convention. The National League communicates with local and state leaders and maintains a variety of materials on its website, lwv.org. It sends out Action Alerts when it is particularly important that members contact their legislators on a certain issue.

There is a State League in all 50 states with its own board of directors. Ours is LWV of Missouri, or LWVMO for short. Each state League advocates its state legislators on priority issues selected at a bi-annual state convention with voting delegates from each local League. LWVMO shares staff and office space with LWV of Metro St. Louis in a Joint Office agreement. It sends legislative bulletins and alerts and a bi-monthly newsletter to members across the state. In recent years, LWVMO has qualified for national grant programs for Making Democracy Work and People-Powered Fair Maps.

Local Leagues are formed to cover a certain geographical area—a city, county, or section of a state—and the names reflect that location. LWVMO supported 10 local Leagues across the state in 2021 (LWV of Metro St. Louis, LWV of Kansas City/Jackson-Clay-Platte Counties, LWV of Southwest Missouri, LWV of Columbia/Boone County, LWV of Greater Joplin, LWV of Tri-Lakes, LWV of Moberly/Randolph County, LWV of Mexico/Audrain County, and LWV of Sedalia/Pettis County).

They focus on voter registration and voter education, with many offering Voters Guides, candidate forums, Speakers Bureau presentations and Lunch & Learn discussions. They also study issues based on the needs of their communities, which might include school district and local government issues, ballot measures, or broader issue studies. Most have committees working on education, environmental quality, health care and other issues.

In 2022, 16 women from St. Joseph became LWVMO Members-at-Large as part of the process of setting up a local League in Northwest Missouri.

A Brief History Lesson

The LWV of Metro St. Louis is a large local League that now encompasses seven counties in the St. Louis area, but that wasn't always the case. When the League was founded in the City of St. Louis in 1919 (the first League organization in the nation, formed even before the National League), local chapters developed where there was interest. There were no League offices; meetings moved from one president's home to another.

As a result, the St. Louis area was a patchwork of local Leagues, each focused on their own agendas. This was good because it allowed them to be extremely in tune with their communities and respond to their needs. However, it also resulted in duplication of effort and resources.

The local St. Louis Leagues merged several times as their populations changed, budgets shrank, and womanpower came and went. Over the years, the St. Louis area has had Leagues in St. Louis City, Brentwood, Clayton, Ferguson, Florissant, Kirkwood, Normandy, St. Charles, University City and Webster Groves. Mergers over the years led to the Leagues of Central County, North County, South West County, and University City dissolving and LWV of St. Louis County being formed in May 1980. You will also see reference to the City-County (Metropolitan) Committee and the Inter League Organization (ILO) that operated from 1971-1985. The St. Louis City League functioned on its own until it joined with the County in 1999 to form LWV of Metro St. Louis.

League members are invited to at least two general meetings each year with a speaker. Members also attend unit meetings for smaller group discussions. Units meet most months at different times for the convenience of members in different parts of the Metro area. Today, the League's units include the City of St. Louis, North County, South County, West County, St. Charles County, Webster Groves/ Kirkwood, and a new evening/Zoom unit.

From 1978-2015, the League had a separate 501(c)(3) organization. It was called the Citizens Information Resource Center (CIRC) from 1978-1989 and the LWV Information Service (LWVIS) from 1989-2015, when it merged with LWV of Metro St. Louis.

Why Has the League Survived for Over 100 Years?

The League's mission of defending democracy and educating and empowering voters is as relevant in 2022 as it was a hundred years ago. Today's League members are speaking out against voter suppression, protecting the right to vote of all citizens, defending reproductive rights, calling for gun safety and environmental protection.

LWVUS President Deborah Turner acknowledged on May 15, 2021, that it's hard to be a nonpartisan organization in hyper-partisan times. She pointed out that Republican Presidents Ronald Reagan signed the Voting Rights Act in 1982 and George W. Bush signed its 2006 reauthorization. She recently reminded U.S. Senator Chuck Grassley (R-Iowa) that his mother was a League member. Former First Lady Eleanor Roosevelt was also a League member.

Calling the League's nonpartisan policy the bedrock of the organization, Turner said, "Wanting every eligible voter to have equal access to the ballot box is not partisan. Wanting a robust democracy in which everyone has an equal voice and equal representation is not partisan. Wanting to see more elected officials that reflect the diverse makeup of our country is not partisan – it is American."[1]

You'll notice as you read this book that many women joined the League because they wanted to make a difference in their communities. Because of this, several went on to run for political office. Many served on local school boards or city councils, as well as state government. Peggy Vickroy served as Mayor of Creve Coeur and Janet Monsey as Mayor of Olivette. Two of the most famous League members to be elected to office are Sue Shear and Harriett Woods, who are profiled later in this book.

A Note on Sources

References for all endnotes and photos may be found online at https://my.lwv.org/missouri/metro-st-louis/about-us. These document came from two major sources: The Missouri State Historical Society Archives at the University of Missouri—St. Louis (UMSL) and the League office at 8706 Manchester Road in Brentwood. The State Historical Society houses the League's historical documents from its beginnings in 1919 through the early 1980s. So all the information in this book from the 1960s and 1970s, and some of the early 1980s came from their archives. The League office recently moved files from the 1980s-2015 to the archives at UMSL.

Cyndy Lenz created the silhouette of five League members on the cover. Finally, Anna Reynolds' recordings and summaries of her conversations with dozens of long-time League members were a wealth of information. Recordings are on file at the League office if anyone needs to access them in the future.

– Nicole Evelina

CHAPTER 1

The 1960s

THE 1960s WERE a decade of rapid change and rebellion against norms. Exploration of space and the 1969 moon landing promised a future based in technology and progress. Race riots and the assassinations of President John F. Kennedy and Martin Luther King, Jr., shook our country's foundation and faith in the status quo. Betty Friedan's *The Feminine Mystique* was released in 1963, the same year Congress passed the Equal Pay Act.

Being in the middle of the "square" Midwest, St. Louis lacked a large hippie population, though Government Hill in Forest Park was known as "Hippie Hill" thanks to an assortment of musicians who would show up, unannounced, to play free concerts.[2] Even in regard to the hot-button topic of race, St. Louis was pretty laid back compared to other parts of the nation. We were "famous for not rioting,"[3] unlike many other cities. For example, in April 1967, more than a hundred young people gathered in Forest Park, not to protest the Vietnam War or rage against outdated social mores, but to celebrate the coming of spring and urge peace. The police found nothing illegal about the "Spring-In," and the *St. Louis Post-Dispatch* reported that at the end of the day, "everybody picked up empty bottles, trash and banana peels and went back home to the suburbs,"[4] like polite Midwesterners.

It's not that St. Louis didn't have any unrest; it simply wasn't on the massive scale seen in other cities. "The most significant area event of the modern civil rights era"[5] began on Aug. 30, 1963, when a group of nine protesters, members of the Committee on Racial Equality (CORE), burst into the lobby of Jefferson Bank, blocked the doors and sat on the floor[6] singing "We Shall Not Be Moved." They demanded that the bank, which at the time had only two Black employees,[7] hire four more in white-collar positions.[8]

When bank executives resisted, the protests continued, taking place almost daily for over a month. Tensions rose until more than 75 people, including two white people and four teenagers, stormed the building on October 7. A truce was supposed to follow, but on October 24, one hundred people sang and prayed inside City Hall, carrying signs that demanded "Remove City Money from Jim Crow Banks." The protests were successful: Jefferson Bank promoted one Black man from a messenger to a clerk[9] and hired six more Black people into executive positions.[10]

Perhaps the most telling event was one that never took place. In the aftermath of the assassination of Rev. Dr. Martin Luther King Jr. on April 4, 1968, cities across the country dealt with violent and costly riots. When a firebomb was thrown at a grocery store near Kingshighway and Page, it looked like St. Louis was headed in the same direction. However, the bomb didn't ignite and neither did the tensions of the citizens. Instead, "local civil-rights leaders, gray-haired veterans and agitated young Turks, met in tense sessions and forged agreement for a peaceful march in response to King's death" on Palm Sunday, April 7. It began with 7,500 people,[11] but ended up including more than 30,000 and stretched for more than 20 blocks.[12]

The St. Louis League During the 1960s

It was against this relatively sedate backdrop that the members and leaders of the St. Louis League confronted the area's ongoing and emerging problems. The League navigated major issues such as education, a growing concern for the environment, an attempt to unify St. Louis City and St. Louis County (again), a push to transition all city/government jobs to a merit system instead of patronage, apportionment and both reactive and proactive efforts to revitalize the city and keep St. Louis relevant for the future. They had the honor of hosting the League's national convention in 1960.

VOTER SERVICES

In addition to devoting their time to issues of concern in the St. Louis region, local Leagues in the St. Louis area continued to advocate for, educate, and register voters as part of their voter service offerings. To this end, the League developed an Inner City Project committee aimed at both improving the lives and living conditions of city residents and helping them become more active voters. The League's position on this matter appeared in a May 1967 newsletter:

> The movement of rural people into urban centers has brought in many residents with no experience in city living, with little formal education or skills necessary for city jobs, and with almost no viable citizenship experience. Because they are poor, they crowd into the deteriorating areas of our core cities, joining the vast numbers already entrapped there. Because many have not voted or participated in governmental processes in the

> past, they need to be motivated to do so now. They need to know how government operates and how they may become participating citizens. Indigenous leaders need to be developed and trained. This is necessary not only as a means of helping the individual help himself, but as a means of keeping the city a vital unit of government.
>
> For our city to survive, political vitality is needed as much as planning, or new building, or better transportation. But political vitality can come about only when all the legitimate interests of the community have a voice in its future and can compete with one another on a fairly equitable basis. Inner city people need to understand how they can guarantee that their legitimate interests will be represented, and their voices heard.[13]

In 1962, James Deakin, a reporter for the *St. Louis Post-Dispatch*, published an article "on a survey of the American public showing appalling political inactivity and the need to emphasize the importance of political knowledge."[14] As the Voter Services and Inner City committees were soon to find out, voter apathy was one of the largest obstacles they had to face. After all, if you've never participated in or been included in the government or decision making, how can you be expected to believe that you can affect change just by casting your vote?

Getting a person registered to vote was the clear place to start. "Voter registration and information are first steps in their finding a voice. Next, the discussion of issues which directly affects them is important, as are their involvement in decision making, practical political skills, and learning by doing," the League wrote.[15]

One example among many of the League's work in the inner city is the partnership it formed with the Human Development Corporation (HDC) in 1967 to help reach the public with basic voting information. The HDC divided the poverty-stricken areas of St. Louis City and County into neighborhood stations and substations, which they canvassed to listen to residents and determine what could be done to help them. Each area had its own needs, and the League tailored its program accordingly.

The first effort was a series of voter registration days in the Wells-Goodfellow area, which included transportation to the site, if needed. There, the League supplied lists of elected officials, brochures on voter law and information on what to expect when voting for the first time. One hundred and forty-three people were registered on that first day.

Another one of the registration dates fell on the 203rd birthday of the City of St. Louis, so they had a special party "with large birthday cakes, cookies, coffee, and soft drinks donated through the kindness of civic minded merchants and the efforts of the Wells-League partnership."[16]

Similar events were held in the Union-Sarah and Chouteau-Russell areas throughout the spring.[17] Over time, the effort expanded to include the Kinloch-Wellston, Yeatman, West End, Carr-Central, Murphy-Blair, and Montgomery-Hyde Park areas.

The League also worked closely with The Women's Job Corps to establish a student government for young women and hold mock elections so that they were prepared to vote in real life. So that the young women could learn about the "mechanics and principles of representative government," they held candidate meetings before "Election Day" and even cast their ballots using a real voting machine supplied by the League.

In the end, the democratically elected student government included seven executive officers and representatives from each dormitory floor of the Women's Job Corps.

Dorothy Harrison, the staff member in charge of the project, explained: "The center believes that, within limits, the Corps woman has a right as a young adult to exercise a determining voice in the regulation of her own affairs. This involvement can help develop skills and attitudes that will permit her to return to her own community and provide leadership for community development."[18]

STATEWIDE PERMANENT VOTER REGISTRATION

Another issue the League fought for in the mid-1960s was the establishment of a statewide permanent voter registry. They believed that "voters and harried election officials would benefit from implementation of a League-supported, uniform, statewide, permanent registration, in place of the various laws now on the books."[19]

The League's involvement came after two years of intensive study of election procedures, problems, and outcomes. In November 1966, they formally announced the beginning of

> a legislative campaign to change election procedures in the state...[including] adoption of a statewide system of voter registration on a permanent basis; the lowering of the present one-year state residence requirement for voters to six months, the establishment of an election laws revision committee, and the support of legislation to allow local option on the use of voting devices.[20]

Other changes the League supported included ensuring "secrecy of the ballot through the use of voting machines, or where it is not possible, through continued use of the black sticker... secrecy in counting of absentee ballots [and] change a primary election to September, with appropriate change in filing date."[21] Many of these issues would continue to be of interest into the 1970s and beyond.

The League's legislation was introduced in the House in 1967 by Rep. Walter L. Meyer (D-27) and assigned to the House Local Government Committee of the General Assembly, where it stalled.[22] As of 2022, Missouri still does not have a system of permanent statewide registration.

EDUCATION

BUSING AND SCHOOL DISCRIMINATION

Education of young people has been a core concern of League members since its inception. In 1947, when the St. Louis League began the practice of adopting formal annual agendas, education was first on the list.

Race and education comingled in our highly segregated city[23] on May 17, 1954, when the Supreme Court ruled in *Brown vs. Board of Education* that state-supported segregated schools were unconstitutional. At first, Missouri made great strides in following the new law, even being praised as one of the top southern or border states in terms of school desegregation. For a town with a history of racial issues and a slaveholding past, early desegregation took place with little resistance, even in large cities like St. Louis where "the burning of two crosses, occasional altercations between white and Negro students, and some mutterings of discontent among white parents indicated minimal opposition."[24]

But fulfilling the law for the long-term was easier said than done. In St. Louis, "housing patterns dictated the racial distribution in schools, creating a de facto segregated education system even after the Supreme Court held that separate schools could never be equal."[25] By the end of the decade, the so-called "Delmar Divide" was in place, with most Black families living north of Delmar and white residents occupying the southern city and county.[26]

With Black neighborhoods clearly defined, schools in these areas were soon bursting at the seams due to an influx of new Black residents relocating to St. Louis from the south, where Civil Rights (or lack thereof) made living dangerous. This, in turn, caused overcrowding in Black schools. Teachers recalled classes of 48 students,[27] nearly twice the number advisable by the Department of Health, Education and Welfare.[28] Some schools were so far beyond capacity that students and teachers had to have class in temporary aluminum structures that lacked heating in the winter and air conditioning in the summer.[29]

At first, the city tried to find alternate locations close to home for the students. In 1960, 2,000 elementary children were taught in high schools and 525 children in rented churches.[30] But it soon became apparent there was not enough existing space; children from the Black neighborhoods would have to be transported to the white schools in south St. Louis where there was plenty of space, thanks to "white flight" into the suburbs.[31] In total, busing cost St. Louis more than $250,000 that year.[32]

In order to help St. Louis schools afford the financial costs of this change and prevent further overcrowding in the future, the school board requested several bond issues in the early 1960s, which the League urged voters to pass. In 1960, they asked for $29.5 million to cover the projected cost of constructing fourteen new schools, "repairing and enlarging"[33] fourteen others and installing fire safety equipment that would bring the schools in compliance with the 1959 school fire safety code.[34] The issue was submitted to voters three times in 1960, three times in 1961[35] and twice in 1962 before finally passing on its eighth time on the ballot in March 1962.[36]

In the first two years of the '60s, while voters continually rejected the bond issue proposals, the school board was legally obliged to do what they could to comply with the desegregation law. In the fall semester of the 1961-62 school year, St. Louis began busing 6,125 students,[37] 90% of whom were Black, from overcrowded Black city schools to less crowded all-white schools.[38]

While this may sound like a reasonable solution to the segregation issue, because of the execution, it was less than effective. These students were transported as entire Black classes, including their teacher, all of whom "entered the white school buildings at a specific allotted time when white students and teachers were in class, assuring there was no interaction between the races."[39] They also learned, ate and played sports at different times from the white students, fulfilling the desegregation law on the surface by their presence in a formerly all-white school, but not in fact. The Board of Education justified this by saying that separate classrooms were easier to administer and recess areas less crowded by keeping the kids separate, an excuse that only enraged the parents of Black students. By 1963, the NAACP was encouraging boycotts of these bused-but-still-segregated schools.[40]

"The Board of Education is doing all it can to seek relief through the changes in state laws," the League told members in a February 1963 newsletter. "The board is seeking changes that will raise Missouri's level of educational support closer to the national average. Such changes would lighten the burden on the property taxpayer."[41]

That month, voters weighed a proposed $0.29 tax increase, which passed by a narrow majority.[42] While waiting for the construction funded by this increase to get underway, the St. Louis School Board authorized construction of 34 temporary classroom buildings, known as "transportables" in the west end of the city, where overcrowding was the worst.[43] While these transportable buildings appeared as sound as permanent structures, they could not be used as such because they lacked toilets and other necessary amenities.[44] Still, to many parents, they were a more favorable alternative to busing,[45] even though they effectively kept Black students in Black neighborhoods,[46] throwing the idea of integration out the window.

Angered by busing, enrollment policies that effectively "maintain[ed] a dual, Jim Crow system of schooling"[47] —and what they saw as minimal attempts by the school board at finding solutions, parents banned together into the organization Parents for Transported Children.[48] They not only railed against the transportable classrooms, likening them to creating a "Negro ghetto"[49] in the city, they demanded their children be taken to other schools in the southern part of the city where they would be properly integrated with white students and urged that school districts be remapped in order to achieve true integration.[50]

Members of the League's Education Committee focused their work on calling "attention to the need for new school construction to accommodate the pupils being bused from overcrowded schools to areas far from their homes where there were rooms available."[51] They investigated claims of discrimination by contractors building transportable structures.[52] They also helped connect people displaced by the construction of elementary schools with services that would find them additional housing.[53]

By 1964, desegregation in St. Louis schools came to a virtual standstill, while the school board pursued the unpopular "neighborhood school" idea even in the face of growing citizen complaints.[54] According to Judge Gerald W. Heaney and educator Dr. Susan Uchitelle, "between 1962 and 1967, the board built nine new elementary schools in all-Black neighborhoods. Soon, Black children were being bused to predominantly Black schools near the housing projects,"[55] which was the opposite of integration.

Beginning in December 1967,[56] the Missouri School District Reorganization Commission worked to develop a statewide master plan for school district reorganization to try to solve this ongoing issue.[57] While neither desegregation nor busing were overtly mentioned in the project criteria, they were certainly implied as a reason behind it, especially given that the criteria stated, "each district should include a diverse population, based on economic, racial, and ethnic characteristics...[and] travel time to school should not exceed 60 minutes each way for secondary and 40 minutes each way for elementary pupils,"[58] an allusion to the significant additional time it took for Black students to get to and from school thanks to busing.

Because the St. Louis League was already deeply entrenched in the issues of desegregation and busing and had a close relationship with the Board of Education, it was only natural that they kept a close eye on the development of this plan.

In its final form, the plan proposed creating 20 regional school districts in the state, reducing the number of local school units from 786 to 132, and fundamentally transforming the way schools were run.[59] On Jan. 7, 1969, the plan received the endorsement of the State Board of Education,[60] but even that couldn't convince the legislature, who rejected the plan in March 1969.[61]

As later chapters will show, busing and desegregation would continue to be matters of concern in St. Louis. They were the subject of legal disputes in the 1970s and came roaring back into public consciousness in the 1980s with the establishment of a formal transfer program between St. Louis City and County schools led by Voluntary Interdistrict Choice Corporation (VICC) that will not officially end until 2023.[62]

Establishing a Junior College System in St. Louis

The American Association of Junior Colleges was founded in St. Louis during a convention held June 30 – July 1, 1920.[63] But ironically, 40 years would pass before the idea of starting a junior (now called community) college system in the city took hold. Junior colleges were differentiated from other colleges and universities by their length of term—two years instead of four—and seen as a more affordable alternative for the first two years of a four-year liberal arts program.[64] Their curriculum was also geared more to vocational and technical training for careers in which a four-year degree was not necessary.

In 1960, the League's Education Committee, led by Teresa Fischer, began to hear rumors about the possibility of St. Louis adopting a junior college system.[65] The following September, the St. Louis School board endorsed the proposal[66] for three locations, one in North County (today St. Louis Community College Florissant Valley), South County (today St. Louis Community College Meramec) and one in the City of St. Louis (today St. Louis Community College Forest Park), which would serve 4,500 students.[67]

On March 12, 1962, the League board voted to support the system.[68] It was approved by voters on April 3, along with a tax of $0.10 for each $100 of assessed valuation to help fund the new district.[69]

Junior college classes began on Jan. 29, 1963, in temporary locations at Roosevelt[70] and McCluer High Schools,[71] while the permanent campuses were being constructed. These locations held about 1,000 students,[72] but demand quickly doubled, then tripled. By 1964, only one in three students who applied could be accepted[73] and temporary campuses had to expand.[74] By February 1965, the district was estimating enrollment of 16,000 full-time students by 1972.[75]

ESTABLISHMENT OF VOCATIONAL SCHOOLS

Concurrent with its work on the Junior College system, the League was also supporting the establishment of vocational schools throughout St. Louis County. This initiative began in 1964, when representatives from each local League attended the White House Conference on Vocational Education. Eight hundred delegates from 185 educational, business, labor, and civic organizations attended to discuss how to provide adequate training and education for young men and women who would enter the labor market after high school graduation instead of attending college.

At the time, St. Louis had only one vocational school, a not-for-profit technical school in North St. Louis County, run by a group of county superintendents, which would only be in operation for another four years because it was being acquired as part of the Lambert St. Louis airport expansion.

This both left a void and created an opportunity in the St. Louis educational system. The League proposed that the board of the Special School District take over the operation of the school on July 1, 1965. Together with the district and other organizations, they estimated that because the proposed schools would include only high school juniors and seniors. They could handle an enrollment up to five thousand students, who would learn both the usual academic subjects for a high school diploma and skills related to their desired career field from teachers who had hands-on experience. The vocational school district and the junior college district would work together to make sure their programs did not overlap, which was especially important because adult education classes would be offered as well.

Working closely with Oral Spurgeon, superintendent of the Special School District for the Handicapped, the League supported a 1965 proposal on the June 22 ballot to establish, maintain, and fund vocational schools in St. Louis County in addition to the current programs for the handicapped. Voters approved the plan, "which entitled the new district to $1.8 million in funds from the 1965 county tax receipts, and to request at least $500,000 from federal funds for buildings," plus possible matching funds by the federal government to cover the cost of teachers' salaries, equipment, and supplies.[76]

The next three years were a transitional period for the county, as they grew from a single part-time vocational school to multiple full-time campuses.

Until those new schools were built, the district leased three classrooms from the Mehlville School District, where two hundred students received education and training during the 1966-67 school year[77] and four hundred the following year.[78] The South County Vocational-Technical School opened in September 1967 and the North County Vocational-Technical School opened a year later, bringing the total number of students up to nine hundred, though it was estimated that total demand was closer to ten thousand.[79]

Studies on University City and Webster Groves School Districts

In 1969, the Leagues of Women Voters of University City and Webster Groves published surveys of their school districts. These surveys were to improve communication between the school systems and their communities. They were designed to help the community understand its school system, curriculum and finances.[80]

ENVIRONMENTAL CONCERNS

Water Pollution and the Metropolitan Sewer District

While the 1960s are synonymous with the beginning of the environmental movement, the League started focusing on the environment in 1950.[81]

Beginning in 1954, water conservation and protection issues were intertwined with the newly developed Metropolitan Sewer District (MSD). League members circulated petitions and took citizens on bus tours of the area so they could smell the problems for themselves[82]—a moment they were sure to remember when they went to the polls. In addition, League records indicate that "after the freeholders were appointed to write a charter, League members were in attendance at every hearing. When the charter was submitted to the voters for approval in February 1954, the League actively supported and campaigned energetically to bring about its adoption."[83]

Established on Feb. 9, 1954, MSD's purpose is "to manage all wastewater and storm drainage facilities and treatment processes within its area, including construction of needed sewers and treatment systems as well as the operation, repair, and maintenance of these facilities."[84] From its inception to 1977, its service area included most of the eastern third of St. Louis

County, approximately 253 square miles.[85] This area includes the Mississippi, Missouri, and lower Meramec Rivers.[86]

In 1956, the St. Louis League formed its first water committee, which studied pollution and sewage issues.[87] At the time, the biggest concern was getting bond measures passed to fund trunk sewers to help in pollution and flooding abatement. The first passed in 1956 in Maline Creek, with 20 more to follow. In November 1962, voters approved a $95 million bond issue, which was "at the time the largest single water pollution abatement project ever submitted to U.S. voters."[88]

The League also pushed for stricter clean water bills than those on the books from the Missouri Water Pollution Board, founded in 1957 and empowered to "require 'necessary, reasonable treatment of sewage... [and] other wastes.'"[89] Five such bills were introduced between 1960-1961 alone,[90] but none passed at the state level, despite severe rebukes from national agencies on the pollution of our waterways. "The U.S. Public Health Service and Missouri State Water Pollution Board gave St. Louis a deadline of January 1, 1963, to meet and comply with its demands to stop dumping 30 million gallons of untreated waste daily into the Mississippi River." By 1965, a representative from the League attended each bimonthly Board of Trustees meeting at MSD headquarters to monitor progress first-hand.

In 1962, MSD, with League support, began planning and building water treatment plants in strategic parts of St. Louis. In 1964, MSD purchased 54 acres for the Bissell treatment plant, which would help with pollution on the Mississippi.[91] The Coldwater Creek treatment plant, the largest in the state of Missouri, was operational by 1966,[92] helping to "alleviate pollution of the Missouri River above the water plant of the City of St. Louis."[93] In 1968, another treatment plant opened in Lemay.

The 1960s

That same year, the Coldwater Creek treatment plant received the Treatment Plant of the Year award from the Missouri Water Pollution Control Association.[94]

Despite these measures, water pollution continued to grow. Studies from 1967 show that "growth and concentration of the population, the increase in industry, the growing complications in industrial processes, increased amount of water recreation and high standard of living have all contributed to mounting pollution."[95] Accordingly, the League came to a consensus in favor of upgrading the water quality in the rivers of St. Louis and to the south and working to improve recreational and wildlife potential out of the reach of the river.[96]

Air Pollution

According to a 1967 League report, "the greater St. Louis area historically has had a reputation as one of the nation's dirtiest metropolitan complexes and has been continually plagued by a contaminated atmosphere. At one time, St. Louis had such a bad smoke problem that the term 'St. Louis throat' was coined to describe certain kinds of damage to the membranes of the nose, sinus and lungs."[97]

St. Louis City passed its first anti-smoke ordinance in 1893, making it illegal to "emit dense black or thick gray smoke into the atmosphere."[98] Many more ordinances followed—all aimed at coal—but few were given sufficient resources to truly enforce them.

In 1961, the Department of Public Safety took over responsibility for air pollution in the St. Louis area through its Division of Air Pollution Control. They initiated an interstate air pollution study two years later. In 1964, the Cleaner Air Act was passed by Congress, laying the groundwork for the Missouri Air Conservation Act the following year and its creation of an Air

Pollution Control Agency.

The League was watching all of this very closely and keeping board members apprised of activities. In 1965, the new East-West Gateway Coordinating Council was tasked by the interstate air pollution study group to coordinate clean air efforts in the area.[99] They quickly found that "aside from the St. Louis-St. Louis County ordinances—which need[ed] revisiting and strengthening—there [wa]sn't at present stringent enough legislation to help abate much of the air pollution."[100]

In 1966, the final results of the interstate air pollution study were released. The report set standards for air quality in the region and made recommendations setting restrictions on types and quantities of emissions, quantity of coal to be burned, outlawed open burning, required anti-pollution devices on automobiles, and more.

These results piqued public interest. The St. Louis League issued a statement urging that "the City of St. Louis again take the lead in air pollution control by passing a strong anti-pollution ordinance based on the Interstate report."[101] This was done by Alderman Peter L. Simpson and passed by the Board of Aldermen before Easter adjournment. The Missouri legislature also passed an anti-pollution law which set air standards for the whole state.

THE BOROUGH PLAN

Anyone who has ever lived in St. Louis can attest that its government is set up unlike others in the nation. That's because St. Louis City and St. Louis County are separate, each with their own government, court system, etc.

This strange phenomenon dates back to 1875 and a provision for the separation of St. Louis City and St. Louis County in the state constitution. As it turns out, the whole thing was never legal[102]— yet it remains in place.

Since well before 1844—the first time the city and county attempted to separate— residents of St. Louis City had been complaining that they had to pay taxes for services in the county, which was mostly made up of farms and small villages.[103] By 1870, the city far out-populated the county and was the center of government and wealth—nearly $148 million in taxable wealth, as opposed to $14 million in the county.[104] Not only that, city residents had a strong suspicion that the county court was corrupt and wasting tax dollars. It was time to do something.

After mulling over various proposals, St. Louis' delegates to the 1875 Constitutional Convention pushed for separation of the city and county and set up a Board of Freeholders to accomplish the task. The following year, "between April and July 1876, the 13 freeholders met 52 times" in closed-door meetings. The result was a new "scheme" or plan for a dual St. Louis city and county and a city charter. Both were submitted—"after midnight on July 3, 1875—on a national holiday, when legal documents cannot be filed," hence making them illegal—for a public vote on Aug. 22, 1876.

On the surface, the measure passed, but not by much— 11,878 to 11,525 in favor in the city and 2,617 to 848 against in the county. With the outcome so close, a recount was held, and officials uncovered ballots containing "partially erased yes votes replaced with nos." Later, election officials admitted stuffing the ballot box at the direction of both city and county politicians, so the Missouri Court of Appeals invalidated those votes, changing the outcome to a victory by just over 1,200 votes.

The split permanently set the boundary between the city and the county, not allowing for population growth or changes in resident migration patterns within or outside of the city. By the 1920s, the city had grown too big for its bounds and tried to convince the county to reunite, but its residents wouldn't hear of it. Reunification attempts failed miserably at the polls in 1926, 1930, and 1959.[105]

After the 1959 loss, the Board of Freeholders revamped their plan, which became the basis for one of the League's most important issues of the 1960s—the Borough Plan. Created by Dr. Karl McCandless, head of the Political Science Department of Washington University,[106] the Borough Plan got its name from its plan to divide "St. Louis City and County into [twenty-two] New York–style boroughs, with eight in the city, seven in the county, and seven straddling the city-county line."[107] It was an ambitious attempt to "correct the mistake of 1875 that has meant the breaking up of our state's major city into many pieces"[108]—115 different jurisdictions in which "tens of thousands of residents of the area lack basic municipal services and existing services are woefully uncoordinated and often wastefully duplicate[d]... [where] the people of what is really one community have no instrument by which they can govern themselves."[109]

In a speech before the St. Louis County Bar Association in November 1961, Richard D. Shewmaker, a lawyer and vice chairman of the Missouri Committee for the Borough Plan, explained that at its core, the plan:

> creates a new government, the municipal county of St. Louis, to replace all governmental bodies except school districts, after a year of transition. The new government will be both a city and a county and perform both municipal and county functions... The amendment gives power to the people of the municipal county to adopt a charter for their own government both as a city and a

county. It gives broader power of self-government than is possessed by either the present city or the present county. It gives about as broad powers of home rule as you can imagine."[110]

The Borough Plan was hotly contested in both political and public circles. As the *St. Louis Post-Dispatch* put it, in the course of a single day, it "was praised as the St. Louis area's means to political unity and economic growth...and condemned as an improperly presented effort to usurp local government in the county.[111]

Proponents of the plan touted that it would force the city and county to work together, reducing duplication and waste and improving efficacy,[112] claimed it would "provide for fair and equal representation of all groups and neighborhoods within the new municipal county," provide "a broader tax base for the growing needs of our state government, help attract new industry to every part of Missouri for the prosperity and growth of the whole state,"[113] and improve public health, land use, and crime, and provide equity in public affairs and taxation.[114] In addition, it would place all St. Louis judges under the nonpartisan court system—instead of just those in the city—removing politics from their election,[115] and enforce the merit system for employees of the municipal county, taking them out of the system of patronage.

As much of a panacea as that may have seemed, the Borough Plan was not without its problems. Critics were quick to point out that it seemed to ignore that the St. Louis Metropolitan Area was more than just St. Louis City and St. Louis County; the area also includes St. Charles and Jefferson counties in Missouri and Madison and St. Clair counties in Illinois,[116] all of which were left out of the plan. It also took away the idea of home rule, which the League had fought so hard to gain.[117]

The part that troubled many experts, including its creator, Dr. McCandless, was that the plan was a constitutional amendment, so if a change was needed it would be necessary to amend the constitution, a long and difficult process.[118] In addition, "a single government would be unduly burdened, if not overwhelmed, by the multitude of petty matters that do not concern the area as a whole."[119] If that wasn't enough, it would create confusion about assessment practices, the boroughs would be of unequal population and could not be realigned until the population reached 120,000, and all municipal elections would be held the same day as state and national elections, which would "make for a long and confusing ballot," not to mention confusing local issues and subordinating local candidates to state and national candidates.

The League was cautious in regard to the plan; they discussed it informally at board meetings and most members agreed that change was necessary but taking a stand on it would take time and additional study.[120] In the meantime, they agreed the League would take on the task of educating the public on both sides of this very complex issue on which they would cast their ballots.[121]

Even though the Borough Plan would just impact St. Louis, citizens from across the state determined its fate,[122] a move justified by the fact that the prosperity of all of Missouri is affected by the prosperity of St. Louis.[123] However, opponents saw it for what it was: the only way politicians could get the plan approved.[124] But they were wrong. On Nov. 6, 1962, the Borough Plan was soundly defeated. The only positive spin that anyone could put on the outcome was that it "again alerted the citizens of the city and county to the need for coordination of activities between these areas on various levels."[125]

MERIT SYSTEM

The League's involvement in trying to persuade the St. Louis government to employ its personnel through a merit system—one that hires and promotes based on a person's tested skill and experience, rather than through the age-old system of patronage, hiring and promoting based on kinship, friendship or political favors—dates back to the 1930s. At the time, Avis Carlson, chronicler of the League's first forty years, called the merit system campaign "the most important program activity of the Thirties (and perhaps of all time.)"[126] That statement would likely have been echoed by League members in the '60s as well.

The League became involved in a merit system when the National League selected it as an item of concerted focus for all Leagues across the nation in 1934. The following year, the slogan, "find the man for the job, not the job for the man"—which endured for decades—was being used.[127] The League proposed several bills over the next few years, but they all failed to pass.

In 1941, when the League began its campaign for a new Missouri constitution, "a large part of its effort was directed toward the inclusion of a section which would provide for the appointment of all administrative employees on a basis of merit."[128] The Constitutional Convention, unfortunately, only approved the merit system for a handful of roles, which voters passed at the polls on July 4, 1941, and over the next two decades the Missouri legislature added a handful more so that by 1964, less than half of state employees were under the Merit System.[129]

The St. Louis County charter, adopted by voters in 1950, also provided for a limited merit system. It went into effect in 1954 and was amended in 1960 to include the Department of Revenue.[130]

In the 1960s, under the leadership of Rodney Harris, the League's expert on the merit system,[131] the League adopted a formal position in favor of getting as many city and county employees covered by the merit system as possible.

Accordingly, throughout the decade, members fought for several bills that would expand the merit system. A flurry of merit-related bills was introduced to the state legislature in 1967 including the controversial SB12, introduced by Senator Albert Spradling, Jr. (D-27), that sought to exempt psychiatrists in the Division of Mental Diseases from the merit system. The League issued an impassioned statement by Frances Olenick, who said:

> We are firmly committed to strengthening, rather than eroding, the merit system for efficient staffing of governmental agencies. …We deplore the prospect of a step backward in Missouri, no matter how well intentioned. The mental health program must be strengthened through a flexible approach within the system itself.[132]

The League was victorious, and the bill died in committee. While better merit bills also failed, the League didn't give up and revised its position for 1967-1969:

> The League of Women Voters believes that a good merit plan not only corrects the evils of the spoils system and avoids the constant turnover of personnel which accompanies each change of political administration, but that it attracts and holds able public employees.

The League position included several tips for operating sound merit systems, including non-discrimination, incentive plans, and well-defined job classifications and salary schedules. The fight for full coverage of the merit system extended into the 1970s and so will be continued in the next chapter.

CHARTER AMENDMENT

Closely tied in with efforts to adopt a merit system for city and county governmental jobs was the idea of home rule for St. Louis County and its municipalities, a concept invented right here in Missouri.

In 1875, at the urging of District 5 Rep. Joseph Pulitzer, Missouri became the first state and St. Louis the first city in the country to adopt a home rule charter,[133] meaning it could not be amended by the state legislature, only by the citizens. The purpose of such a form of government is to allow local citizens to take care of their local needs and form their own local governments without having to seek permission from the legislature and to keep the legislature from overreaching into local affairs. The exception is "matters which affect the entire state, [in which] the legislature should be supreme."[134]

When the city and county split in 1876, home rule didn't follow into the county. As a result, "the county government was not allowed to develop in the same way as the municipalities within its territorial limits" resulting in "development of a confusing 'jurisdictional jungle' of separate governmental units which…hampered area progress."[135] The county had 96 municipal governments and nearly 150 local taxing authorities, each of which had independent powers and provided variable quality in services, police and fire protection, and taxes levied. This left the St. Louis County government with very few countywide functions; instead, it was given the authority to provide services only in the unincorporated areas or cities which contracted for them.

By the time the merit system became a desired change in 1939, it was clear that St. Louis's charter was in need of an overhaul. "From then on, there has never been a time when Leaguers were not saying to whomever would listen, 'We need a new Charter,'"[136] League historian Avis Carlson wrote.

Still, change was slow in coming. By 1950, even though St. Louis had grown and expanded to be nearly unrecognizable by 1875 or even 1939 standards, its government had barely changed. That year, St. Louisans approved a limited home rule charter that gave it legislative powers in four areas: public health, police and traffic, building construction, and planning and zoning. This enabled the government to better handle modern issues that couldn't have been foreseen 75 years before; it was amended sparsely, only in 1954 to set up a police department and in 1960 to establish a Department of Revenue.

However, as time progressed and needs increased, the people of St. Louis grew more confident in the use of their powers to bring about change. In 1966, after a lengthy League study of city government, a number of charter amendments were submitted to voters, including extending the merit system to "approximately 300 employees in the department of planning and revenue, and in divisions of highways and data processing and to permit future extension by council ordinance," a measure that voters approved.[137]

The following year, voters made a push for "complete home rule," to free the County government from its nearly century-old restraints. They called for a charter amendment because they wanted to be able to decide for themselves just how much power the government should have and in what matters. The League was behind them, as this idea upheld League "principles

[that] state that the democratic government depends on the informed and active participation of its citizens. Responsible government should be responsive to the will of the people. Efficient and economical government requires competent personnel with clear assignments of responsibilities."[138]

Not surprisingly, officials in the smaller municipal governments were opposed to the idea of complete home rule because they feared the county would take over their roles, putting them out of not only a job, but political power. They had enough sway that when home rule measures were brought before the state legislature in 1963 and 1965, they were allowed to die (1963) or were not passed (1965).

But in the end, the voters had their say, with full League support. On Nov. 8, 1966, they approved Amendment 1, also known as the "Missouri St. Louis Plan for Partial or Complete Government Amendment," which "authorized St. Louis County and City to adopt a plan for partial or complete government of all or any part of the county or city." [139]

In 1967, the League endorsed a plan for further amendment to allow the county government, with voter approval, to provide or create services such as public health and safety, recreational facilities and construction and regulation of arterial roads across the area. In addition, the League identified 13 offices that did not fall under the current definition of home rule or under the merit system, including the circuit attorney, collector of revenue, the coroner, prosecuting attorney/public administrator, treasurer, sheriff and several clerkships.[140] A charter revision was proposed and passed by voters in a "landslide" victory during a special election on April 2, 1968.[141]

At the 1969 LWVMO State Convention, delegates adopted a county government study item. This came out of the understanding that with St. Louis's victory, other counties would be adopting charter governments and pushing for home rule as soon as they reached the 85,000-person population threshold required by law—including Boone, Buchanan, Clay, Greene, Jackson, Jefferson, and St. Charles.

Amendment SJR 12 was placed on the November 1970 ballot that "would allow citizens of a charter county to determine what services shall be supplied to their incorporated and unincorporated areas by local and city governments."[142] What this meant in practice was that if the amendment was passed, it made two major changes: 1) the county could exercise legislative power pertaining to all services in the unincorporated part of the county, except school districts, without going to the legislature and 2) incorporated areas would retain the provision allowing the county to contract with municipalities or political subdivisions for services. The Amendment passed with 57% of the vote statewide.[143]

This was a major victory for home rule in the area that emboldened many smaller townships to fight for home rule. Over the following decade, the League also followed efforts in Clayton, Kirkwood and governments outside of St. Louis, such as St. Charles County.[144] It also supported an amendment to lower "the population and signature requirements for county home rule,"[145] which passed in 1971.[146]

REDISTRICTING

Closely tied to the League's work with the merit system and home rule in the 1960s is the idea of apportionment, also called redistricting. The U.S. Census Bureau defines apportionment as a method that "measures the population so that seats in the U.S. House of Representatives can be correctly apportioned among the states."[147] The Bureau also notes that because the Constitution doesn't specify how apportionment is meant to take place, it varied after every election until a set method was declared on Nov. 15, 1941, that "provided for the automatic reapportionment of the House of Representative's 435 seats following each census, using the Huntington-Hill/Equal Proportions Method."[148]

The League became involved in apportionment in June 1964 after the U.S. Supreme Court ruled that both houses of the state legislature were required from then on to be apportioned on a population basis. The League immediately began studying various options that the state could use, published a pamphlet and trained discussion unit leaders on how to talk to their members about it.

In October, in partnership with the University City and Central County Leagues, the St. Louis City League reached a consensus that later became the official position for all of St. Louis: The League supported "reapportionment of the lower house [House of Representatives] on a population basis, and also supported the principle of a one-house [unicameral] legislature." They believed a unicameral legislature "would be a more economical and efficient form of government for Missouri."[149]

Headed by Virginia Deutch, future St. Louis League president, the St. Louis League continued to study what other states were doing —especially Nebraska, which adopted a unicameral legislature in 1934[150]— and speak with unit members of the various Leagues. Finally, they moved to recommend that the State League support a unicameral legislature, despite anticipated resistance from citizens outside of the two major metropolitan areas of St. Louis and Kansas City.[151]

Invoking the merit system slogan of "one man, one vote," members set about convincing lawmakers to uphold the Supreme Court decision rather than supporting various measures aimed at getting Congress to reverse the Court's decision and allow the states to apportion one house "on factors other than population."[152] However, less than three months after the League took a stand, the Missouri House, led by Speaker Thomas D. Graham (D-Jefferson City) joined 21 other states in passing a resolution (HRC 2) that used the lack of specificity in the United States Constitution to argue that they should be able to apportion their seats as they see fit.[153]

As the two sides continued butting heads, the deadline set by a directive of the Federal District Court for the Missouri General Assembly to reapportion itself before the session ended approached. To try to get around it, a constitutional amendment (Amendment 3) was proposed and put on the ballot; if passed, it would have allowed the House to reapportion itself without a bipartisan commission.[154]

When it was defeated in a special election on Aug. 17, 1965, Democratic Governor Warren E. Hearnes had no choice but to call a special legislative session in October. The result was an apportionment proposal that provided for a House of 163 members and a Senate of 34 members, "with districts for both senators and representatives to be drawn by bipartisan commissioners from lists submitted to the governor by the two political party state committees. All Missouri legislators will henceforth represent the new districts which have recently been drawn by these redistricting commissions."[155]

It wasn't their ideal solution, but the League felt they could endorse it and they did, speaking to groups and distributing LWVMO flyers. The constitutional amendment was put to a public vote on Jan. 14, 1966, and passed.

As for the idea of a unicameral legislature, other Missouri Leagues didn't share St. Louis' enthusiasm, so the idea was tabled. As Ginny Deutch wrote at the time, "Hope springs eternal—and someday perhaps we will complete the formula of one man equals one vote equals one house."

CITY REDEVELOPMENT

Every city goes through periods of decline and renewal as it ages. For St. Louis, the aftermath of World War II pointed out many of its flaws. Not only was there a housing shortage, but it became clear that minimum housing standards were needed, especially as more mostly white families began to abandon the city in favor of the county and areas of the city fell into disrepair.[156]

In the late 1940s, the League helped get a new zoning ordinance passed and worked with the city to combat areas turning into slums. By the early 1950s, they were fighting for new zoning ordinances to combat neighborhood decay and fighting against the displacement of 200,000 Black people when the down-on-its-luck Mill Creek area, a historically Black neighborhood, was demolished in 1959 to make way for new development.[157] It was the largest single area in St. Louis ever to be bulldozed at one time.[158]

In 1960, the League's City Redevelopment Committee studied proposed revisions to the building code in St. Louis City that were "the result of many long hours of collective thinking, study and argument by about two hundred men representing all segments of the building industry, including union representatives, architects, city officials and Realtors."[159] The League voted to support them,[160] arguing that the 1945 code was not only antiquated, but downright obsolete[161] thanks to advances in materials, construction methods and increased standards of safety, especially related to the annual peril of tornadoes and constant threat of fire.[162] At a public hearing on the matter, the League was loudly and rudely challenged by opponents from the masonry, bricklayers and steamfitters unions,[163] stirring many present from a position of apathy into action.

"It seemed to trigger a determination on the part of those

supporting the code to see that there would be no further delay," one Leaguer reported.[164]

League members immediately began a concerted telephone and mail campaign to educate lawmakers about the proposed code, as well as new zoning ordinances that would support a new master plan for downtown St. Louis. On March 17, 1961, the Board of Aldermen passed the new code with only a single dissenting vote, despite threats by the opposition to load the bill with "crippling" amendments. A week later, the board passed the zoning amendments,[165] paving the way for a brighter future for the city.

Next up for the League was supporting a minimum housing standards bill that was in the hands of the Board of Aldermen. SaLees Seddon, chairman of the City League's Redevelopment Committee, spoke for the League at an October 24 meeting, "pointing out the inadequacy of the present minimum housing ordinance and urging the aldermanic committee to report favorably on this proposed revision."[166] She also expressed support for the changes in substitute bill number 80, though the League later issued a statement suggesting "that professional groups who oppose the amendment are better qualified to judge them than the two organizations that are backing the proposals.[167]

The bill languished for months before finally being passed 21-3 in January 1963. In the end, it provided for "bathtubs, running water and 70 feet of living space per person"[168] to be enforced in both current and new residences. Property owners were also to be given seven days' notice under the bill before a visit by a city inspector. This was "one of the most controversial amendments to the bill," Mrs. W. Parker Burns wrote in the League newsletter. However, "we believe that with [it]...city inspectors will be better able to enforce the provisions of the minimum housing and zoning ordinances."[169]

HELPING THE INNER CITY

In 1964, St. Louis celebrated its 200th anniversary and many felt it was showing its age. Ruth Moore, a St. Louis League member, journalist and authority on city planning, was the speaker at the League's 1965 annual meeting. She said:

> There are three ways to cope with the space problems as housing gets older: to tear down the worst of the old; to renew and rebuild the old; and to find new places to build....Repaired streets, new parks, and effective lighting would improve the general environment, thereby encouraging individual property owners to improve also...We should not forget our landmarks but should work effectively to save them.[170]

For the rest of the decade, the League would work with various agencies and lawmakers to try to reverse blight and prevent future deterioration. After in-depth study of the local housing needs, the committee chose to focus on three areas: "ensuring the minimum housing standards we fought so hard to pass were enforced; beautification projects that increased the health, environmental quality and enjoyment of local residents; and projects that would spotlight St. Louis to the rest of the state and nation, especially those along our famed riverfront."[171]

In the area of minimum housing standards, one concerning issue was the demolition of old housing, which was leading to a shortage of quality residential units in the city affordable to low-income residents. According to the National Commission on Urban Problems, in 1965, around 13,600 families in St. Louis were unable to afford adequate housing—these included 66,300 children; only 3,118 residential units were available, enough to shelter only 23% of families.[172]

League member LaDonna Green stressed how demolition of condemned property disproportionately hurt those in low-income, pre-dominantly Black areas:

> There were 257,800 housing units in the City of St. Louis—5,200 less than in 1960. In the five-year period 1960-1965, 12,000 housing units were demolished but only 6,800 were constructed. While 2,000 of the new units were in urban renewal areas, only about 300 were for low- and moderate-income groups. Almost 89% of the units demolished were in multifamily structures and were occupied by low-income families.[173]

If that wasn't enough, between 1965-1967, an additional 3,400 demolitions were scheduled—3,100 in the city and 300 in the county. Green estimated that even on the conservative side, "12,000 additional housing units were needed...and an additional 13,000 such units will be needed by 1975."[174]

While one may think that the low-rent public housing created by the Housing Act of 1937 should prevent problems like this, the reality was that the federal government provided little money to maintain the buildings, forcing tenants to contribute the bulk of needed funds in rent. Because operation costs kept increasing and income did not, housing authorities were faced with a choice that defeated the whole purpose of the low-rent housing in the first place: either raise rents on those who couldn't afford them or let the buildings decay.

Many landlords opted for the latter until their properties were no longer safe, but others chose to keep raising rents. In February 1969, a group of tenants, angered by the third rent increase in three years, had enough. Over half of the residents were paying more than 25% of their income for rent—some as high as 75%. Unable to stand the strain any longer, they went on strike, demanding that rent be restored to a level below 25% of income, the creation of a tenant affairs board, and that three residents be appointed to the Board of Commissioners of the Housing Authority.[175]

Nine months later, the strike ended, and the St. Louis Civic Alliance for Housing was created. As the strikers demanded, it was comprised of tenants, but also labor, business, religious, and Black community leaders. This was not only a win for the residents, but also a first in the nation; never before had a group of private citizens taken over the operation of public housing.

The League felt that the possibilities of this new organization were "tremendously exciting. They opened the door for St. Louis to become the show place for the best, rather than the worst, in public housing."[176] So they joined the organizations supporting the St. Louis Civic Alliance, promising to support legislation that would enable them to succeed.

Beginning in the autumn of 1969, the League's Human Resources Committee, led by Marjorie Pharis, and its Inner City Committee, led by Susie Philpott, held joint meetings to tackle the subject of inner city housing. One of the first subjects they studied was the omnibus Housing Act (HUD) of 1969 because of its wording that related to the rent strike in St. Louis. The committee held a large letter-writing campaign and "strongly endorsed the rent subsidy amendment to the housing bill."[177]

In January 1970, several members of the committee attended a meeting of the housing committee of the Wells-Goodfellow Neighborhood Center on minimum housing code enforcement in St. Louis. The Wells-Goodfellow group had been working for over a year, trying to get the code enforced in their area, so they called upon the League for help. League members observed court proceedings and interviewed officials to better understand the situation and then sent letters to all city officials immediately responsible for housing code enforcement informing them that the League was involved, and they were being monitored for legal compliance. They continued to regularly attend housing court, document the procedure and disposition of concerning cases and follow up on bench warrants issued for known slumlords.

BEAUTIFICATION

The League's first step in working with the St. Louis County Park System was to support a bond issue on the ballot on March 3, 1964, that would finance a 51,000-acre comprehensive park plan based on the standards set up by the National Recreation Association in 1963. The expansion was needed, they argued, because attendance at local parks skyrocketed by 265% in the previous five years and was expected to keep increasing. The plan would more than double park space in the St. Louis area by adding 24 new parks and improving existing parks and scenic roads.[178]

The bond was defeated, along with all the other bond issues on the ballot, as voters shied away from tax increases,[179] but the League didn't give up. It was put back on the ballot at every opportunity, no matter how many times it was voted down. By August 1966, the defeat had narrowed to a small number of votes.

The $25 million plan was again put before voters on Nov. 8, 1966, The League once again emphasized their support, citing professional studies that proved the need for parks and open space for the physical and mental benefit of citizens; that the time to establish park land was now, before suburbanization made it more difficult to find open land; and that plans for such park expansion would qualify the county for federal grants.[180] Unfortunately, it was rejected yet again.

Three years later, however, voters were more willing to listen. On June 3, 1969, they passed a bond issue supported by the League for $19.3 million to buy about 2,800 acres of land for seven new parks in areas where such facilities were not conveniently available and make improvements at 23 existing parks.[181] The new parks included Queeny Park in West St. Louis County; Spanish Lake and Bellefontaine Parks in North County; Cliff Cave Park in South County; a 400-acre addition to Creve Coeur Lake Park; a 40-acre addition to Jefferson Barracks Park; and a 120-acre annex of Grant's Farm to form a park.[182]

Five and a half million dollars of the bond issue also provided for "development of major recreational facilities to include three ice skating rinks, three golf courses and three year-round swimming pools...in the north, west-central, and south county areas."[183]

LEAGUE ACTIVITIES

50TH ANNIVERSARY

The League turned 50 in 1969 and kicked off celebrations with a once-in-a-lifetime national campaign, called "Does she look her age?" which aimed to raise $11 million nationally. In St. Louis, the local goal was $200,000.[184] One of the many fundraising and celebratory events was a party in the Windsor room of the Cheshire on May 19, 1969, including lunch and a speech by Glenn D. Pratt, Chief of Enforcement for the Federal Water Pollution Control Administration, Upper Mississippi River Basin.[185]

1964 REGISTER AND VOTE PARADE

In 1964, President Lyndon B. Johnson, St. Louis Mayor Raymond R. Tucker, and St. Louis County Supervisor Lawrence K. Roos declared the week of Monday, September 14, as Women Voters Week. [186]

League co-founder and former state and St. Louis president Edna Gellhorn suggested the St. Louis League hold a parade to mark the week, much like they had in 1916 when women protested the lack of the vote to the Democratic National Convention. Edna, Ella Stinson and Ginny Deutch co-chaired the committee.

The result of their hard work was the 16-mile "Your Vote Makes a Difference—Register So You Can Vote" Parade,[187] led by Grand Marshall Adolph Vedder, who was also marshal of the Shrine Circus Parades. Following him came the American flag with the Scott Air Force Base Band close behind.[188] League members were next, identified by a large sign. Comprising the group were seven cars carrying women who won the vote in 1920—including Edna, Erma Stix, Luella Sayman, Elsie Rauh and Eleanor Hardy—followed by nearly 1,000 League members, some wearing bloomers and suffrage costumes, stretching more than five blocks. The parade also included marching bands from Cleveland High and Sumner High and two floats. As the parade passed 8th and Locust, balloons with the word "vote" printed on them were released into the sky.[189]

When the parade ended at the Visitor Center, several League officers spoke to a crowd of about 150, urging them to vote. Other speakers included Frankie Freeman, a local attorney and member of the United States Commission on Human Rights, LWVMO President Esther Osborne, and Luella Sayman, chair of Women as Citizens, a subcommittee of the Governor's Commission on the Status of Women. Entertainment was provided by actor Jack

Murdoch of the Municipal Opera, who served as master of ceremonies, and St. Louis singer Perri Moreno.[190]

METROPOLITAN LEAGUE ORGANIZATION (ILO)

Within the Leagues, times were changing as well. By early 1965, some members felt strongly that there was a need for a Metropolitan League that would coordinate matters that concerned both the county and the city so that local leagues could focus on local issues.

But many in the St. Louis County local Leagues such as Kirkwood, Webster Groves, and North County were against this idea because they feared "they would be swallowed up and lose their identity."[191] Others felt that the County-City Committee served this purpose just fine and did not need expanding.

Despite these opposing viewpoints, the suggestion to explore if it might be beneficial to reorganize the St. Louis City and County Leagues on a metropolitan basis was taken up and a committee was formed on Aug. 30, 1965. They began by studying what other locations—such as Baltimore, Cincinnati and Dade County in Florida, areas that had similar issues—were doing. After consultation, the committee proposed that St. Louis form a Metropolitan Council like the one in Cincinnati: five elected officers: chairman, two vice chairmen, secretary and treasurer, one representative from each of the local leagues, elected by each league at its annual meeting, and appointed directors as needed.[192] Each director would have a specific responsibility (publicity, TV/radio, newsletter, etc.) as needed.[193]

The formation of the Council was really just a way of making the Committee's work official. Very little would actually change from the way things were currently run—the Council would only take up county-wide and metropolitan area problems, with occasional meetings to plan for activities involving state or national items. The Local Leagues would become units of the parent organization.[194] "It gives recognition to the fact that lines of local governments crossed increasingly often in these days of more complex problems," wrote Jeanne Blythe, president of LWV of St. Louis.[195]

On March 21, 1965, delegates from all the local Leagues in St. Louis City and County met and accepted the proposal and new bylaws. They were charged with sharing information with their local membership before a final vote was taken at the annual meeting in April. But the vote was delayed, with opponents voicing concern that:

> Because it operates under the principle of unit voting rather than one woman-one vote, we consider it to have inadequate membership representation, with unclear authority and weak lines of communication. Any expansion of its powers would seriously weaken the Leagues by building a superstructure without base support and would further drain our limited womanpower.[196]

In April 1965, the membership voted to approve, and the Metropolitan Council of the LWV of St. Louis and St. Louis County was born. Ginny Deutch, League vice president, issued the following statement of explanation on October 11, "Since the trend today is toward a greater interplay between geographic areas, we feel that the League should establish a flexible plan within which all members can work together on governmental problems affecting the metropolitan region. The current need for a metropolitan administration in American urban centers is the same need that exists in League organization; we should point the way by setting our own house in functional order."[197]

ST. LOUIS LEAGUE'S ROLE IN CHINA'S ADMISSION TO THE UNITED NATIONS

From 1966-1969, members the Central County League's China and Foreign Economic Policy Committee, under the leadership of Sydell Shayer, turned their attention across the world to China. They helped the National League evaluate the United States' relations with the People's Republic of China[198] and support of the Nuclear Nonproliferation Treaty.[199]

For two years, the Central County League members immersed themselves in learning all they could about the country, its history and government, its relationship with the U.S. and U.N., and more. They held annual workshops for up to 300 people. In 1967, the League and 21 other organizations sponsored a St. Louis conference on China, involving five experts from all over the country.[200]

On Feb. 14, 1969, their work culminated in a meeting to help guide the LWVUS in its efforts to influence Congress and present an educated viewpoint to the executive branch of government. Almost 1,200 Leagues participated in the study. The consensus was:

> We favor improvement of relations between the U.S. and China in areas such as communication, trading in non-strategic materials, postal, telephone ... [201]

On April 27, 1969, Lucy Wilson Benson, the National League president, announced that the LWVUS had arrived at a consensus to ask the United States to normalize relations with the People's Republic of China. The League also called for specific policy changes such as the establishment of cultural trade and diplomatic relations with Peking and that the United

States no longer oppose representation of the Chinese People's Republic in the United Nations.[202]

Conclusion

The 1960s were a decade of great advancement for the League; actions taken during this time—such as supporting school desegregation, establishing the St. Louis junior college system and focusing on city redevelopment—set up policies and infrastructure that would positively impact the St. Louis region for decades to come. Many of the issues the League took on carried over into the 1970s and beyond, as members fought for the merit system, fair redistricting, and protecting voter rights and access, especially in St. Louis City. As the following chapter will show, the need for the League's advocacy only increased as local municipalities fought for independent rule and more political pressure was exerted by the city and county.

WOMEN WHO MADE AN IMPACT IN THE 1960s

Ida Perkins Johnson West
Nov. 24, 1936-March 1, 2021

Ida Perkins was born on Nov. 24, 1936, in St. Louis, the only child of John Marshall and Estella Mae Perkins. She grew up in the 4600 block of Kennerly in a segregated city and in a neighborhood that could be hostile to Black people.[203] Ida graduated from Charles Sumner High School in 1952 and St. Louis University, where she earned her degree in physical therapy.[204]

Ida had the distinction of being the first Black woman in the state of Missouri to head a State Hospital's therapy department and continued to practice her profession years after retirement. She was deeply saddened when the State Hospital released hundreds of our most vulnerable people in the 1970s and remained an advocate for health care her entire life.

Ida married Dean Johnson, with whom she had one son, Philip, born June 20, 1959. She later married again, this time to schoolteacher Donald West.

In 1977, Donald ran for the school board, but failed to gain enough votes due to low voter turnout in North St. Louis. "Low voter turnout, just twelve years after the historic 1965 Voting Rights Act did not sit well with my mother," Philip recalled. "One can trace that election as the moment in which she became activated."[205]

She joined the League because she loved history. "My father was a history buff...Growing up...with all that history, I didn't have anything else to do but to join the League. I wanted to get more involved, knowing what Black people had to go through to vote," she said. "I had especially concerns for voting rights for Blacks...I knew when I joined the League I was going to be actively involved. I wasn't going to be just a member, sitting like a bump on a log."[206]

And active Ida was, for more than 50 years. At each League meeting when she introduced herself to newcomers, she told them, "I have been a League member almost all of my adult life."[207]

Described by friends as a warrior, it was in the mid-1970s that Ida began her quest to educate voters—especially Black voters—out of a state of victimhood by teaching them about voting and the law. She conducted large voter registration efforts and "deputized ordinary citizens" to register people to vote until St. Louis Board of Elections Commissioner Jerry Wamser took that power away from the League. Ida was enraged and responded by waging war with him in the media, in the courts and by testifying in the House.[208]

In 1984, Ida became the first Black president of the LWV of St. Louis City. In that role, which she held for six years, she was instrumental in recruiting women of color as members, mentoring them as future League presidents, and leading several voter initiatives. "She singlehandedly changed the flavor and color of the League," one mourner recalled at Ida's memorial service.[209]

Ida particularly enjoyed nonpartisan intelligent discussion and protecting the precious right to cast a vote – hopefully an informed one. She was still an active League member two weeks before she died, when she insisted on writing postcards to St. Louis voters encouraging them to participate in the upcoming city elections.

Ida walked three miles every morning. She read and traveled widely, to Europe, Israel and Cuba and made friends all over the world. In addition, she loved playing cards—especially bid whist—doing crossword puzzles, learning about history and politics and watching football.

Ida passed away on March 1, 2021, after a brief illness. The family held a memorial service in her honor on Aug. 14, 2021, at Exodus Gallery in St. Louis.

Teresa Fischer

May 17, 1911-Feb. 27, 1995

Teresa "Terry" Mayer was born in St. Louis in 1911.[210] She attended Soldan High School in downtown St. Louis and then Washington University and the University of California, Los Angeles. She studied for a year in Europe, specifically in Berlin, Munich, and Paris. That was where her interest in education began. "I didn't learn much academically — despite all the praise given European schools," she told the *St. Louis Post-Dispatch* in 1960, "but I learned a great many other things. And my interest in democracy was aroused when I saw the effects of inflation on Germany and the events leading to the Second World War."[211]

Teresa worked as a nurse-secretary before and after her 1932 marriage to Aaron Fischer, an industrial consultant. The couple had one son, Peter.[212]

After joining the League, she joined the education committee. She served as its chair and later as president of both the St. Louis (1945-1947) and the Missouri League (1953-1957).[213] In 1950, while on the board of John Burroughs School,[214] she joined the Missouri Lay Citizens Committee, which was appointed to study the needs of the public schools throughout the state. Their report, "Better Public Schools for Missouri's Children," eventually led to the adoption in 1957 of the School Foundation Program.

Terry's work to better the educational opportunities in St. Louis continued as a delegate to the 1955 White House Conference on Education, where she was inspired to action. Upon her return to St. Louis, she founded the St. Louis-St. Louis County White House Conference group, which held annual conferences on local education.

In 1958, she was one of ten women honored by the *Globe Democrat* as a Woman of Achievement for "their outstanding contributions to betterment of the community's way of life in 1958."[215] In honoring Terry, the *Globe* noted she "paved the way for better administration of our schools and better education for our children....By her service and energy Mrs. Fisher attracted about 600 delegates to the St. Louis conference on education in 1956. She developed a well thought out agenda that made possible the success which came out of that conference."[216]

In 1960, the Conference looked at the local educational

needs beyond high school and found that St. Louis lacked options for those who didn't want or couldn't afford to attend a four-year college. This was the impetus for legislation that eventually led to the Junior College program, a two-year alternative to traditional colleges and universities.[217]

Terry later headed the Missouri Citizens Committee for State Aid and for Junior Colleges and was co-chairman with Oscar Earnhardt of the Citizens Committee for the St. Louis-St. Louis County Junior College District.[218]

In December 1962, she was presented with the St. Louis Award—becoming the first woman to be awarded the honor on her own and only the second woman ever to receive it—for her crucial role in developing the St. Louis Junior College system. Ever civic-minded, Terry immediately donated the $1,000 in prize money back to the St. Louis Junior College Scholarship Loan Fund.[219]

In 1967, Terry help found Citizenship Education Clearing House (CECH),[220] which helps young people in Missouri become informed about and involved in government and community affairs and was an active board member until 1995 when health issues forced her to step down. She was also a member of the Webster University board from 1970-1986 and volunteered with the Missouri Botanical Garden.[221]

Along with her husband, Aaron, Terry started three foundations for the betterment of the St. Louis Community: The Deer Creek Foundation, a national civil rights and government accountability group; The Gateway Foundation dedicated to St. Louis arts and culture; and The Litzinger Road Ecology Foundation, which uses land around the Fischer home to teach young people about ecology.

Teresa died on Feb. 27, 1995, at age 84, only three months after her husband.[222]

Virginia Deutch

Feb. 23, 1916 – April 20, 2011

Virginia "Ginny" Loeb was born Feb. 23, 1916,[223] to Tess and Virgil Loeb in St. Louis. Ginny attended Washington University and the University of Chicago. She worked as an advertising copywriter before World War II. When war broke out, she joined the American Red Cross, serving in Australia and Manila from 1944-1946.[224]

Once peace had come and she was once again stateside in 1946, Ginny married Dr. Max Deutch. They later had a son, Tony, and a daughter, Deborah.[225]

When Ginny said she wanted to join the League of Women Voters, her husband gave her his full support. He told one newspaper that he "feels as strongly as his wife the responsibility of citizens to give public service."

To which Ginny retorted, "Besides, he is a superb cook, so I know our household will survive."[226]

The League of Women Voters was in Ginny Deutch's blood. Her mother Tess was president in 1926 and helped influence the fledgling organization on the local, state and national levels. Because of this, Ginny joked that she'd been in training as a member her whole life.

"My brother and sister and I were under the impression that it was a normal part of life," she told the *St. Louis Post-Dispatch* in 1967 when she became St. Louis League President. "One joined as soon as one was old enough. If you were voting age, it was just good sense to learn which you were voting for or against; and the place to do this was through the discussion units of the League."[227]

The following January, when a fire destroyed the League headquarters on Delmar Boulevard, *The Post* reported that "the fires were still burning," when Ginny showed up to survey the damage and make a plan. Equipment and soggy records were moved to her basement, and she volunteered for phone calls to come to her home.[228] By 9 a.m. the following Monday, the League was back up and answering phone calls.

Fortunately, the League's valuable historical records were in the building's basement, so they weren't damaged by the fire,[229] but Ginny did have the foresight to have them moved to the Missouri Historical Society in June 1969,[230] where they still reside today.

Outside of the League, Ginny served as a board member for the Planned Parenthood Association of St. Louis, Adult Education Council of Greater St. Louis, the St. Louis Council on World Affairs, and the Committee on Nuclear Information. She also worked as an election judge from 1972-1992 and volunteered at the KTVI Call for Action consumer helpline.

Ginny passed away on April 20, 2011. She donated her body to Washington University School of Medicine for research purposes."[231]

Main Sources Chapter 1 – 1960s

Annual Reports of the President, League of Women Voters of St. Louis, 1960-1969

Books
- Carlson, Avis. *"The First 40 Years: 1919-1959. The League of Women Voters of St. Louis."*
- Davis, Wylie H. *Civil Rights U.S.A.: Public Schools, Cities in the North and West, 1962.*
- Federal Constitutional Convention: Hearings Before the Subcommittee on Separation of Powers...90-1, on S. 2307, October 30, 31, 1967.
- Gore, Lilian. *A Survey of Early Elementary Education in Public Schools: 1960-1961*
- Heaney, Gerald W. and Dr. Susan Uchitelle. *Unending Struggle: The Long Road to an Equal Education in St. Louis.*
- Rias, Hope C., *St. Louis School Desegregation: Patterns of Progress and Peril.*
- Vaughan, George B. *The Community College in America: A Short History.*

Board and Council Meeting Minutes, 1960-1969

League of Women Voters County-City Committee

Metropolitan Problems Committee of the County-City Committee

League Proposed Local Current Agenda for 1964-1965

Newsletters
- *Central County Bulletin/Central County Scene,* January 1966-January 1976
- *League Reporter/In League Reporter,* September 1960-November 1969

League documents regarding
- Air Pollution
- The Borough Plan
- Education, Vocational Schools, Special School District
- Home Rule
- Inner City work
- Merit System
- MSD
- Redistricting Missouri Schools

Memorial and Obituaries for Ida West and Virginia Loeb Deutch

Periodicals
- *Journal of the Illinois State Historical Society*
- *The Journal of Negro Education*
- *Missouri Law Review*
- *Riverfront Times*
- *The St. Louis American*
- *St. Louis Globe-Democrat*
- *St. Louis Jewish Light*
- *St. Louis Magazine*
- *The St. Louis Post-Dispatch*

Thesis/Dissertations
- Brown, Michael, "An Examination of Disingenuous Deeds by St. Louis Public Schools 1945-1983." University of Missouri-St. Louis Dissertations, May 2019.

Websites:
- Ballotpedia
- Decoding the City
- St. Louis Government
- United States Census Bureau

For a complete list of sources, please see the endnotes at https://my.lwv.org/missouri/metro-st-louis/about/our-history.

1960s

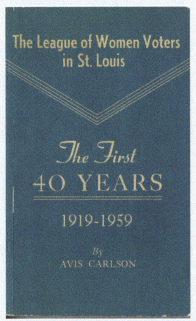

Avis Carlson wrote a history of the League's first 40 years.

Leaguers led a GOTV parade downtown in September 1964 (photo courtesy of Mercantile Library St. Louis Globe-Democrat collection).

CHAPTER 2

The 1970s

THE 1970s WERE a decade of reform for women, as they demanded change and greater rights than ever before. This was especially visible in the decade-long fight for the Equal Rights Amendment (ERA). The feminist movement celebrated the formation of women's studies programs in colleges and universities and *Roe vs. Wade,* the Supreme Court's landmark abortion decision in 1973.

This was also a period when many single-issue women's groups were created such as the National Organization of Women (1966, civil rights/ERA), the National Women's Political Caucus (1972, politics/voting), Coalition of Labor Union Women (1974, workers' rights), Women's Action Alliance (1971, local action/women's rights), etc. Many League members were attracted to these new organizations, and as a result, League membership suffered. Records show that 1974 and 1975 were particularly tough years financially for the League. There was even talk about if the St. Louis League would make it through the year.

For many years, League funding was provided by dues and contributions from corporations and individuals to its Metropolitan Finance Campaign (MFC). As part of its fundraising effort, the MFC adopted the slogan "Help the League Survive in '75."[1]

Despite this downturn, the League rallied to have a successful decade. Some of the highlights included:

- Welcoming men as members for the first time.
- Establishing a desegregation/busing study committee.
- Supporting the ERA, welfare reform, environmental issues and property tax reform.
- Winning an Emmy for "outstanding achievement in broadcasting" for the 1976 Presidential debates.

VOTER SERVICES

The League continued its focus on registering and educating voters in the 1970s. Members supported ratification of the 26th amendment to the U.S. Constitution, which lowered the legal voting age from 21 to 18. Missouri ratified the amendment on June 14, and it became part of the constitution on June 30, 1971.[2]

One form of education was how to use a new type of voting machine that employed punch cards instead of levers.[3] While such a device had been used in selected areas of St. Louis County in the 1970 general election and a 1971 special election,[4] its use was broadened to all of St. Louis County in 1975.

The League demonstrated how to use the new voting machine at meetings, festivals and shopping centers. The suitcase-like devices were small compared to the lever machines—they were only 21 pounds compared to 1,000 pounds—and were easier to transport to events so they could help as many voters as possible become familiar with the new machine.

By 1973, the League's relationship with the Board of Election Commissioners of St. Louis was so strong that the League was invited to attend the board's regular meeting on June 15. That evening, the commissioners requested that the League help them with a new program to register patients and residents in hospitals, nursing homes and senior citizen homes,[5] places in which voter registration had never taken place before.

CITIZENS INFORMATION/RESOURCE CENTER (CIRC)

As the decade reached its half-way point, it became clear that "the public needed a single place from which to get information about government and politics."[6] Janet Becker came up with the concept for a Citizens Information/Resource Center (CIRC) in 1975. This 501(c)(3) organization would provide "nonpartisan information about governmental operations, issues and services, politics and elections."

The CIRC was staffed by volunteers from the St. Louis County and St. Louis City Leagues who worked thousands of hours every year. One service members provided was a telephone line citizens could call to ask questions such as "How do I register to vote?" "Who is my Senator and how do I contact him?" "What district am I in?" and so on. On average, 50 volunteers answered over 10,000 calls like this annually.[7]

Similarly, the League ran a voter hotline that was open from two days to two weeks—depending on the election—prior to registration deadlines for the primary and general elections and in the weeks leading up to and on every election day. During this time, volunteers answered questions from 500 to 5,000 voters about voting, registration, election laws, and ballot issues.

The CIRC also published various publications on voting, government, and similar topics. The best known of these was the Citizen's Handbook, which grew out of the thousands of phone calls the CIRC received each year. It provided answers to the most frequently asked questions about legislation, taxes, social services, and even consumer and environmental concerns. It was made available for free at libraries, public agencies, government facilities and through organizations and corporations.[8]

In 1978, CIRC was awarded a $13,000 grant from the Danforth Foundation to develop materials and training for its community leadership training workshop project which helped citizens' groups gain organizational skills and knowledge of practical politics and lobbying.[9]

CAMPAIGN FINANCE

The Watergate scandal of the mid-1970s brought the idea of limits on campaign spending into the national spotlight. The Federal Election Campaign Act of 1971, the first legislation since the 1925 Corrupt Practices Act to address finances in politics, was a good first step, but the League felt it needed to go further, and mechanisms to enforce it needed to be put into place. In 1973, the League took the position that

> changes must be made in the methods of financing campaigns, supplying free government services such as mailing, television, printing, travel, office space and staff...campaign financing [must be] representative and responsive. It should ensure the public's right to know, and by limiting the size and type of contributions, eliminate corruption and undue influence and so enable candidates to compete more equitably.[10]

During the summer of 1974, as part of a coalition for campaign finance reform, the League helped circulate a reform petition, which resulted in Proposition 1 appearing on the November ballot in Missouri.

> Proposition 1: "Provides for new campaign financing and election law to replace part of the present Corrupt Practices Act; Limits contributions and expenditures for public office; Requires reporting of such contributions and expenditures; Requires disclosure of economic interests of a candidate and his family; creates a bipartisan Commission to administer the act; Provides penalties for violations."[11]

Despite Missouri voters passing the proposition by an "overwhelming"[12] margin, change was slow in coming. One particularly harsh blow came in 1976, when the U.S. Supreme Court struck "down limits on independent expenditures, overall spending limits on congressional campaigns, and limits on the candidates use of his/her own money" as violations of the First Amendment.[13]

As a result, we saw the rise of Political Action Committees (PACs). Because these groups aren't directly affiliated with a party or candidate, they can skirt campaign finance laws and make unlimited independent expenditures. By joining PACs, corporations, labor unions, trade associations, and other organizations can legally collect and make contributions to candidates, committees, or political parties.

In 1977, the Missouri League began a year-long study of progress in campaign finance reform, which found that there was a conflict of interest between the individual right of privacy and the public right to information when it came to knowing who was financing political campaigns. For these purposes, conflict of interest was defined as a situation in which "an elected or appointed official or candidate is or will be in a position to vote or issue rules or regulations on anything that will result in financial gain or loss for himself, his immediate family or any business with which he, or a member of his immediate family, is associated."[14]

Subsequently, the League came to the consensus that it would "support a financial disclosure to expose potential conflicts of interest among public officials and candidates."[15] They pushed for legislation to apply to all "elected or appointed official[s] or candidate[s] of the state and any political subdivision thereof, and...judges and commissioners of a court of law as well as persons holding appointive offices whose appointment requires confirmation by municipal or County Council or assembly or board of any political subdivision." In addition, financial disclosure should extend to spouses, dependent children and any interests controlled by the candidate or official.

EXTENSION OF THE 1965 VOTING RIGHTS ACT

In 1975, Congress faced a choice: whether or not to renew the special provisions of the Voting Rights Act of 1965, which provided special protection for Black voters, or to expand the law?[16] The League was strongly in favor of expanding the law, but the House and Senate had passed very different versions with conflicting coverage and lengths of renewal.[17] The Senate version was favored as a stronger bill because it would extend the provisions for another five years as well as end the use of literacy tests. It also retained a provision that enabled the attorney general to appoint federal examiners and registrars where valid concerns were raised over residents being denied the right to vote on account of race.[18]

After months of debate in both the House and the Senate, an amended bill was signed by President Gerald Ford on Aug. 6, 1975. The bill went even further than the League could have hoped: it extended the provisions for seven years, created a permanent, nationwide ban on tests or devices and expanded voting rights and protection to other minority groups such as Latinos, Asian Americans, Native Alaskans, and Native Americans.[19]

ELECTION REFORM

In 1972, Democratic Secretary of State James C. Kirkpatrick told League members in Jefferson City, "Today the weakest link in the chain of our democratic process is the administration of our elections." Members were probably thinking, "We've been telling you we need election reform for more than a decade!" Despite several bills sitting in the House and Senate—all encumbered by needless amendments—Missouri remained one of only seven states without statewide permanent voter registration for all elections. At that time, 76 of Missouri's 144 counties (or about 25% of Missouri voters) still lacked county-wide voter registration, much less state-wide.[20]

In June 1973, John H. Poelker, the new Mayor of St. Louis, asked the League for suggestions to improve election procedures. In addition to statewide voter registration, the League called for the elimination of the old practice of numbering ballots and putting black stickers on them, in favor of detachable numbered stub ballots in places where paper ballots were still used. More than half of voters used lever-based voting machines, so a numbering system was no longer needed.[21] In addition, the League supported reform to the order of the names on the ballot, supported assistance for blind or disabled voters, and agreed with the provision that on Election Day any person whose name was stricken from the registration list should be permitted to cast an absentee ballot.[22] Five months later, in November, the League was pleased to see Republican Governor Christopher "Kit" Bond sign legislation that did all that they asked—including finally establishing a statewide voter registration law, which the League had been advocating for 21 years—and then some.[23]

After this victory, the League went back to fighting for additional reforms, including establishment of a permanent election laws revision commission; training of poll workers; open primaries; and change of the primary election date to September. They actively opposed bills that would have limited or made referendum petitions more difficult.

With the passage of the Missouri Comprehensive Election Act of 1977, the League won more long-fought-for victories. "This recodification of Missouri election laws accomplished long sought goals to simplify, clarify and harmonize the laws governing elections."[24] Major changes included:

- Setting specific dates for elections.
- Enabling mail voter registration for specified reasons.[25]
- Barring people convicted of a felony or a misdemeanor connected with the right of suffrage from voting, without a pardon or discharged from probation or parole.
- Enabling employees of schools or libraries or other persons to be appointed deputy registrars in the city and county, providing residents with more than 300 permanent registration locations.
- Allowing registrars in the city to register people in the county and vice versa.
- Permitting voters to vote one time under their old address if they have a change in name or address between when the books close and election day.
- Allowing applications for an absentee ballot to be made in person, by mail, or by a relative within the second degree.[26]

Open Primaries

Open primaries are primaries at which voters do not have to publicly declare their party affiliation—Democrat or Republican are the only options—before entering the voting booth.[27] Instead, "in the secrecy of the voting booth, [the voter can] throw a switch that will permit them to vote for candidates on either the Democratic or Republican ticket."[28] The League had supported this idea since at least 1965[29] for both state and city elections because it upheld the privacy and freedom of choice of the voter and allowed them to be of any party (i.e. independent, etc.) or none at all.

When the League found out that the Board of Election Commissioners was open to the idea, they wasted no time getting it in front of membership for a vote. The open primary was presented as an emergency item at the general meeting on Oct. 29, 1973. It was considered, discussed, and approved by the members in attendance at this meeting. The question, "Do you favor open primary elections in the City of St. Louis?" was immediately presented for consensus and letters were sent to Leagues across the state asking them to consider the idea.[30]

While the St. Louis Leagues were in favor of open primaries, the rest of the state did not follow suit, and so the item failed to be adopted at the 1973 state convention. The following year, however, the State Council voted to extend the St. Louis League position to other local Leagues to support open primaries in city elections.

The St. Louis Board of Election Commissioners had the ability to make the change to open primaries through ordinance or charter amendment, but they had to get the state to agree in order for voting machines to be modified to make the new system possible. Any change to the voting machines would be permanent; they couldn't be adapted to allow open primaries for city elections and then switched back to allow closed primaries for state elections. In order to get the permission needed, the Board filed suit in the Supreme Court of Missouri. Secretary of State James Kirkpatrick ruled against them because he believed it would cause confusion for those still using paper ballots because they would think they could vote for people of both parties, which would invalidate their ballot.[31]

As the next several chapters will show, the League's fight for open primaries continued throughout the next four decades.

EQUAL RIGHTS AMENDMENT (ERA)

Section 1. Equality of rights under the law shall not be denied or abridged by the United States or by any state on account of sex.

Section 2. Congress shall have the power to enforce, by appropriate legislation, the provisions of this article.

Section 3. This amendment shall take effect two years after the date of ratification.

These three seemingly simple lines, adapted in 1943 from Alice Paul's 1923 original wording, asking for women to be treated equally with men under the United States Constitution, set off a firestorm during the 1970s and early 1980s. Already, they had been passed and defeated multiple times in the Senate, but it did not appear that lawmakers thought it necessary to declare women equal under the law. "'We imagined that all the women's organizations would support the measure,' 88-year-old Paul told the *Los Angeles Times* in 1973, 'but almost all of them opposed it.' Many organizations felt the ERA threatened all that they had worked for."[32]

Although many people believed the Equal Protection clause of the Fourteenth Amendment[33] gave women equal protection under the law—especially when taken together with the Civil Rights Act of 1964 and Equal Pay Act of 1972—even those did not provide as much coverage as the ERA would. The ERA was needed for three main reasons. First, once enshrined in the most powerful document in the United States government—the Constitution—it would end the questions surrounding equality of rights of men and women under the law once and for all, giving women equal status to men for the first time in our country's history. Second, it would provide much-needed clarity for the courts in lawsuits against sex discrimination. And third, and, perhaps most importantly, it would make sex "a suspect classification like race. It would require the same high level of 'strict scrutiny' and have to meet the same high level of justification—a 'necessary' relation to a 'compelling' state interest—" to be denied, just as race is now.[34]

Not willing to settle for less, in 1970, a group of feminist leaders from the National Organization for Women (NOW) disrupted hearings of the Senate Subcommittee on Constitutional Amendments, demanding the ERA be heard by the full Congress.[35] Over the next two years, with the help of Congresswoman Martha Griffins, the Senate and then the House passed the deceptively simple measure, releasing it to the states for ratification in 1972 with an arbitrary deadline of seven years to get the required 2/3 ratification before it would become law.[36]

ADVOCATING FOR THE EQUAL RIGHTS AMENDMENT: 1969-1977

As in many other issues, the League in St. Louis was ahead of the rest of the country. Members helped create the Missouri ERA Coalition in 1969 to support the ratification of the ERA[37] and advocate for its passage.[38]

Leaguers were well prepared when the ERA landed in

Missouri's General Assembly in 1972. The League hoped that Missouri would jump on the bandwagon with the 31 other states who were quick to ratify it. However, their enthusiasm dimmed a little when the Missouri Senate Judiciary Committee voted 7-3 against it. In the House, the ERA was amended on the floor to make ratification subject to a statewide vote, which the League supported, but the bill was defeated.[39] Senator Raymond Howard (D-5) promised to introduce the bill again the following year.[40] Rep. Sue Shear (D-76), a League member elected in 1972, would soon become the ERA's strongest advocate.

League members spent the intervening months calling and writing to legislators asking them to vote in favor of the ERA. Those who could hosted coffees and other public events where they were urged to ask candidates for the Missouri House and Senate: "If elected, will you vote for the ratification of the Equal Rights Amendment to the United States Constitution?" Members were encouraged to push until they got a clear answer so there would be a public record of where each person stood.[41]

League board member Mary Greensfelder was appointed the St. Louis area coordinator of the Missouri ERA Coalition in 1973.[42] The 44 organizations in the coalition included the National Council of Jewish Women, the Mid Missouri Chapter of Hadassah, and the National Women's Political Caucus.

Missouri native Phyllis Schlafly led the opposition to the ERA, founding the organization STOP ERA in 1972 (renamed to The Eagle Forum in 1975).[43] In an editorial reply that aired on St. Louis television station KMOV-TV 4 on Sept. 1, 1972, Schlafly claimed that the ERA "is a fraud which will take away from women ... the right to not take a job, the right to care for her own baby in her own home, and to be financially supported by her husband." She claimed it would make women subject to the draft and for combat duty.[44] Schlafly and her followers continued to make false claims. The League, with the help of Osta Underwood, a women's rights organizer in Nashville, Tennessee, refuted each point[45] of a flyer commonly known as "Adam's Rib."[46]

Despite the misinformation being circulated, the LWVUS saw favorable momentum and predicted that the ERA was likely to be law by May 1973. LWVUS President Lucy Wilson Benson said, "Leagues have not forgotten their suffragist roots and in state legislatures where action is still to come, they'll be working for women's rights just as hard as their predecessors lobbied for the right to vote." [47]

Governor Bond was a strong supporter of the ERA and helped launch a ratification campaign in 1973. A House subcommittee headed by DeVerne Calloway (D-St. Louis City) held public hearings on sex discrimination in eight Missouri counties. However, the Senate Judiciary Committee voted in 1973 not to send the amendment to the Senate floor.[48]

Not to be deterred, 30 women's organizations,[49] comprised of more than 400 women—some dressed in old-fashioned costumes and others in modern clothes to show they were working to get the rest of women's rights—marched in 100-degree heat down Olive Street from the Public Library to Kiener Memorial Park on August 25. There, U.S. Congresswoman Martha Griffin (D-MI) and St. Louis lawyer and activist Frankie Freeman spoke at a rally in favor of the ERA.[50]

Around the same time, the Missouri Equal Rights Coalition, a group of organizations—including the Missouri League and all the St. Louis-area Leagues—united in an effort to get the state to pass the ERA and established an office in Jefferson City to house a trained lobbyist funded by the National League. This lobbyist not only fought for the ERA before the Missouri General Assembly but also held special training sessions to teach coalition members and other interested parties about lobbying techniques.⁵¹

Just over a month later, on October 18, STOP ERA founder Phyllis Schlafly took on LWVUS President Lucy Benson on the *Today* show. This was a turning point for the movement in that it took the issue of the ERA from just being a concern of feminists and legislators into America's living rooms and opened the eyes of voters across the country to the issue. After the holidays, the battle in Jefferson City started up again when the legislature convened on Jan. 2, 1974, for a four-month legislative session. The ERA was at that time being discussed in the Senate Rules Committee and the House Constitution Committee. As the ERA was expected to come to the floor in February, the Missouri League held a "legislative day" on January 29. Women from Leagues across the state, including St. Louis' six Leagues, piled into a charter bus to spend the day talking with legislators about why Missouri should ratify the ERA.⁵²

Around this time, opponents of the ERA added to their argument that passage would affect abortion laws and legalize same-sex marriage. Kay Jones of Columbia, Missouri, and other concerned citizens began writing their representatives. As U.S. Senator Marlow W. Cook (R-KY) was quick to reassure Jones, the effect of the ERA on the abortion issue would be:

> None whatsoever. Until men conceive and bear children, any legislative regulation concerning abortions will not offend the Equal Rights Amendment, because until that time women are not being classified for legislative purposes because of their sex, but because of their childbearing capacity... As I see it, any confusion between the Equal Rights Amendment and the

abortion issue results from a misunderstanding of the underlying principle of the ERA.[53]

As for the issue of homosexual marriage, the League issued a clear answer that the word sex in the amendment connotes gender—male or female; it does not connote sexual behavioral patterns.[54]

Committee hearings were scheduled for late February in both chambers. As reported by the Missouri League, "immediately after the Senate hearing the members of the committee voted not to send the resolution to the floor of the Senate. The vote was 7-3, with one member absent. This meant that 21 of our 34 state senators had no opportunity to participate or hear any debate on the issue, or to cast a vote—either for or against—on something as important as a proposed amendment to the U.S. constitution."[55]

In the House, the ERA was finally sent to the floor for debate on May 2. Opponents got an amendment added that required statewide voter approval for ratification, even though many lawmakers and lawyers thought it unconstitutional. At least in part because of this amendment, the ERA was defeated a week later 81-70.

The opposition was certainly gearing up for a fight. In addition to their previous arguments, they were now saying that Section Two of the amendment— "Congress shall have the power to enforce, by appropriate legislation, the provisions of this article"—violated states' rights. The League argued this was a ridiculous notion, given that the exact same wording appears in the 13, 14, 15, 19, 23, 24 and 26th Amendments. As they pointed out, "the 26th Amendment is the one lowering the voting age to 18 that was ratified just last year and some legislators who are concerned about this section in the ERA voted to ratify the 26th Amendment and thought nothing about that state rights part."[56]

By 1974, two more states had ratified the ERA, leaving only five more before it became law. However, the anti-ERA factions launched a powerful campaign, calling the ERA "a subversive communist ploy," despite the fact that four years earlier, the Communist Party USA stated publicly that they were against it.[57] In addition, several powerful groups with millions of dollars at their disposal were founded to defeat the ERA: the Scaife Foundation began the American Legislative Exchange Council; the National Conservative Political Action Committee (NCPAC) was established to elect conservatives to Congress; and Committee for the Survival of a Free Congress was founded by Joseph Coors with the goal of promoting conservative values in the government.

Proponents had new groups supporting them as well. In February 1974, Catholic Women for the Equal Rights Amendment (CW/ERA) was formed with the goal of showing the nation that not all Catholic women were against the ERA. They visited bishops across the country, mailed prayer cards to state legislators, and held "pray-ins" outside the state capitol buildings in unratified states, to show their support and "enlighten the hearts and minds of state legislators to the idea of justice and equality for women so they will have the vision to see that the Equal Rights Amendment is enactment of the deepest Judeo-Christian beliefs."[58]

While these groups worked nationally, back home in Missouri League members were still doing all they could to sway lawmakers, even though the chance for a vote that year was slim. The Missouri Equal Rights Amendment Coalition designated March 18-24 as Missouri ERA Week, seven days of events and meetings with lawmakers in Jefferson City designed to raise awareness of and excitement for the ERA. Activities included boxed lunches with legislators and a rally on March 20 at the Hotel Governor in Jefferson City that was a "show of strength for women across the state."[59]

The year passed with the usual activities, but the ERA didn't even come close to a vote in Missouri. Surveys taken under the direction of Governor Bond showed that the people of Missouri differed in opinion from their representatives who kept blocking the ERA. The first survey taken in August showed that "65% of people favored ratification, 26% opposed, and the remainder had no opinion." By November, that number jumped to 81% in favor of ratification, 14% opposed, and 5% with no opinion.[60] The November elections offered a glimmer of hope that the legislature might finally align with the will of the people when three new female Representatives—all Democrats from Kansas City—were elected to the House: Dotty Doll, Della Hadley and Doris Quinn.[61]

Before the year was even over, the National League declared its goal to be "Ratification by 5 in '75," putting pressure on the remaining non-ratified states. "The year 1975 will be crucial for ERA," said LWVUS President Ruth Clusen, noting that only two other constitutional amendments, the 16th and 22nd, took four years to ratify. 1975 will be the fourth year for the ERA. "We must maintain our momentum,"[62] she said.

The Missouri Equal Rights Amendment Coalition formed a political action committee, the Missouri Citizens for Constitutional Democracy, in 1975. This committee provided financial support to pro-ERA candidates for the Missouri state legislature, especially those in five districts with anti-ERA senators.

Groups such as Phyllis Schlafly's newly-renamed Eagle Forum and the newly established National Right to Life Political Action Committee began emphasizing fear-based tactics in their messaging and in newspaper advertisements, a tactic the League "expressed deep concern" about, saying:

> Inflammation of fears through distortions, half-truths and false statements is unforgivable regardless of one's point of view. Our whole system of government is based on the principle of legislators voting their convictions. If we disagree with those positions, the proper place to seek redress is the ballot box—not by physical threats or harassment. We deplore the actions of those who have resorted to such tactics. [63]

In addition, STOP ERA activists in Missouri participated in the "Bread Project," in which members baked loaves of bread and presented them to legislators with the note, "to the breadwinners from the breadmakers," to emphasize their traditional roles as women and homemakers. Apple pie and jam were also handed out with the message, "Preserve us from Congressional jam; vote against the E.R.A. sham."[64]

But those weren't the only dirty tricks going on. According to the Central County League newsletter: "It seems that some members of the opposition have been calling ERA supporters, saying they were writing articles for national publications, but asking questions regarding strategy and plans" in order to gain information. They urged all members who are contacted to take down the name and affiliation of the person and call the publication to verify the caller was real before answering any questions. [65]

In Jefferson City, Governor Bond and the Missouri Equal Rights Amendment Coalition were working hard to get the ERA up for a vote. To supporters' joy, the House voted to ratify it

82-75; the Senate however, voted no, just as they would each year it came to them through 1982.[66] Disappointment among League members was palpable. The Central County League shared the strong reaction from the editor of the North County League newsletter: "There had been a discussion about whether or not to put a word in this bulletin about the recent defeat of the ERA in the Missouri Senate. After considerable thought, I decided that the word I wanted to say on the matter was socially unacceptable. I wish us better luck in 1977."[67]

The League spent 1976 planning and fundraising for the fight that was sure to come in 1977. In addition to selling ERA T-shirts, bracelets and necklaces, on May 16, the St. Louis County League hosted wine and cheese fundraising events. One at Millie Cohn's home on Westmoreland featured none other than actor, feminist and ERA supporter Alan Alda. In addition to charming the crowd, he impressed attendees by reminding them that the ERA is important to everyone, men and women. "We must remind others that the ERA is not a woman issue, but a people issue," he said. The events raised $7,000.[68]

Meanwhile, more groups were forming to press for ERA ratification. Chief among them were Missouri Citizens for Constitutional Democracy, a multi-partisan organization founded to support pro-ERA candidates for the state legislature in the 1976 election—something the ERA Coalition was barred from doing by law. Together, the two groups decided on a change of strategy; since changing minds wasn't working, they would change the people in office. The coalition had "shadow senators"—all female—in each state Senate district who kept them up to date about the Senate race and its candidates.[69]

The fight for Missouri came to a head in 1977, and the eyes of the nation were watching because it was a "top target state" in the battle to get four more state ratifications. This is because the vote in 1975 was only four short in the Senate. When Indiana closed the gap to only three more states needed, the pressure mounted.

The leading advocates and opponents in the Senate that year were both women: Democrat Harriett Woods from St. Louis (pro) and Republican Mary Gant from Kansas City (against). Another Missouri woman crucial to the 1977 outcome was Doris Quinn, a one-term state representative who ran as an independent in the special election held in February 1977. She was not reelected, a blow to proponents and to the cause because she was expected to be a strong advocate. "'It looked like the amendment had an excellent shot if we could win those three vacancies,' Senator Woods observed. 'But when we lost two of them, that started a slide. If you don't have the momentum, people dive off the ship.'"[70]

Lobbying and fundraising activities were common that year and included parties, letter writing and persuasion campaigns, local fundraisers, phone banks, and canvassing. In addition, the "Show Me Equality Caravan," modeled after a successful campaign in Indiana, toured every county in Missouri, was a gathering point for public meetings, and provided educational materials and assistance to smaller coalitions. The Coalition worked with labor unions and groups such as the Teamsters Joint Council 13, the Communications Workers of America, the UAW, and the Missouri State Labor Council to help with fundraising, lobbying, and raising awareness of the Amendment.[71]

On Feb. 2, 1977, both sides of the ERA debate testified before the Missouri Senate Committee on Constitutional Amendments. Two weeks later, when the ERA came to a vote on March 15, it lost in the Senate 12-22, with six more votes than it had in 1975. This essentially spelled the end of the ERA campaign in Missouri, even if the rumored extension were to pass. It was the last time the amendment went to the floor of the Senate, though the League and other advocates continued raising money and pushing for ratification in other states.[72]

1978-1982: SUPPORT AND FUNDRAISING

In 1978, 10,000 women marched in Washington D.C. (along with an estimated 100,000 more in their hometowns) to demand equal rights. The ERA was granted a deadline extension from March 22, 1979, to June 30, 1982.[73] NOW urged organizations that host conferences to boycott states that have not ratified the ERA, which Missouri Attorney General John Ashcroft said was illegal but that a judge later allowed.[74] The St. Louis Leagues supported the boycott but also understood not everyone could honor it, so they offered their homes as "ERA Bed and Breakfasts" to about a dozen travelers so that they wouldn't have to spend money on hotel rooms and food in an unratified state.[75]

The St. Louis Leagues also planned a full slate of fundraising activities, including a non-party where people paid not to attend, a sing along, a cocktail party with a Las Vegas theme, and a June 1 "Homemakers for ERA" kitchen tour.[76] The tour was by far the biggest draw, selling 700 tickets and bringing St. Louisans into the homes of eight women who support the ERA to look around and learn. The event, which also included a bake sale and plant sale, netted $4,000.[77]

Other events the League participated in during 1978 and 1979 were the Missouri Equal Rights Amendment Coalition grand rally in Jefferson City on April 30,[78] a lunch and reception with U.S. Senator Barbara Mikulski—where she asked, "If the people of Missouri could give us Harry Truman and the Fair Deal, why can't they give us ERA and a square deal?"—[79] and two major fundraising dinners with special guests, actress/

singer Polly Bergen and humor columnist Erma Bombeck.[80]

The Democrats continued to support the ERA while the Republicans, led by future president Ronald Reagan, reversed their 40-year stance in 1980 to come out against it.[81] After the Missouri ERA Coalition failed to oust enough Senators who voted against the ERA, the amendment's state sponsors officially removed it from Missouri's legislative calendar because they didn't have the needed votes - but not without a last word from sponsor Senator Harriett Woods: "A body dominated by men should not deny a vote on this issue, which is so significant to both men and women."[82]

For the next two years, the League worked with the Missouri Equal Rights Amendment Coalition,[83] until they disbanded in 1982 when the ERA deadline expired three states short of ratification.[84] While the ERA appeared to be dead, it would be revived in 2005 when it was reintroduced to Congress. The most recent push for ratification will be chronicled in Chapter 7.

CITY REDEVELOPMENT

As St. Louis moved into the 1970s and more citizens fled to the suburbs, concern over the fate of the City of St. Louis increased. Under the leadership of Ann Burns, familiar concerns such as building code enforcement, minimum housing standards, zoning ordinances and relocation of families due to highway construction/housing demolition carried over from the previous decade. New items such as reorganization of the city housing division, disposition of tax delinquent properties, lighting and public housing were taken up for study.[85] Two related areas dominated the League's attention: housing and redlining.

Housing

Advancements in the early part of the decade included legislation signed into law by St. Louis City Mayor Alfonso J. Cervantes in 1969 and 1970 to increase the city's housing inventory, redevelopment of the West End and a land utilization law.[86] In addition, "Operation Breakthrough," a program of the U.S. Department of Housing and Urban Development, built two "model cities," displacing Black residents in the Mill Creek area of St. Louis.[87] League records showed members supported adding 464 new townhouses and apartments to the city's housing inventory.[88] Old neighborhoods such as Jeff-Vander-Lou, LaSalle-Park, and DeSoto-Carr were rehabilitated. This included new construction, as well as turnkey units for the elderly and families, all of which added up to thousands of new homes in the city.

Toward the end of the decade, the League intervened in a dispute between St. Louis County Supervisor Gene McNary and the U.S. Department of Housing and Urban Development (HUD) over the use of $8.9 million in community development funds in St. Louis County. HUD refused to release the funds after finding the county's plan to provide low- and middle-income housing unacceptable because McNary wouldn't guarantee his plan would include at least 400 new subsided housing units to help solve the area's housing crisis.[89] Against League advice, McNary countered by filing a lawsuit requiring HUD to release the funds, which only resulted in the money being tied up and future planning stalled, a situation that didn't help anyone. HUD Secretary Patricia Harris responded that she welcomed the suit, saying she would be interested in "having [it] brought to the attention of the entire country and having its outcome serve as a guideline for National Housing policy."[90]

On Aug. 9, 1979, the League urged both sides to remember the greater good and their shared commitment "to work for fair housing and expansion of the housing supply for low-income families... at every level of government." The League also advised that McNary call a meeting of mayors, housing officials and local and county officials to "cooperatively plan for fair disbursement of low- and moderate-income housing throughout the county, [with] the goal [of creating] a mutually acceptable plan that would also meet federal requirements."[91] In the end, it took the intervention of U.S. Senator Thomas Eagleton (D-MO) to resolve the issue. The senator had heard from representatives of municipalities caught in the middle of the dispute and appealed to HUD on their behalf. HUD released the funds under the condition that municipalities be allowed to apply for them, rather than the county receiving it all and allocating it as it sees fit.[92]

The decade ended on a high note when St. Louis was one of 35 cities to compete for funds to address urban crises from the National Endowment for the Humanities. Thanks in part to the League, St. Louis was one of the 21 winning cities. The League used the grant "to educate citizens about the root causes of urban problems and ways to improve the urban condition by developing humanistic approaches to urban problem solving." Their focus was on the conflict between St. Louis City and County and how they could work together "to improve revitalization, planning and stabilization of the metro area." The two groups came together for a series of talk shows on KSD radio to discuss topics like housing, transportation, education, employment, history and how the city and county could work together better.[93]

REDLINING

Racial discrimination in housing and lending practices in St. Louis dates back to 1915 when a petition was presented to the Board of Election Commissioners asking them to pass an ordinance creating separate housing blocks for white and Black residents. Though the stated reason was "to prevent ill feeling, conflict and collisions" between the races, it clearly was nothing more than thinly veiled racism.[94]

As time wore on, mortgage brokers and banks began color coding maps "according to their racial composition and the supposed risk of lending in each of them...they were coded red ("hazardous"), yellow ("definitely declining"), blue ("still desirable") and green ("best")." Because areas in the red—predominantly Black neighborhoods—were to be avoided, the word redlining developed into a term for any "policy that further segregates minority groups through government-issued zoning and programs."[95] The result of these policies was that Black "homebuyers often had difficulty getting access to lower interest rates and down payments. The bravest fought the barriers with legal maneuvers, by using straw buyers, or by passing for white," wrote Jeannette Cooperman in a *St. Louis Magazine* article on the history of segregation in St. Louis.[96]

Although the Federal Fair Housing Act of 1968 was supposed to put an end to the practice of discrimination in lending, redlining continued unabated. The LWV opposed the practice, speaking out rather forcefully in the mid-to-late 1970s. For many years, they had been conducting meetings with the Savings Service Corporation, which gave high risk loans, and with other companies unafraid to bridge the color divide to help people identified by Consolidated Neighborhood Services Corp, a community coalition that collected cases in which people of color were denied home loans due to their race. They also worked closely with local HUD Director John Bullock and with the East-West Gateway Coordinating Council to monitor how block grants were being planned and used.[97]

On Sept. 9, 1977, the League testified before the Missouri Senate Urban Affairs Committee against the Home Mortgage

Disclosure Act of 1975 because it did not include how many loans they refused to make among the information lending institutions were legally required to make available to the public. They explained:

> We see [redlining] as part of the urban disease of decay. It stands in the way of city dwellers who seek to improve their neighborhoods. It causes some people to leave the city and discourages others from moving into the city. We appreciate the recent state legislation which was aimed at control of redlining in the insurance area. However, we fear there are loopholes in this bill which allow insurance rates to rise to prohibitive highs, which will prove to be as destructive to interest in city property as before.[98]

Not long after, the Missouri Human Rights Commission became involved and supported the League's efforts to "eliminate discrimination because of race, creed, color or sex in the categories of employment, public accommodations and housing." They succeeded in getting three bills into the legislature as "do pass" that not only enforced this idea but added discrimination on the bases of disability or sex as well.[99]

While these and other efforts were noble, nothing has yet fully stopped practices like redlining in the mortgage industry in St. Louis. Even 50 years after it was supposed to legally end, loan discrimination persists. According to the *St. Louis Post-Dispatch*, in 2018, Black people who applied for a conventional mortgage were still "2.5 times more likely to be denied than non-Hispanic whites."[100] The League continues to oppose such practices and will continue to do so until all people, regardless of color and other identifying factors, have an equal opportunity to finance their home in the St. Louis neighborhood of their choice.

TRANSIT

The St. Louis LWV began studying transit issues in the area in the 1960s. Thanks to a $300,000 rapid transit study, the League and area transit officials had known since the mid-1960s that St. Louis was in need of some kind of mass transit system beyond its current bus service. The two main authorities in the area were the Bi-State Development Agency, which was formed in 1949 to run St. Louis's bus system and function as its Port Authority, and the East-West Gateway Coordinating Council, which was formed in 1965 to "facilitate area-wide planning in such matters as can be solved effectively by local governments acting in concert." [101]

In 1968, the six metropolitan Leagues reached a consensus to "support...upgrading the present mass transit system and the need of a rapid transit system...[that] guarantees these criteria: increased speed, comfort, safety, convenience, reliability, reasonable fares, preservation of community character, and compatibility with future rapid transit options."[102] To this end, League members were asked to write letters to their congressmen urging them to vote for passage of the urban mass transit bill, which was approved in October 1970. As a result of this bill, the Department of Transportation put Bi-State in charge of developing a $38 million plan for the future that would upgrade the current transit system in the area as a stop-gap measure until a rapid transit system could be built—in 10-20 years.[103] After study, the League's Metropolitan Council Transit Committee approved the program but suggested it could go further by including more all-transit streets and extending controlled curb lanes and park-ride routes.

In 1971, the League voted to study current mass transit proposals and develop criteria for evaluating future ones. In 1972, the position statement on mass transit was updated to add specifics supporting the criteria, explain why government funding and participation is desirable, how such a system should be financed and include consideration for the environment so that there is as little disruption as possible.[104]

The League also participated in a massive public relations and education effort to help restore Bi-State's poor reputation and earn the trust of voters who would need to pass bond issues, especially in predominantly Black areas of St. Louis and East St. Louis, where residents were likely to be unhappy about higher taxes and possible displacement during construction of a rapid transit system.[105]

Over the next few years, all agencies involved were busy. Bi-State purchased a fleet of new buses, which went into service during the summer of 1973 and participated in studies on the expansion of service lines; the St. Louis County Public Transportation Commission began a pilot program of a demand-response bus system (DIAL-a-RIDE) with a recommended 11 park and ride express routes;[106] and the East-West Gateway Coordinating Council began a new one-year transit study (1975-1976) aimed at defining the mass transit needs of the St. Louis region and determining the best possible alternative transit systems for the area.[107]

On Sept. 7, 1977, League representative Merle Goldstein spoke before the Missouri Senate Urban Affairs Committee to affirm the League's ongoing support of a mass transit system:

> An adequate transit system is essential for the life of an urban area such as St. Louis. No longer is it

just the transit dependent—that is, the poor, the elderly, the handicapped, the young and those who have limited or no access to the use of an automobile—who need to use a transit system, but larger numbers of people should have access to such a system. Recognition of our need to conserve energy and our need to protect our environment makes the case for mass transit that much more compelling. We have no alternative but to limit the use of automobiles by increasing the availability of mass transit. The state must share in this responsibility.[108]

With no easy answers or quick changes in sight, League members continued to serve on the East-West Gateway Coordinating Council's transit action committee, on a Bi-State committee studying county routes, and monitor County Transportation Commission meetings.[109] Advocacy for mass transit would continue into the 1980s and 1990s, when St. Louis finally got a light-rail system, which will be discussed in subsequent chapters.

WELFARE

In the first half of the 1970s, the League focused on finding alternatives to the welfare system. Through study, members found that most welfare recipients still live in poverty; the system excludes many poor people, especially working poor and those without children; standards and eligibility requirements vary widely across the country; and the way the system is structured gives recipients no real incentive to earn money.[110]

Instead, the League favored a system of income maintenance, regardless of whether it provided payments based on need (guaranteed income) or to everyone regardless of income (credit income tax or children and family allowances). Members closely watched debate on welfare bills before the U.S. Congress. In early 1973, a new system of federalized minimum income for the aged, blind, and disabled passed with an effective date of January 1974, so the League switched focus to educate people on it.[111] Meanwhile, the League supported tax relief for the elderly and others in need. Repeals of taxes on intangibles for individuals and nonprofit organizations as well as a personal property tax on household goods were passed in November 1972.[112]

In 1975, the League spoke out against a government plan to cut back on spending by reducing the food stamp program by $325 million. "Under the new guidelines, all families receiving food stamps, regardless of size or income, will have to pay a flat 30% of adjusted net earnings for stamps, the maximum allowed by law. Elderly persons or single persons on fixed incomes would be hurt more than persons with large families."[113] Much to everyone's relief, this plan was blocked.[114]

CHARTER EFFORTS

OLIVETTE HOME RULE

In August 1974, the city council of Olivette in St. Louis County decided that, since the area had grown beyond the population of 5,000 threshold, they wished to have home rule—and thus a more independent government—and voted to create a charter commission.[115] Six months later, council members sought the League's support to help win over voters in preparation for the April 1, 1975, municipal election.[116] Voters agreed and approved the creation of the charter commission 784-197.[117] Over the next nine months, the commission met to draft the Olivette City Charter. On March 23, 1976, voters approved it by a vote of 788-158.[118]

Creve Coeur Home Rule

Several League members in Creve Coeur supported home rule on a similar schedule to Olivette. In December 1974, the Creve Coeur Citizen's Government Review Committee submitted a report recommending the city try to become a charter city.[119] In February 1975, the Creve Coeur Board of Aldermen called for an April 1 election to put the issue to the voters.[120] Voters approved creation of a charter commission 850-145.[121] After seeking public input and considering several types of government—some controversial— the charter was turned over to voters on Dec. 30, 1975.[122] In a Feb. 10, 1976, special election, voters approved home rule 760-170.[123]

St. Louis County Charter Revision

In 1979, the League followed with great interest the St. Louis County Charter Commission's study of the charter which was adopted April 2, 1968. The impetus for the study was concern from the Democrats on the County Council—who held the majority—that the governing body wasn't set up properly. They alleged it was too small, underpaid, and lacked necessary legal and professional advice.[124] Moreover, they said the Council did not have additional powers, which were held by the supervisor.[125]

In response, a 14-member commission, including former County Supervisor Lawrence K. Roos, was appointed to investigate the matter. The League was "the only organized group to take special interest in the commission's work...other special interest groups...were determined to maintain the status quo."[126]

After conducting its own study on the charter, the League offered a set of 14 proposed recommendations to the commission, including increasing the size of the County Council from seven to somewhere between nine and 11 to provide better citizen representation, filling vacancies by election instead of appointment, and setting Council member salaries independently of what the county supervisor is paid.[127]

A final set of amendments appeared on the November 6 ballot. Voters approved minimum training standards for fire fighters, approved a raise for Council members and that vacancies on the council be filled by election, much to the League's delight.[128]

NON-PARTISAN COURT PLAN

The League's involvement in a non-partisan court plan began in the 1940s when one was first adopted by Missouri voters. The idea was to ensure "judges would be appointed on their merit and once selected, be assured freedom from political influence and threat and freedom from conducting campaigns so they could devote themselves full-time to the work of being a judge."[129] But there was one catch: the plan applied only to the Missouri Supreme Court; the Court of Appeals and St. Louis City Circuit Court; criminal corrections and probate courts, and the circuit and probate courts of Jackson County. St. Louis County and smaller areas were left out on the theory that because everyone knew everyone in those areas, they could decide for themselves who was suited to be a judge.[130]

The League believed that all area judges should be included. In 1961, members voiced their support for an extension of the non-partisan court plan via petition as proposed in House Bill 28.[131] Citing the fact that the urban populations of St. Louis County and Kansas City were growing, it only made sense to include them; not long after other urban areas in the state would catch up, so why not cover everyone now?

As usual, the government was slow to act. In late 1965, the U.S. Citizens Conference was "held to examine the Missouri judicial system under the nonpartisan court plan. A broad plan for reorganizing the Missouri court system was approved in December by a citizens' committee." The League was particularly interested in the proposals related to how the plan would extend the non-partisan system to St. Louis County, what provisions it made for the retirement, pensions and salaries of judges, and how judges found to be doing wrong would be disciplined and, if needed, removed from the court.[132] The required 25,000 petition signatures were gathered, and the issue was put to voters. Unfortunately, the wording on the ballot was very obscure and so the plan did not get the majority vote needed at the polls, failing 81,683 to 91,630.[133]

In 1970, the League again took up the issue. As before, members gathered the required number of signatures, and the question was placed on the ballot. While the wording was the same, the League undertook a vast educational campaign to ensure voters understood what they were being asked[134] and this time it passed. Three years later, voters approved a second extension covering judges in Clay and Platte counties. When the Missouri Constitution was amended in 1976, the plan and both amendments were enshrined in its wording.[135]

EDUCATION

Many of the educational issues the League was involved in in the 1960s continued into the 1970s. For example, as the Junior College system continued to grow—from 700 students in 1962 to over 18,000 in 1970—tax increases and bond issues to fund it repeatedly came before voters with full League support.[136]

In addition, the League continued its commitment to raising the educational standards of St. Louis schools by seeking out ways the community could be involved with St. Louis Public Schools.[137] In Kirkwood, the League went so far as to gain consensus on the issue of education, supporting quality staffing and equal education opportunity for all students—the gifted and the "slow learner" alike—including those not going to college."[138]

LOCAL COUNTY SCHOOL DISTRICT STUDIES

In 1972, the Central County League conducted school study surveys of the Clayton, Rockwood and Ladue School Districts.[139] They focused on seven key questions:

1. What are our goals for public education?
2. What should be included in the school curriculum to help meet these goals?
3. What should be included in the school physical facilities to meet these goals?
4. What special services should a school provide to help meet these goals?
5. How can the staff effectively meet these goals?
6. What should the role of the school board be? How can it be fulfilled?
7. What should we as citizens do to meet the school districts' goals?[140]

As each survey was completed in 1973, it was published, with distribution of between 300-1,500.[141] Parkway was supposed to be part of the study, but a coordinator couldn't be found, so its school district wasn't surveyed until 1976.[142]

The following year, the League secured funding to expand upon this work by undertaking a mammoth two-year study of

44 school districts of St. Louis City, St. Louis County, Jefferson County, and St. Charles County. The goal was to "show availability of curriculum, school financing, enrollment data, and special services provided." The committee's findings were published in a free booklet in late fall 1974.[143]

SPECIAL SCHOOL DISTRICT SURVEY

Beginning in fall 1976, the Metropolitan Council undertook a unique survey to learn more about the County's Special School District, the only district of its kind in the U.S. The goal was to be able to teach citizens about this valuable resource, which includes area special and vocational-technical schools. They began by conducting interviews with administrators, parents, and teachers, observing classes, and other forms of research.[144]

It quickly became clear that this project would be of value to all areas of St. Louis, so the five local Leagues all agreed to participate.[145] The bulk of the research was conducted during the fall of 1976 and winter 1977.

The Special School District agreed to have the survey results printed by one of their vocational technical printing classes as a real-life learning experience. More than 25,000 copies of the 28-page booklet were distributed to the League's mailing list, and copies were available to the public at libraries, doctors' offices, realtors, and community organizations.

The results included "information on the history of the...district, state and federal laws regarding the special education, the district's administration, all programs for the handicapped, the vocational technical program, various services, district financing, facilities, and school-community relations."[146]

Funding of Public Education

Noble as this commitment was, like so many other things, its success came down to one thing: money. After nearly a year of extensive study of financing and availability of educational opportunities in Missouri, the League recognized the vast inequality of funding across the 596 school districts in the state.[147] In 1974, they came to consensus favoring increased state funding for education, but also realized that people were not necessarily willing or able to support tax increases. The state of Missouri was then pondering if there was a way to raise and distribute education monies on a statewide basis. The League supported this so long as there was no time limit imposed, local districts were able to control the funds they were given, and that the state set a comprehensive K-12 standard for all school districts, including established minimums for graduation.[148]

Over the next three years, League members did all they could to raise awareness of the funding inequities. In 1977, the Missouri General Assembly approved a new formula for distributing state aid to local schools that included many of the items advocated for by the League, including "guaranteed per student income, and a pupil count based on enrollment and attendance with the inclusion of hours attended by part time and summer school pupils."[149]

Busing

Busing, the area's "solution" to desegregating schools, continued to be an issue. On the April 7, 1970, ballot—the same one as a major Junior College tax increase—was a $4 million bond issue from the St. Louis Board of Education for critical construction of 12 schools. At that time, approximately 1,200 students were being bused. Passage of the bond issue would prevent another

600 students from being moved to other schools.[150]

The Kirkwood League was particularly active on this issue, knowing as they did that "the federal government has cited Kirkwood as one of several Missouri districts having de facto segregation and warned of possible action."[151] In that school district alone—one in a mostly white, affluent area of St. Louis County—only seven schools could be considered fully integrated; eight others had less than a dozen Black students in total.

Results like these were partially due to the positions of leaders such as Missouri Senator Earl Blackwell, a Democrat from Hillsboro. They supported a national constitutional convention to amend the constitution to stop any student from being "assigned to, nor compelled to attend, any particular public school on account of race, religion, color, or national origin."[152]

While Blackwell was known to be "a flamboyant maverick"[153] and such a petition was unlikely to ever become law, the League spoke out against it, citing the "hysteria developing around the question of busing school children," as a potential flashpoint for violence. The League believed such measures were dangerous as they violated "our strong belief in constitutional government and the separation of legislative, executive and judicial powers" and undermined "a commitment to a free public education system which provides equal opportunity for all."[154]

The debate over busing in St. Louis moved to the courts in February 1972, when *Liddell vs. Board of Education* brought the issue into the national spotlight. The case was a class-action lawsuit filed by five Black St. Louis families in the U.S. District Court for the Eastern District of Missouri.[155] The families argued that the St. Louis public school system was segregating its schools on purpose and providing fewer resources to schools with a large number of minority students.

The case went on for three years—during which most of the 69,500 Black students remained segregated.[156] The state government attempted to put an end to the need for the case by proposing legislation commonly known as "the anti-busing bill," but the House and the Senate could not come to a resolution. After being "talked to death"[157] in the Senate, it was put aside, much to the League's dismay. *Liddell vs. Board of Education* was finally settled in 1975 by U.S. District Judge James Meredith. The result was a plan that included increasing the number of Black teachers in the school system, rezoning school districts to make them more diverse, and adding magnet schools in St. Louis. That wasn't enough for the St. Louis chapter of the NAACP. It filed objections and sought to intervene,[158] even going so far as to suggest that a third of St. Louis' Black students be bused into the county from the city.[159] In 1980, a judge agreed, beginning a busing system that would last for more than 40 years.

ENVIRONMENT

The League's concern for environmental matters, while not slight by any means in the 1960s, grew considerably in the 1970s as it expanded from water and air pollution to encompass emerging issues such as solid waste, energy and land use. Pollution took center stage nationally as well, when President Richard Nixon kicked off the decade by signing a bill creating a three-person Council on Environmental Quality to help guide national policy on water, air and land pollution.

WATER POLLUTION

Betty Wilson chaired the League's very active environmental quality committee and was appointed by Governor Hearnes to serve on the Missouri Clean Water Commission.[160] She made sure the League remained steadfast in its commitment to the Metropolitan Sewer District and doing what they could to help MSD improve the St. Louis area's water supply.

The League worked to help MSD move up opening of its secondary treatment plants on the Mississippi to comply with an aggressive new deadline from the Federal Water Pollution Control Administration. The second primary treatment plant at Bissell Point was way off schedule when it finally began operations on Oct. 19, 1970.[161]

In 1972, the U.S. government signaled for the first time since 1948 that it was taking pollution seriously with the Clean Water Act of 1972, a set of federal government standards everyone had to meet for wastewater treatment. As a result, MSD was required to make major, expensive changes in its treatment system. Despite federal and state grants, some of the cost had to be passed on to customers, who were vocal in their opposition. The League stepped in, urging better communication between MSD and St. Louis residents and recognition of citizen perspectives. The League was clear that people had to have a voice in decisions and a way to appeal those they could not live with.[162]

At the same time, the League lobbied in support of bills to bring Missouri clean water laws in compliance with federal requirements, to allow third- and fourth-class counties not served by MSD to establish their own sewer districts, and to require factories and businesses producing waste that shouldn't go into sewers to provide their own holding tanks.[163] They also educated members and the public about changes in acceptable wastewater standards under the Clean Water Act.[164]

From 1973-1974, the League, along with the East-West Gateway Coordinating Council, St. Louis County, and the federal government, undertook a comprehensive study of how wastewater management was handled in the St. Louis area and the problems facing residents, especially the severe water pollution problems in west, southwest and north St. Louis County.[165] They found that there were eight private sewer companies and five municipal sewer companies in St. Louis County alone. Two of the watershed areas, Grand Glaze Creek and Fish Pot Creek, were classified as "the worst effluent pollution problem in the state" in 1970 by the Missouri Water Pollution Board.[166]

As a result of the study, the League concluded that the area essentially had two options: establish a new sewer district or annex the areas currently not covered by MSD into their service area. As either would take time, for the present, they suggested a regional approach to stormwater and wastewater management in the area, unified standards and developing methods for cooperation with surrounding counties and locations outside of MSD's jurisdiction.[167]

Ultimately, though, the League believed that extending MSD's coverage area was the best solution."[168] The next step was to try to get MSD's annexation efforts placed on the ballot in the areas of St. Louis County that would be affected. MSD deemed the League "the most 'credible' organization favoring annexation" and asked it to lead a petition drive and education campaign on behalf of the measure. Citizens agreed with the need, and the measure passed 6-1 on May 10, 1977.

While the League's county-wide work on wastewater is what got the most press, it also focused on local issues. One such example was the dire need for a solution to water pollution along Deer Creek in Webster Groves. In October 1977, the Webster Groves League held a public meeting to address the waterway's infestation of rats, fecal coliform bacteria, and mosquitoes, which could be considered a public health crisis. Working with the Webster Department of Environmental services and local government, the League advocated for limited governmental financial aid to help stop abuses by business and expedite clean-up efforts.[169]

Air Pollution

Major victories for cleaner air in the late 1960s included a new regional control system established by the Air Quality Act of 1967, the establishment of air quality control standards for the Missouri portion of the St. Louis Air Quality Control Region, court-ordered enforcement of clean coal burning regulations for Peabody Coal, a new law against leaf burning in all but the outlying area of St. Louis County, the adoption of methods for notifying citizens of air pollution alerts, stricter air quality standards for sulfur dioxide and particulate, and a crackdown on air pollution by jet planes using Lambert-St. Louis International Airport.[170] The League still had a lot yet to do in the 1970s.

As with the regional approach to water, the League quickly realized that tackling air pollution problems was going to be easier if the St. Louis area worked with its neighbors to develop an interstate approach. As such, the League supported the establishment of national industrial emission standards, as well as regional air pollution emission standards that could be legally enforced on the entities doing the polluting. They also advocated for a single regional agency to set and enforce these standards,[171] to require top-notch control technology for new fuel burning installations in the Mississippi portion of the St. Louis Air Quality Control region and for the state of Illinois to mirror Missouri's standards.[172]

In 1974, the League established an Environmental Quality committee comprised of members of all six local Leagues to monitor and be spokespeople in their communities on environmental issues. Not long after, Esther Clark, a League member who served on its metropolitan Environmental Quality committee, was successful in gaining enforcement of the ban on leaf burning in St. Louis County, even when representatives of several municipalities pushed for it to be lifted at a Missouri Air Conservation Commission meeting.[173]

The following year, the League's attention turned to major environmental problems caused by area cement plants.[174] At issue were the practices of Portland Cement, a company with facilities in both north and south St. Louis County, and their compliance (or lack thereof) with St. Louis County emission standards and their reluctance to be open with the public. In their role as citizen advocates, the League provided the Air Appeal Board and the Missouri Air Conservation Commission with information to inquire into the company's handling of required testing, their reluctance to place a continuing monitor device on their main stack, and the status of dust control equipment they had agreed to purchase.

The result was a nearly year-long investigation that resulted in court action, including by Esther Clark and her husband, Jim, a chemist and former employee of the air pollution control division of the County Health Department. Although Portland Cement claimed new monitoring devices were not necessary, citizens who lived near the North County plant reported being "snowed with cement" from the plant. Eventually, due to constant pressure from the Clarks and Irma Bosley, the head of a citizen group monitoring the company's activities, Portland Cement agreed to fix issues with five of its six stacks.[175] An unexpected outcome of this advocacy work is that the St. Louis City Air Pollution Control Department invited Clark and Bosley to attend smoke observer school. They became the first women ever certified as smoke observers in St. Louis City—and possibly in state history.[176]

Another local company who was in hot water with the

League for trying to skirt air pollution regulations was National Lead Industries, Inc. In September 1977, the League filed a brief as amicus curiae (friend of the court) with the St. Louis County Air Pollution Appeals Board against National Lead's appeal of the revocation of the operating permit for their #6 boiler, which was not in compliance with air pollution laws. They promised it would not be used except in case of emergency while the company changed their processes. The League argued National Lead should either be forced to bring the boiler into compliance, or the board should uphold the revocation; the industry shouldn't be allowed to "bank" pollution.[177]

SOLID WASTE

In the 1970s, landfills became more than just places to store unwanted trash and forget about it. An August 1969-July 1970 survey conducted by the Division of Health of Missouri raised public awareness with its startling findings. Results "indicated that Missouri residents are generating 4.2 million tons of solid waste per year (excluding uncollected agricultural and mining wastes) for an average of 4.9 pounds per person per day. St. Louis County residents generate 5.5 pounds per person daily."[178] What was worse, only 13 of the 457 solid waste disposal areas in St. Louis met health standards (not including 2,600 roadside dumps). Despite its illegality and potential air pollution problems, open burning was found as a regular practice at three of every four managed dumps; similarly, despite water pollution from seepage and runoff, solid waste was placed directly into groundwater at one of every five dumps.

When these results were released, the Central County League took a firm stance that "improved solid waste management should be a prime importance to the citizens of our area," and implored citizens to join them in educational programs aimed at reuse, or reclamation, and recycling.[179] They called for "state and regional standards for storage, collection, transportation, processing, and disposing of solid wastes [to] be stringent and strictly enforced; long range, flexible solid waste management plans [to] be mandatory, approved by the appropriate governmental body, and implemented with expediency," as well as oversight by an existing agency to be put in place.[180]

After studying the matter—including how solid waste might be used as a fuel to generate electricity—the other five local Leagues took consensus on the members' thoughts about potential national or state laws governing solid waste management.[181] The result was a commitment to reduce solid waste in any way possible.

To that end, LWVMO engaged in a project funded by the Environmental Protection Agency (EPA). The goals were three-fold: to educate the public on the problems of solid waste and on landfill alternatives, to develop programs and financing of short-term and long-term solutions, and to encourage the formation of citizen coalitions to carry on for the League in the future.[182] One example of a public education event spearheaded by the League as part of this work was a year-long tree-saver project that LWV University City completed in September 1977. It was aimed at encouraging University City residents to use the community's recycling program, which was pioneered in 1971 to collect newspapers at residents' curbs to sell to the Alton boxboard company for recycling. Efforts included door-to-door canvasing and mailing of "tree saver calendars" with city trash collection bills to nearly 10,000 residents as follow up.[183]

Leaguer Betty Wilson was part of a six-month conference on hazardous waste in 1976. She worked with Senator Wayne Goode (D-13) to draft the state's first hazardous waste management bill in 1977 (HB 660).[184]

Land Use

In 1975, after a year-long national study, LWVUS reached a consensus on land use:

> Recognizing that land is a finite resource, not just a commodity, [we] believe that land ownership, whether public or private, implies responsibilities of stewardship. In decisions about land use, public as well as private interests should be respected, with each consideration for social, environmental, and economic factors. Each level of government must bear appropriate responsibility for planning and managing land resources. It is essential, at a minimum, that an appropriate level of government determine, regulate, guarantee responsive and responsible government decisions. Citizen participation must be built into the planning and management of land resources at every step.[185]

Part of upholding this position involved encouraging the management and preservation of parks in the area. In the 1970s, the League came out in support of creating a Parks Commission to oversee this work in the city and county. Tied into this was a master plan for the future of Forest Park and the League offered suggestions for improving it by pushing for clarification of certain points. Another park that was closely watched by the League was Creve Coeur, which was looking to expand by acquiring part of the Creve Coeur golf course. In February 1970, the Creve Coeur Parks and Recreation Study Committee presented the results of its research and the League supported the expansion as well as future plans for a swimming pool and sports complex.[186]

The League also was involved in a debate about rezoning the Gumbo Flats floodplain in Chesterfield. In March 1978, the St. Louis County Planning Commission wanted 1,500 acres removed from floodplain zoning so building could occur, but the Army Corps of Engineers and the League were wary. The Corps conducted a new study of flooding frequency while the League emphasized that "conflicting development pressures on this land still exists...[and] development in a manner which protects property from flooding is very expensive."[187] The Corps' report resulted in the levee system in the area being improved in the early 1980s against a 100-year flood and certified by the Federal Emergency Management Agency.[188]

Another highly publicized land issue of the decade was what to do with the Weldon Spring area, which was "used by the Department of Army in the 1940s for TNT and DNT production and by the Atomic Energy Commission in the 1960s for uranium ore processing. The affected portions were all part of a federal environmental cleanup project and required to meet certain environmental, health, and safety standards," after which it was found to be safe for recreational use as well as for wildlife.[189] The League supported using the land for public recreation while protecting wildlife and keeping environmental concerns in mind.[190] In 1978, UMSL purchased 7,230 acres to establish the Weldon Spring Conservation Area.[191]

ENERGY

The energy crisis of the 1970s made many Americans conscious of the economic and environmental dangers associated with overreliance on oil consumption. In early 1978, during the height of the crisis, the League came to a consensus on wise use of energy that urged St. Louisans—members and citizens alike—to conserve and embrace new forms of energy. "Public understanding and cooperation are essential to the success of any program of energy conservation," the League said in a statement. "Citizens should be involved in the difficult choices that must be made." It suggested taking full account of economic consequences; distributing costs and hardships as fairly as possible without bearing unduly upon the poor; [and] giving full consideration to the environment."[192]

The St. Louis League was instrumental in writing the official Missouri state energy conservation plan and in ensuring citizen input from across the area was included.[193] The crisis also made their "support for a viable public mass transit system in order to save energy, preserve the environment, and provide the public with a transportation alternative to the automobile" all the more relevant. It would be another 20 years before the area would see a light-rail system.[194]

Educational articles and suggestions for members on conservation were printed in each edition of League newsletters from 1978-1980. Penned by Mary Foreman, who took the lead on energy matters, these pieces taught members how to become more aware of the operating costs of major appliances, how to read the new energy labels on appliances,[195] offered updates on national and international policy ("start getting out of oil now"),[196] and even member-submitted tips in the form of an "energy cookbook."[197]

May 3, 1978, was declared National Sun Day, and the League partnered with other local organizations to sponsor activities promoting the use of solar energy in St. Louis.[198]

LEAGUE ACTIVITIES

St. Louis League Welcomes Male Members

The 1970s dawned with a growing awareness of the need for equality between men and women. With that thought in mind, on Aug. 14, 1970, SaLees Seddon suggested that the St. Louis League "start a movement to open LWV to men members" because it would be consistent with the concept of equal rights, which they were fighting for.[199]

Although she suggested the St. Louis League take the idea to the National League, it would be another three years before Seddon's call was heeded at the National Convention in May 1974 and all Leagues were allowed to admit male members. Following League tradition, delegates discussed "the pros and cons of admitting men to full voting membership in the League...[and] members presented their views by a paper ballot. By a margin of two to one, our members favor[ed] this move."[200]

At the same time, members were also very clear that they did not want to change the name of the organization even though men were now allowed to be members. "There is a legacy with the name," Agnes Garino said. "We didn't want to give that up." "Most members' husbands were very involved and supportive. Some were members, once that was allowed," said Emma Lee Chilton. Her husband Steve joined the Webster Groves League and became a long-time League Treasurer. Esther Clark's husband, Jim, was deeply involved even before men could become members. He risked his job as an environmental scientist for the St. Louis County Health Department to serve as an expert witness for the League in the court case against Portland Cement. He became a member once they settled in St. Louis for good. Together, the couple worked in voter registration. She did data entry for membership for several years, and he continues to help deliver Voters Guides.

From 1974 on, it wasn't uncommon for membership in the League to become a family affair and the League even offers family/household memberships. Garino was one member whose whole family was involved. "There is nothing similar in men's organizations," she said, remembering how her husband Dave and son Tony used to help prepare mailings. Dave would take them to the downtown post office because it was close to where he worked.

When asked why men were drawn to the League, especially since it was traditionally a female organization, Mickey Hall responded, "I think [men join] for the same reason as women do—because they see the League as a source of impartial information, an organization that does careful study before it takes a position on any issue, and I think that they see that the League has had some impact."

But just as the women who joined the League tended to be a notch above, it wasn't just any man who became a member. "A man would have to be very sharp to keep up with League women," Maxine Gilner said. Fortunately, her husband, Frank, was one of those.

60ᵀᴴ ANNIVERSARY

The League kicked off its 60th anniversary celebrations in 1979 with a proclamation by Governor Joseph Teasdale that the week of March 25- 31 was League of Women Voters Week in Missouri. League Day was March 28, so members from across Missouri met at the capital in Jefferson City, representing 2,400 members of Missouri's 23 Leagues.[201] The party continued on May 1 with a coffee at the home of member Milly Cohn to honor past presidents.[202]

METRO NEWS

The first issue of the *Metro News* was mailed to members in January 1970. Besides featuring news on League/CIRC meetings and activities and election/voting information, quarterly issues highlighted member civic accomplishments. Editors over the next 45 years included Suzanne Topham, Gerry Friedman, Barbara Shull, Amy Barker and Agnes Garino.

CONCLUSION

This was a decade of reform and advocacy for the League, as local members stepped beyond the boundaries of St. Louis and the state of Missouri to take on issues of national significance, including the ERA and much-needed additions to the 1965 Voting Rights Act. Careful studies of campaign finance and election reform, as well as issues affecting the racial make-up of St. Louis, prepared the League for even larger battles to come in the next decade, when they would focus on these issues as well as working to ensure fair voting practices.

WOMEN WHO MADE AN IMPACT IN THE 1970S

JANET ROSENWALD BECKER
AUG. 25, 1931 - JAN. 30, 2017

The daughter of Sears, Roebuck and Company Chairman Lessing Rosenwald,[203] Janet was born and grew up in Philadelphia, Pennsylvania. Community service came naturally to her, and by her teenage years she was volunteering in the inner city. When Janet attended Sarah Lawrence College, she worked with the NAACP and met Civil Rights leaders Thurgood

Marshall and Roy Wilkins. From these experiences she realized her calling in life: "helping people find dignity through decent housing and racial justice." [204]

Janet married Dr. Bernard Becker, an ophthalmologist, with whom she had six children. When Janet and her family moved to St. Louis, she wanted to make a difference, so she began volunteering with Freedom of Residence, a fair housing group. She would later serve on the board. In 1958, Janet joined the University City League where she focused on human rights, quality low-income housing, and voter education. Long-time friends Agnes Garino and K Wentzien described her as "a fearless activist ahead of her time and not to be underestimated."[205] She served as the University City League's president before serving as ILO president from 1975-77. Also in the 1970s, Janet worked for seven years as a community liaison for Missouri State Senator Harriett Woods, whom she met through the League.

In 1976, Janet founded CIRC as a 501(c)(3) arm of the League dedicated to voter services and education. CIRC provided voter hotlines, publications, a year-round telephone information service, citizen participation workshops and much more. CIRC was later renamed the LWV Information Service.[206]

From the late 1970s on, Janet devoted her time to housing issues. In 1979, she co-founded Ecumenical Housing Production Corporation (now called Beyond Housing), which helped families find affordable homes and good schools, and offered job training and parenting classes. In 1987, she helped establish Adequate Housing for Missourians (AHM), which fights for housing for low-income families at both the legislative and grass-roots levels. She also worked on a committee to create a nationwide housing trust fund and served on the board and executive committee of the National Low Income Housing Coalition.[207]

In 1999, Janet was recognized with the Women of Achievement's Social Responsibility Award for her dedication and commitment to improving the quality of life in the St. Louis community. Janet and her husband Bernard were lifelong philanthropists, supporting many causes, including higher education, medical science, and social justice. In 2009, they donated bonds (estimated at $300,000) through their Horncrest Foundation to the CIRC.[208] The interest on that gift has been instrumental to keeping the St. Louis League open over the years.[209]

When she wasn't volunteering, Janet enjoyed playing tennis, listening to local blues bands, and knitting. Janet passed away at the age of 86 at her home in Webster Groves on Jan. 30, 2017, after a long struggle with Alzheimer's disease.[210]

JANET HELEN ATLEE SHIPTON
FEB. 25, 1923 – FEB. 13, 2019

Janet was not your average LWV member. Born Janet Attlee in 1923, she is one of four children[211] of British Prime Minister Clement Attlee (1945-1951)—who was well known as Winston Churchill's deputy for most of WWII[212]— and his wife, Violet.

Like most wealthy British children, Janet attended boarding school. Unlike many women, she served in the Women's Auxiliary Air Force (WAAF) during World War II. After the war, she worked as a psychologist in Bristol, where she met Harold William Shipton, a professor of biomedical engineering. The couple married on Nov. 20, 1947, in a society wedding and reception at Chequers attended by many Labour Cabinet members.[213]

The couple had two daughters, Ann and Susan. The family moved to the United States in 1957 when Harold was offered a position at the University of Iowa,[214] settling in Iowa City. Janet was a League member in Iowa, where she used her writing and speaking skills to advocate for better health care in America. According to one profile, she was an early organizer of the Hoover Health Council and active in the Johnson County Health Council. A four-plex she owned in West Branch, Iowa, was occupied by low-income renters.[215]

Janet was also active in local politics, running for Johnson County Supervisor in 1976, a race she lost, but won in 1978. She was preparing for a third bid in 1980 when her husband received a job offer from Washington University in 1980 and they moved to St. Louis.[216] Janet joined the League shortly thereafter. By 1983, she was advocating for equal rights as ERA Chair for the St. Louis League and equal pay as Women's Issues Chair the following year. In the late 1980s, she chaired the tax committee for the League.

Janet also managed the ABC Condominiums on Kingshighway and volunteered with First Unitarian Church, the Missouri Older Women's League and the Missouri Women's Network, where she established a voter registration project. It was this latter organization that would have her heart in her retirement years. She served as president in the mid-1990s[217] and continued to lobby for laws that will "improve the quality of life for older women," such as raising Social Security payments for women, better managed care, and increasing Medicaid payments for home health. In 1990, she was recognized by the Older Women's League with the inaugural Wonderful Woman Award.[218]

When she wasn't volunteering, Janet enjoyed bowling as a form of stress relief and putting on lavish holiday parties that incorporated customs from her native Britain beside American traditions.[219] She passed away in 2019 at the age of 95. She had seven grandchildren and 12 great grandchildren.[220]

Pat Rich

January 1943 to present

Pat Elkins grew up in Detroit, Michigan, in a middle-class family. She had one sibling, a younger brother. She was active with the Girl Scouts until she graduated from high school. In high school, she also was involved in helping with theatre productions and loved English and writing.

When she entered college at the University of Michigan – Ann Arbor, her parents made her promise to get a teaching certificate, which was a safe job option for a woman at the time. In addition to English, Pat studied French and Latin, having discovered a talent for languages. After graduation, she and a friend moved to California, where she taught English for a year before going back to Michigan to get her master's degree in English, with a minor in French.

In 1966, she married Dr. Leslie Rich, a dentist with a love of cars, sports, hunting and dinner parties. The two met on a blind date the previous year when Pat was passing through St. Louis, having been set up by a friend of her mother's. The couple settled in St. Louis and soon she was hired to teach French in middle school in the Ladue School District.

After two years, Pat decided to stay home to take care of her children, daughters Barbara and Kathryn. For the next dozen years, she volunteered heavily with the Junior League, where she served as treasurer, and later, vice president, and the League of Women Voters. Pat joined the League in 1969. She served as chairman of the Area-wide International Relations Committee and Representative Government Chairman, and then president of the League's Metropolitan Council from 1977-1981. She was particularly passionate about voting rights, campaign reform, international trade, the ERA and the arts. While in this role, she participated in the second Leadership St. Louis class.

When her daughters were 10 and 13, she went back to work, taking a job at the Metropolitan Association for Philanthropy (now Gateway to Giving). Her work with the League on the Zoo-Museum District put Pat in touch with Dr. Peter H. Raven, director of the Missouri Botanical Garden. In 1981, he hired her as his special assistant and then as the construction manager, working on completion of the Ridgway Center. In 1984, she was promoted to director of planning and development.

In the early 1990s, Pat became president of the Arts & Education Council, retiring in 1999. In 2002, she and two partners founded EMD Consulting Group. The company first focused on fundraising and strategic planning, and now consults on a variety of issues that have an impact on nonprofits. The company works with all types of nonprofits, mainly in St. Louis, but Pat has consulted with nonprofits throughout the country, including other botanical gardens. She led a group of forward-thinking women to found the Women's Foundation of Greater Saint Louis in 2007. She taught fundraising for nonprofits at UMSL from 2000-2015.

Always active, in the past Pat has been a member of the board of Craft Alliance and on the advisory board of the Organization for Tropical Studies. She also served a three-year term as the first woman Police Commissioner of St. Louis County.

Pat has received numerous awards, including the Association of Fundraising Professionals Fundraiser of the Year Award. She has published two books on membership programs with co-author Dana Hines, the latest being *Membership Marketing in the Digital Age*, published by Roman and Littlefield.

Main Sources Chapter 2 – The 1970s

Annual Reports
- Annual Reports of the President, League of Women Voters of St. Louis, 1970-1982
- League of Women Voters Citizens Information/Resource Center Annual Report, 1985-1986

Books
- *The Missouri Almanac, 1993-1994.*

Board and Council Meeting Minutes, 1970-1979
- Board of Directors of the League of Women Voters of St. Louis Metropolitan Council

Newsletters
- *Central County* Bulletin/*The Bulletin/Central County Scene*, March 1970-December 1979
- *League Reporter/In League Reporter,* March 1972- December 1978
- *Metro News,* January 1971-Spring 1989
- *Nutshell*, LWV Kirkwood, December 1972

League documents regarding
- Air Pollution
- Education
- Election Laws
- Election Procedures
- Equal Pay
- ERA
- Extension of the Voting Rights Act of 1965
- Home Rule
- MSD
- Natural Resources and Land Use
- New League Office
- Mass/Rapid Transit
- Nonpartisan Court Plan

- Tax Increases
- Welfare/*SNAP*

Periodicals
- *The Atlantic*
- *The New York Times*
- *The Riverfront Times*
- *St. Louis Post-Dispatch*

Websites
- Civil Rights Litigation Clearinghouse, University of Michigan Law School
- Equal Means Equal
- Historical Context of the ERA in Missouri
- #Redlined: A St. Louis Story
- Missouri Courts Judicial Branch of Government
- United States Department of Justice

For a complete list of sources, please see the endnotes at https://my.lwv.org/missouri/metro-st-louis/about/our-history.

1970s

Janet Shipton advocated for pay equity and the Equal Rights Amendment (photo courtesy of Iowa Women's Archives, U of Iowa Libraries, Iowa City).

League member and ERA sponsor Sue Shear served in the Missouri House from 1972 to 1998 (photo courtesy of David M. Henschel/*St. Louis Jewish Light*).

Janet Becker founded the League's Citizens Information/Resource Center in 1975.

St. Louis Mayor Jim Conway signing a proclamation in 1979 with Helene Saymen, Deborah Patterson, Ida West, Debby Waite, Julie Hale, Mary Greensfelder.

CHAPTER **3**

The 1980s

EVERYTHING WAS BIGGER in the 1980s—the hair, the shoulder pads, the nighttime soap operas, the political drama, and amount of change in the world. This is the decade when the Berlin Wall came down, MTV launched, and Congresswoman Geraldine Ferraro became the first woman nominated for Vice President by a major political party.

The achievements of the St. Louis LWV were also big. In the 1980s they:

- Formed a single St. Louis County League, uniting the North County, Central County, Southwest, and University City Leagues.
- Successfully sued the state over gerrymandering congressional districts in 1981.
- Televised candidate forums and a weekly cable TV show called *Impact on the Issues*.
- Started League in The Loop, a flea market and book sale with items donated by League members. This fundraiser and voter registration drive started in 1983 and continued until 2011. Organizers included Brenda Banjak, Agnes Garino, Barbara Elbrecht, Elise Joerger and Julie Behrens.

Under the leadership of city presidents Debby Waite (Howard), Lucy Hale, Ida West and Cay Thompson, and county presidents Rosanne Newcomb, Mary Kirkpatrick, K Wentzien, Vivian Schmidt and Mary K. Brown, the League made major changes to the St. Louis landscape over the course of the decade. The public learned about campaign finance reform and election procedures; stricter environmental laws were enforced; the Missouri Botanical Garden became part of the Zoo-Museum District; the League promoted pay equity for women, and much more.

VOTER SERVICES

In addition to their usual activities of registering and educating voters, four large projects dominated the League's voter service activities in the 1980s: campaign finance reform, bidding to host the 1984 Reagan-Mondale debate, changing Missouri from a caucus to a primary state, and new election laws.

VOTER HOTLINE

In fall 1980, the League installed six extra telephones—a new voter hotline—to answer voter calls about registration, ballot issues, absentee voting, and other voting and election-related issues. It was advertised on billboards, in League publications and at registration events. The hotline was open before the primary registration deadline before the August primary election, netting some 3,000 calls. A general election hotline ran from October 27 to November 4. The hotline was made possible by contributions from corporations, unions, foundations and individuals, including the League of Women Voters of Missouri Trust and Tribute Fund for Education.[1]

The phones were quieter after the election, but in 1984, they fired back up again at the League's new location. The hotline was open five times that year: leading up to the April municipal elections, before registration deadlines in July and October, and of course, leading up to and during the primary and general elections.[2] While online information, email and social media now handle the bulk of questions, the League still answers calls from voters.

"Vote Smart" Campaign

One of the most important parts of the League's voter service work is educating voters in a non-partisan way on the issues and candidates that will be on the ballot. In 1986 and 1988, through CIRC, the League launched a "Vote Smart" campaign to help voters "not only vote but vote intelligently." The campaign urged voters to educate themselves by reading about the candidates and issues, listening to the radio or watching candidates on TV, and attending candidates forums, many of which were sponsored by the League.[3]

Several elements worked together to help make Vote Smart visible throughout the St. Louis community. In partnership with Gannett Outdoor, a billboard reminding voters of the voter registration deadline was placed at Highway 40 and Oakland; Gannett sponsored a billboard design contest for St. Louis students that was won by Tammy Knepper of Honors Art High School. Posters were on display at thousands of locations around the area including grocery stores, banks, business schools, and libraries. In addition, radio stations played public service announcements supplied by the League. Schnucks grocery stores branded their shopping bags and advertising with the Vote Smart logo.[4] KDSK anchor Karen Foss served as moderator at a forum for candidates for U.S. Congress co-sponsored by the League.[5] Volunteers answered thousands of questions through the voter hotline.

Televising Local Candidate Forums

For the election of 1982, KETC Channel 9 partnered with the League to broadcast a public meeting between candidates for U.S. Senate in the first, second, and third congressional districts. At the October 14 event co-sponsored by the League, Junior League, and the National Council of Jewish women, candidates debated for an hour and then answered questions from the audience. Participants included U.S. Senator John Danforth and his Democratic challenger, Harriett Woods, a state senator and League member, as well as congressional candidates William "Bill" Clay (D-MO), William "Bill" White (R-MO), Robert Young (D-MO), Harold Dielmann (R-MO), Richard Gephardt (D-MO) and Richard Foristel (R-MO).[6]

Urban Concerns Radio Program

Thanks to a grant from the League of Women Voters Education Fund and the National Endowment for the Humanities, the League partnered with KSD Radio 550 to present five one-hour radio programs the week of March 10, 1980. Each night examined a different urban concern of the St. Louis metro area, looking at it through the lens of the past, present, and future. Topics discussed by academic humanists and prominent civic, business, government and educational leaders included the relationship between the city and county, housing, education, transportation and employment.[7]

Campaign Finance Reform/The "Big Vote"

The League had been following campaign finance reform since the mid-1970s. With campaign spending still on the rise, from 1983-1984 the League conducted a campaign to educate the public on the election process. Called the "BIG VOTE," it asked more than 5,400 St. Louisans, both volunteers and recipients of random telephone surveys,[8] a series of questions on eight election issues, including campaign finance, presidential debates, the role of the media in elections, election projections and the delegate selection process to gauge their thoughts.[9] About campaign finance reform, the League asked people how they thought the presidential campaign should be financed. Approximately 44% of respondents said it should be paid for by the federal government and private contributions should be outlawed. They also felt that PACs made campaign finance reform laws moot.[10]

1984 Presidential Debates

Another aspect of the "BIG VOTE" was asking voters what they thought about televised presidential debates. After all, the previous two (1976 and 1980) had attracted more viewers than ever before—an estimated 120 million.[11] Three out of four participants told the League they believed television debates should be a regular part of presidential campaigns, and 35% said only the major party candidates should be included. They felt that "debates offer exposure to the views and personality of each candidate. Debates are also an opportunity to observe contenders on common ground and in comparatively unrehearsed circumstances. They afford a base for judging the leadership capabilities of candidates." Those against televised debates stressed that the events are more about who wins than on the issues and that any kind of gaffe could ruin an otherwise qualified candidate's image.[12]

The League tried and failed to get a November 1983 ruling by the Federal Communications Commission reversed that allowed broadcasters to sponsor "limited participation debates without being required to grant equal free time to all other candidates." This was a reversal of past practice, which treated debates as non-partisan news items, a philosophy that the League endorsed with its own policy.

During the 1984 Presidential campaign, the League was vocal in its desire to sponsor a presidential debate between Republican incumbent Ronald Reagan and his Democratic rival Walter Mondale. St. Louis was one of four cities vying to host the debates, and the League's members were eager to bring it to town; Kansas City was chosen instead. But the League was still the sponsor, as they were for the vice-presidential debate between Vice President George Bush and Geraldine Ferraro, the first woman to ever run for that seat.[13]

Media Projections

Two additional questions that were part of the "BIG VOTE" had to do with media projections, long a subject of controversy among politicos. In 1964, one network predicted Lyndon Johnson's victory four hours before the polls closed on the west coast and NBC called the 1980 presidential race for Reagan while California voters still had two hours left to vote.[14]

Because of situations like this, the League asked voters if they thought early projections influenced voter turnout/outcome of elections. They also asked if voters thought broadcasters had a journalistic responsibility to "report facts only as they happen" or if the use of technology to project winners was justified.

After the 1980 election, several legislative proposals were introduced in Congress designed to eliminate or lessen the probability that projections would affect election turn out. These included prohibiting network projections; establishing a uniform poll closing time across the nation; changing election day to Sunday; or having it extended over a two-day period. But each potential solution had its own problems from increased chances of voter fraud to voter confusion and violation of First Amendment rights, so they failed to move forward.

Considering this, another popular suggestion was that networks voluntarily abstain from broadcasting early projections. On May 4, 1981, "32 national organizations including the LWV sent letters to major television, radio and cable networks and to wire services asking that the media report only the official results of the presidential vote in each state and not project the results when the polls were still open elsewhere."[15] Not surprisingly, their request fell on deaf ears. In the quest for ratings and bragging rights, 40 years later networks are still projecting winners long before the polls close in western parts of the country—there are just more of them, and they are using ever more advanced technology to do it.

PRIMARY SYSTEM SELECTED FOR PRESIDENTIAL ELECTIONS

On the heels of the BIG VOTE, the League chose to study Missouri's process for selecting presidential candidates. At the time, Missouri was a caucus state, which meant the selection process began with large, in-person meetings at the township or ward level among party members where discussion and votes for delegates took place. Then, at state conventions, delegates, either committed to a particular candidate or uncommitted, chose national candidates.[16] In contrast, primaries (officially called presidential preference primaries) allowed voters to directly indicate their preference for a candidate to be their party's presidential nominee by secret ballot. Delegates to the conventions would then select the party nominee, ostensibly based on the will of the people.[17]

The League had been pressing for primaries since at least 1965. They argued that primaries made it easier for more voter voices to be heard, reduced the influence of special interest groups, put candidates from smaller parties on an equal playing field with those from the two major parties, increased voter interest, eliminated the peer pressure that could be felt at caucuses and overall was a simpler, quicker and more straightforward process. Conversely, they also acknowledged that because candidates don't visit the states in person, the media can have a tremendous influence over primaries. Primaries also "take away a party's power to select delegates at caucus," are more expensive and also "emphasize popularity over realistic view of skills needed to lead."[18]

In July 1985, the League sought public opinion on the matter[19] and held a public meeting on Sept. 9 to discuss the topic at St. Louis City Hall. Though the panel of political experts was in favor of primaries 3-1, the League met significant resistance when they proposed that Missouri change to a primary system.[20] During the previous legislative session, a bill to establish a primary in Missouri was passed in the House but died in the Senate, so the outcome of the 1986 session was far from certain.[21] The Missouri Republican Party came out strongly against the change in February 1986, accusing Democrats of using the change to benefit their candidates.[22] However, it quickly passed both houses and Governor John Ashcroft signed the Presidential Primary Bill on March 18, setting the first Missouri primary date in decades for Super Tuesday, March 8, 1988.[23] After 1988, state Republicans pressed for a return to caucuses, citing the cost of holding a statewide primary." Missouri held caucuses in 1992 and 1996 but went back to a primary again in 2000.[24]

New Election Laws

The League was instrumental in getting a new law passed that sought to clarify any proposed ballot language. The new law required the Secretary of State and Attorney General to:

approve the form of a petition before it is circulated, thereby protecting it from being rejected later for technical reasons. Furthermore, the description of the measure that will appear on the ballot (the ballot title) must be drafted at the beginning rather than at the end of the petition process so that criticism of the wording may be dealt with early and voters may identify the issues they will be voting on if the petition succeeds.[25]

A second new state law required voters to present valid Missouri identification before they could register; this had previously been an informal practice in many locations, but now it was mandatory. The League supported a provision making it easier for those whose permanent disability required them to vote absentee by removing the notarization requirement and allowed election board representatives to execute ballots for the hospitalized regardless of location (i.e. a county election board member could help someone hospitalized in the city).

REDISTRICTING

Redistricting is the process of drawing the lines for districts within each state from which public officials are elected after each decennial census. Current Speakers Bureau Chair Nancy Price says, "When it's conducted fairly, it accurately reflects population changes and diversity, and is used to equitably allocate representation in Congress and state legislatures."[26] When it is not and is done to favor one political party or class, it is called gerrymandering.

The process of redistricting or reapportionment based on a state's population can change district boundaries for the U.S. House, Missouri Senate, Missouri House, county and city councils, and aldermen.[27] The League took an active role in the redistricting process in the 1960s, and it became a major issue again 20 years later. The results of the 1980 Census required Missouri to drop one of its Congressional districts, bringing its total from 10 to nine.[28] The House easily agreed on a plan for new district boundaries, but the Senate was another story.[29]

A 10-person bipartisan commission was created to redraw the 34 Senate districts in Missouri. In May 1981, the commission held three public hearings across the state to listen to voters in St. Louis, Jefferson City and Independence before they began their work. The League urged the commission to keep working with voters in mind and hold some hearings at night. Some people at the hearings believed redistricting was an opportunity to gain more minority and female representatives, while others questioned why federal civil rights laws allowed gerrymandering for minority seats under the guise of equality but not others.[30]

The commission ended up recommending a merger between the first and third congressional districts in St. Louis due to population loss in the city. This would force Democrat William Clay, the state's first and only Black Congressman, to run against Democrat Richard Gephardt, a white politician. Black Democrats objected and formed their own solution which involved merging districts in DeSoto. The Senate commission quickly abandoned its merger plan. The idea was taken up by the Missouri Farm Bureau, who sued to preserve rural representation, and was favored by Republicans because it pitted two powerful Democrats against one another.[31]

In July, the Missouri League chose to file a lawsuit seeking to turn responsibility for redistricting over to the courts, since the legislature had failed so miserably. "We would be pleased if the [federal] judges wiped the slate clean and started from scratch," LWVMO President Sydell Shayer told the *St. Louis Post-Dispatch,* emphasizing that while members were not endorsing any particular plan, the process needed to take into consideration public opinion, as well as social, economic and geopolitical factors.[32]

This action struck a nerve with Missouri Republican Party Chairman John Powell from Rolla who called the League a "pious-acting group...[that] is nothing more than a farce...by calling themselves bipartisan they are either deliberately deserting the truth or incredibly naïve...they [said they] wanted a fair plan but what they wanted was a Democratic plan." Used to being called all sorts of things, the League shrugged off the accusation, reminding Powell that "the federal court will draw the district lines, not the League."[33]

In August, the panel of three judges overseeing the League's suit chose to combine it with the Missouri Farm Bureau suit.[34] In a joint statement, both the Missouri House and Senate said they agreed that the redistricting should be left to the courts,[35] as the League asked.

In September, only two weeks before a hearing on the combined suits was scheduled in Jefferson City, the National Association for the Advancement of Colored People (NAACP) filed its own suit "asking that Missouri's congressional districts be redrawn in a manner that will not dilute black voting strength."[36] This suit was quickly combined with the other two[37] and the panel of judges agreed to act if the special session of the legislature called for November 1981 didn't produce a resolution.[38]

The 60-day special session began on Nov. 6, 1981, and considered several options: The Dirck plan, which was essentially what the Senate commission had proposed; the Heflin plan, which took away one of St. Louis City and County's three representatives; and the Griffin Plan, which maintained St. Louis' three districts, but put the ability to draw them in the hands of political leaders from the area and encompassed a larger geographic area, including St. Charles County and most of Franklin County.[39] Two additional plans were added later. One was a revised plan from Democratic Senator Edwin Dirck, eliminating the Democratic showdown and pitting Gephardt against Republican Wendell Bailey of Willow Springs. The other was the Griffin-Ribaudo plan, which preserved St. Louis' three districts and called for the creation of a 350-mile-long district that stretched across the northern part of the state and divided Kansas City's fifth district.[40]

Debate continued into December, with the House approving a bill in late November and the Senate dragging its feet as more versions and amendments were added. As of Dec. 1, approximately halfway through the special session, the Senate still hadn't considered a plan even though the holidays and a Jan. 4 deadline were looming.[41] The special session ended for the holidays on Dec. 17 without a resolution.

The three federal judges were ready for this outcome and set a goal of establishing new districts by Jan. 12, 1982.[42] They rejected all previously submitted plans because they didn't meet their criteria for population equality, compact and contiguous districts, and state policies on reapportionment.[43] They created a plan that combined the eighth and ninth districts in southeast and south-central Missouri and made minor changes to the lines of other districts.[44] This allowed them to ensure all districts had a relatively similar population and avoided breaking up rural counties.[45] In St. Louis, it also expanded Clay's district to include some predominately white areas, which pleased Black Democrats and the NAACP.[46]

Reapportionment appeared again on the Nov. 2, 1982,

ballot under Amendments 5 and 12.[47] Amendment 5 to move the responsibility for reapportionment from the Legislature to a bi-partisan commission did not pass. Amendment 12, which did pass, made the Missouri Senate reapportionment procedures the same as those of the House.[48]

FREEHOLDERS PLAN

The League continued advocating for and monitoring St. Louis City and County government. One of its first victories in this decade was getting a city charter amendment put on the ballot to remove the salary cap for city workers. The League worked with the city employees' Fair Pay Committee and sent educational materials and sample ballots to all League members asking them to share with their friends and neighbors.[49] When the measure passed by 64% on Aug. 5, 1980,[50] the Fair Pay Committee called the League "the fair pay angels" and credited them with getting the extra votes necessary for passage.[51]

The League was also interested in reducing the number of municipalities in St. Louis County. In 1987, a Board of Freeholders—a group of 19 homeowners "authorized by the state constitution to make changes to governance and service delivery only if city and county voters approve its proposed plan"[52]—was appointed to reorganize the governments of St. Louis County.[53] The Board proposed merging the county's 90 municipalities into 39, changing the way fire and emergency services were handled, changing the tax structure for St. Louis County, and setting forth a uniform economic development plan for St. Louis City and County.[54]

In 1988, the League completed its own separate three-year study of the organization of St. Louis County and its municipalities. While doing this, the League also "followed the freeholders' work, participated in the freeholders' process, and analyzed the completed plan and the issues it involves." Members ultimately supported the plan "on its merits, in relationship to the structure of government now in place, and in light of trends occurring in the county's governmental structure."[55]

The League helped the freeholders hold public meetings throughout St. Louis County in August 1988 to educate the public on what was being proposed and what it would mean for their area.[56] By December, six other groups joined the League to form the Coalition for an Informed Electorate to continue education through March 30. An opposition group, Countians Against High Taxes and Loss of Local Control, formed shortly thereafter.

The plan was due to be voted on by residents on June 20, 1989, but in November 1988, Rep. Robert J. Quinn, Jr. (D-80) and Patricia J. Kampsen filed a class-action lawsuit challenging the legality of the makeup of the board because of the stipulation that they had to be homeowners. They argued that this created a two-class society where wealthier people who owned land had greater rights. The Court ruled that the qualification was valid, but this was overturned by the U.S. Supreme Court on appeal just four days before voters were due to go to the polls. The high court ruled unanimously that the Equal Protection Clause of the 14th Amendment applied, and the Board of Freeholders was invalid, bringing an end to yet another attempt to fix St. Louis' ongoing governmental issues.[57]

In the aftermath of the end of the Board of Freeholders, a 19-person Board of Electors was formed as required by the Missouri Constitution. Among the nine citizen members nominated by St. Louis County Executive H.C. Milford was League member and past president K Wentzien, who was confirmed by the County Council and went on to serve on the board until it dissolved in 1991.[58]

EDUCATION

By 1980, the *Liddell vs. Board of Education* desegregation case had dragged on for almost a decade. It was then in the hands of the St. Louis Circuit Court, which reversed previous rulings on the case, including a 1979 decision by Judge Meredith that "the city school board had not intentionally segregated Black students," finding that it was indeed the city school board and the state that allowed the school system to remain segregated. As a solution, the Court proposed a student exchange program between the mostly Black city and the predominately white county. Accordingly, school officials developed a plan to bus 7,500 students beginning in September 1980.[59]

The St. Louis City League did not comment on the ruling or the plan but did all they could to comply with it, helping "in several citywide programs to make sure that students would have the opportunity to continue their education in a climate free of disruption and the fear of violence."[60] League volunteers also staffed the "Straight Story Line," a telephone bank located at the Board of Education office and open throughout the summer and early fall to answer questions from the public about things like school assignments, bus schedules, problems, and other issues.

The Metropolitan LWV was one of several local organizations and individuals that endorsed the Coalition for Peaceful Implementation's Statement of Community Concern, which appeared in newspapers on August 31. The statement urged parents, teachers, students, and community members to do all they could to create a calm, peaceful school environment in which all students, regardless of race, could receive a quality education and urged the community to keep student welfare in mind and to resolve differences "in a proper and lawful manner with the best interests of the children always uppermost in our minds."[61]

Once the school year began, 30 League volunteers joined a citizens' advisory committee in monitoring the opening of schools. They checked to be sure that buses were running on time, were clean, and that the exchange of students took place peacefully.[62] They also visited schools every two months to "interview staff and students concerning the areas of progress and problems in their schools." This information was then submitted to the monitoring committee, who wrote a report submitted to the Federal Judge overseeing the implementation.[63]

The following year, in 1981, Judge James Meredith stepped down from the case and U.S. District Judge William Hungate was selected to oversee the case. He proposed a regional voluntary desegregation plan—which would eventually come to be run by Voluntary Interdistrict Choice Corporation (VICC) and boast more than 70,000 students, the largest and longest running such program in the nation.[64] School districts had until August 6 to respond.[65]

The League, meanwhile, established a citizen education coalition to inform the public about voluntary school desegregation. It was comprised of community groups and individuals who were trained as speakers to go out and explain the history and issues around voluntary desegregation. They also created a publication in which they could address questions from the public.[66]

When August 6 came and went, only four of the 30 St. Louis school districts—Clayton, Kirkwood, Ritenour, and University City—had approved the court's plan. Pattonville joined soon after and when school started in September, 124 students chose to become part of the voluntary busing program.

In 1982, five League members (Patty Appel, Brenda Banjak, Lois Bliss, Agnes Garino and Jan Schoenfeld) and St. Louis education and desegregation leaders attended a Yale University desegregation seminar. The seminar focused on policy and planning and what desegregation looked like in school districts across the country.

Over the next two years, the program was the subject of multiple changes, including, at one point, a threat by Judge Hungate to merge the city and county school districts and make desegregation mandatory. While that did not occur, it did force many school districts to participate in the voluntary plan. By March 30, 1983, all 23 districts were compliant, and more than 2,500 city students were attending school in the county. Within a year, that number more than doubled to 5,500.[67]

In February 1984, having done its job, the Coalition for Information on School Desegregation closed its office and disbanded, knowing it could be reformed if needed in the future.[68] Indeed, it would be about a decade before desegregation made headlines again.

PAY EQUITY

By the mid-1980s, the number of mothers working outside the home was increasing steadily each year. As *The Atlantic* noted in a 1986 article:

> From 1890 to 1985 the participation in the work force of women between the ages of 25 and 44 soared from 15 to 71 percent...At the end of the Second World War only 10 percent of married women with children under the age of six held jobs or were seeking them. Since then mothers of preschool children have thronged the job market: by 1985 the census had classified more than half of these young mothers as participants in the work force.[69]

Pay equity in employment was supposed to be assured by the 1963 Equal Pay Act and Title VII of the Civil Rights Act of 1964.[70] Yet, nationwide, when the salaries of male and female employees were compared for jobs for which they were equally qualified based on education, skill and experience, women made $11,001 or 25% less than men ($32,976 for women vs. $43,686 for men).[71] In Missouri, the gap was slightly less at 19%; according to the *St. Louis Post-Dispatch*, "the average annual salary of male state employees was $16,644, compared with the average of $13,542 for women, who comprised 62% of the state's merit workforce."[72] By 1985, it was estimated that women in the United States earned $0.62 for every dollar earned by men.[73]

While some argued that a difference in pay was fair due to the time away from the workforce women took when they became mothers, League member Janet Shipton found that "less than half of the difference in pay between women and men can be accounted for by differences in work record due to such things as time out for pregnancy. The rest is due to culturally determined discrimination."[74]

It's little wonder, then, that pay equity became an issue that took the media, and the League, by storm. In 1984, several bills to establish pay equity between male and female workers of the state government were in the Missouri General Assembly, sponsored by female politicians, Senator Harriett Woods, and Rep. Sheila Lumpe, both League members from University City. Supporting them were around a dozen groups from labor, professional, political and civic groups in Missouri, including the League.[75] "Our state cannot claim a commitment to equity when it discriminates in its wages against half of its employees," Rep. Lumpe said. "This is the Civil Rights issue of the 80s."[76] These groups felt great urgency at getting equal pay legislation passed, as they believed Missouri law, as it then stood, left the state vulnerable to lawsuits over wage discrimination. In fact, one group, the American Federation of State, County and Municipal Employees (AFSCME), was already hinting at a lawsuit.

The League issued a statement in February 1984 endorsing equal pay for work of comparable value for all state employees[77] and supporting HB 436, the bill sponsored by Woods and Lumpe, which had been edited to "authorize a job evaluation of all positions in the state over a three-year period."[78] At the same time, the Federal Pay Equity and Management Improvement Act of 1984 (HR5680) was being debated in Congress. The House approved it 413-6 on June 28, but the Senate version—the Civil Service Amendment Act of 1984 (S958), which didn't include a comparable worth provision—failed.[79]

Less than six months later, Missouri had its first pay discrimination lawsuit, filed with the Equal Opportunity Employment Commission (EEOC) and the Missouri Human Rights Commission. AFSCME made good on its earlier threat by suing the state of Missouri on behalf of 15,000 employees, charging that they "deliberately maintain a sex-segregated workforce and pay employees in female dominated jobs less than it pays employees in male-dominated jobs which require equivalent or less skill, effort and responsibility."[80]

In 1985, female employees of the state of Washington became the first to sue their employers in federal appeals court for pay discrimination. This led to proposals being considered on the national level as well as in 30 states, including Missouri, to study and/or raise salaries for jobs which are predominately female. In support of such legislation, the League joined the National Coalition on Pay Equity. As with the Equal Rights Amendment, one of the loudest voices of dissent was Phyllis Schlafly's Eagle Forum. The conservative group not only opposed the legislation being considered in Missouri but filed a brief in the Washington state pay equity case.[81]

Debate between pro and con groups continued for years without federal or Missouri law changing. Nationally, the Lily Ledbetter Fair Pay Act, signed by President Barack Obama in 2009, is as close to an equal pay law as the country has. Similarly, Missouri has no equal pay legislation beyond one from 1963, though the Missouri Human Rights Act, as modified in 1986,[82] provides some protection from gender-based discrimination. In 2015, "Governor Jay Nixon signed an executive order aimed at eliminating the wage gap in the Missouri executive branch and strongly encouraged private employers to 'identify and address any gender wage gap in order to ensure that all Missourians receive equal pay for equal work.' But attempts to pass equal pay reform on a statewide level have stalled amid calls to address root causes instead of mandating compliance."[83]

RIVERPORT DOME

In the mid-1980s, one of the biggest challenges to the environment was the proposed Riverport football dome. On Nov. 26, 1985, the St. Louis County Council approved $4 million for land and levee improvements so that a 70,000-seat domed football stadium could be constructed on floodplain farmland in Maryland Heights. A new stadium was believed to be key to keeping the St. Louis Football Cardinals in St. Louis.

Proponents of the plan praised its positive economic influence on the area, the number of jobs it would create and the fact that keeping the football team in the city would make it more attractive to businesses and investors. They also pointed to the number of other events it could be used for, from soccer, hockey and basketball to circuses, rodeos and conventions.[84]

But the League wasn't one of them. "The area is an aquifer for the Missouri and Mississippi Rivers," League President K Wentzien said, "We thought it should be located in the city for the environment and to strengthen the city." The League believed an environmental study by the Army Corps of Engineers would back up their position, so they requested one. In a letter published in the *St. Louis Post-Dispatch*, Wentzien and Barbara Shull pointed out that building a levee could even be more damaging than helpful, citing negative effects on sewers, storm runoff and overall maintenance cost.[85]

As plans for the stadium solidified, County Executive Gene McNary began talking about using money from a half-cent sales tax that was supposed to be funding Bi-State to fund the stadium instead. "We object when money is used to build roads and bridges. We definitely don't see how using those funds to build a levee can be justified," members said in a letter to county officials.[86]

The League quickly became part of a "No Dome" committee to oppose the plan.[87] Wentzien recalled a local TV reporter appeared unannounced in the office to ask about the campaign. "When I saw him, I jumped up and with arms open wide walked over to him and said, "Elliot Davis, I'm so glad to see you!!!' He sobered up immediately and said, 'No one is supposed to be glad to see me'. . .and then we both laughed."[88]

In 1986, the League joined with the Missouri Coalition for the Environment and the Open Space Council for the St. Louis region to file a suit in the Circuit Court of St. Louis County[89] challenging the legality of using revenue from the transportation sales tax to fund a levee. News of the issue reached even the ears of lawmakers in Washington D.C., where the Tax Reform Act of 1986 was on its way to being passed; it "specifically excluded sports facilities from eligibility for tax-exempt revenue bonds." That didn't stop St. Louis lawmakers from trying to get St. Louis exempted from the law.[90]

In August, the Army Corps of Engineers dealt a blow to opponents, concluding in their study that the Riverport wetlands were "not a valuable public resource," and giving their permission for building to take place.[91] With that victory, proponents began touting that their project would actually *benefit* the environment by forming more bogs and marshes, a theory that opponents scoffed at, pointing out that wetlands are made by nature, not by man.[92]

The lawsuit continued into 1987, with more and more people joining the League in opposing the Riverport Dome. St. Louis Mayor Vincent C. Schoemehl, Jr. turned against the plan and went public with an alternative outline to build the stadium downtown, just as the League had suggested.[93] His vision was to expand the existing Cervantes Convention Center[94] so that St. Louis would have a one-stop-shop for its meetings and attractions rather than competing venues in the City and County.

In July, Mayor Schoemehl convinced the Estimate Board at City Hall to join the League lawsuit "saying the city would lose thousands of jobs, up to $105 million in yearly sales, up to 55 percent of the profits of businesses affected and up to $3.9 million in city tax revenue annually." Support for the Riverport stadium soon dried up, and with it, vital financing.

Frustrated with the political back-and-forth, Cardinals owner Bill Bidwell began quietly looking for other cities to move his team to, finally doing so in March 1988. Construction on the Mayor's plan, which the League did not oppose, began in 1992 and a year later St. Louis was home to the (formerly Los Angeles) Rams.[95]

ENVIRONMENT

WATER POLLUTION

The League continued its strong partnership with the Metropolitan Sewer District on all issues related to water in the 1980s. This close relationship resulted in compliance with state and federal environmental laws and advances for St. Louis residents, including in the areas of the sewer system, sewage treatment, and stormwater drainage.[96] Projects undertaken from 1980-1984[97] included installation of a secondary treatment facility at MSD's Lemay treatment plant; a sewer system evaluation study related to stormwater to identify issues that cause basement sewer backups, flooding, and treatment facility overload; pretreatment for "exotic" wastes; and projects to eliminate pollution of the Meramec River, Caulks Creek and Coldwater Creek by raw and inefficiently treated sewage.[98]

In 1984, the League supported a $60 million clean water revenue bond issue on the August 7 ballot. Voters passed it 63.9% in favor even though it meant a monthly sewer fee increase of $1.16.[99] The bond issue helped finance eight major MSD projects necessary for compliance with the Clean Water Act of 1972. The League was especially supportive of projects for secondary treatment facilities, which remove nearly all pollutants from wastewater before it flows back into rivers and streams. In addition, having a secondary treatment facility at the Bissell Point plant would help prevent toxic waste from leaking into the Mississippi River.[100]

The League was asked to be part of a pilot project on clean water education in schools during the 1988-1989 school year. Together with Mallinckrodt and MSD, the Partners in Protecting the Environment (PIPE) project educated 5th graders in St. Louis

City and County on the importance of clean water and what was being done to keep it that way. In addition to live presentations, educational materials included background information, worksheets and assignments teachers and students studied before PIPE visits. The project was well received and saw favorable press from the *St. Louis Post-Dispatch* and KETC Channel 9. While participation was modest that first year, reaching only about 20 classes, growth would skyrocket over the next decade until it reached around 1,000 students each school year by 1998.[101]

Safe drinking water became a subject of public discourse in May 1989 when the Missouri General Assembly took up competing proposals (SB112 and HB 124, 133) to "require more frequent testing for an expanded list of contaminants in public drinking water supplies."[102] Over the previous year, Leagues in all 50 states conducted studies on their drinking water systems. The Missouri survey found that across the state there were 1,084 community public drinking water systems, 88% of which "serve[d] fewer than 3,300 people, but together...supply drinking water to more than 700,000 users," making legislation to provide funding for such testing crucial to the state.[103]

On May 12, the legislature passed a bill to require "annual testing of drinking water for 134 contaminants," a 100-item increase from previous legal requirements. The law changed little for St. Louis City and County, where MSD already tested for most of the items, but was a huge change for smaller areas of the state. The bill also required the public to be notified any time their water failed a test.[104]

AIR POLLUTION

In the late 1970s, lawmakers began seeing a link between auto emissions and air pollution. In 1977, Congress passed the Clean Air Act amendments, which included "detailed methodology for attaining clean air standards designed to protect the public health and welfare."[105] Part of that involved reducing the amount of carbon monoxide and ozone, so in June 1979, Missouri passed a vehicle emissions inspection/maintenance program, which went into effect on December 31, 1982. The program involved annual vehicle emissions testing and repair for vehicles that emit amounts of pollutants above established standards. The League took up the responsibility of informing the public and talking to legislators about the importance of inspection/maintenance of vehicles.

In 1981, the League supported renewal of the 1970 Clean Air Act as part of a national clean air coalition. On March 14, the Missouri League sponsored a meeting in Columbia for all state League leaders and members to learn more about the issues. In the end, even though the President's Council on Environmental Quality found 395 counties in the country were in violation of the minimum federal health standards for total suspended particulate matter (St. Louis was ranked as having the 6th dirtiest air in the nation), the bill never left the house.[106] The next amendments to the Act took place in 1990.

A hot topic in 1984 was acid rain, which was being greatly increased by man-made pollution, especially sulfur dioxide from coal burning utilities in the Midwest. The League supported HR 3400—co-sponsored by 107 lawmakers, including Missouri's Reps. Richard Gephardt and William Clay—to "provide national cost sharing for 90% of the cost of installing scrubbers at the 50 dirtiest plants in the nation, thus cutting sulfur dioxide emissions by 7 million tons a year, over 1/2 of the present level of pollution."[107] Unfortunately, the bill did not pass. Missouri's air would not improve until after the U.S. passed acid rain regulations as part of the Clean Air Act of 1990.[108]

In fact, the EPA had threatened the state with sanctions that would take away millions of federal dollars because Missouri's Air Pollution Control Program submitted an inaccurate air pollution reduction formula to the EPA. The result was that the state had to impose new measures for reducing pollution. The League endorsed five possible solutions and helped to host public forums before a decision was made.[109] The Missouri Air Conservation Commission ultimately approved the installation of air pollution control equipment on all gasoline pumps by 1987.[110]

Nuclear Power and Hazardous Waste

In January 1980, the St. Louis League formed an Energy Committee to study "alternative energy sources such as solar, nuclear, wood, water, wind, and geothermal. [They also] investigat[ed] the technology of recycling industrial waste and possible alternative forms of transportation."[111]

One of the emerging forms of energy was nuclear power, which came with serious questions about how to properly dispose of the dangerous waste it generated. The League supported environmental legislation to create a hazardous substance/materials bill. The Comprehensive Environment Response, Compensation, and Liability Act of 1980, or "Spill Bill,"[112] as it was colloquially named, "establish[ed] a procedure and process for the regulation and control of the transportation, storage and disposal of hazardous substances or materials and the regulation of hazardous substance emergencies."[113] It also created the Missouri Interagency Council of Hazardous Substances as coordinator of hazardous substances regulation.

In 1984, the Resource Conservation and Recovery Act of 1976 (RCRA) was amended to include the Federal Hazardous and Solid Waste Amendments that regulate the use and disposal of the nation's hazardous substances.[114] This change "establish[ed] a comprehensive hazardous waste management system, set advanced design standards for hazardous waste disposal facilities, and regulate[d] small hazardous waste producers and underground gasoline storage tanks, closing loopholes that have plagued the RCRA in the past."[115]

The League took the position that the law should be amended so that each state's Department of Natural Resources could manage and enforce the hazardous waste program for that state. In addition, they called for revisions to Missouri's solid waste legislation to bring it up to date because technology had advanced significantly since it was written in 1972.[116]

In addition, Missouri joined five other states (Indiana, Iowa, Minnesota, Ohio and Wisconsin) as a member of the Midwest Interstate Low Level Radioactive Waste Compact, a Congressionally supported group of states that pledged to abide by proper management and disposal of low-level radioactive waste.[117] The League supported the bill that made Missouri a part of the compact, which was passed by the Missouri legislature during a special session.[118]

Later that same year, the topic of building a nuclear plant in Callaway County came to the fore, even as the site itself was nearing completion. The League opposed it "because they had not seen sufficient evidence that the government knew how to properly dispose of nuclear waste," a position that was considered "ahead of its time."[119] The plant was put into operation anyway on Dec. 19, 1984.

Four years later, Missouri's hazardous waste preparations were put to the test when "the U.S. Department of Energy reported that radioactive material was found to be present 'in and along'"[120] Coldwater Creek. It was traced back to two local dumps owned by Mallinckrodt, who had produced weapons-grade uranium at a factory north of downtown in the late

1940s. The creek was placed on the National Priorities List of the Superfund Program of the U.S. Environmental Protection Agency and work on an Army Corps of Engineers flood-control project was ceased. This project went silent after that, but it would come back to haunt everyone involved in the 2010s.

TRANSIT

The League's second full decade of studying transit issues in St. Louis and advocating for an upgrade was stymied by the financial issues facing Bi-State. Like other transit systems across the nation, they were dealing with cutbacks in federal aid and subsidies combined with astronomical fuel prices—diesel was up by 800% from what it was in 1973. Additionally, sales tax revenues were down, and consumers were loudly voicing their displeasure with service.[121]

Even in this dire situation, the League continued to support Bi-State, making two recommendations for changes the organization could make in 1981 to survive. The first was to do all they could to get the Missouri Transportation Sales Tax Extension Authorization (SB163) passed to keep the half cent sales tax that benefited Bi-State in place through Dec. 31, 1983. This bill was passed, but County Executive Gene McNary ended up using a surplus that should have gone to Bi-State for roads instead, claiming, "it is unconscionable to put everything into a bus service that is mainly in the city and then raise county property taxes."[122] He also vetoed another measure which would have given Bi-State $25.2 million from the transportation sales tax.

Second, the League recommended the hard choices of cutting service, raising fares during peak hours (leaving non-peak at a lower rate that unemployed and transit dependent people could still afford),[123] and cutting administrative costs. Bi-State ended up eliminating some routes at the end of April, adding a

10-cent fare increase for rush hour service in July, and cutting $1.2 million in administrative costs.[124]

As for the public's complaint about service, Bi-State believed that it would be improved by a new garage program that began in spring 1981. It included a $26.2 million main repair shop at Compton and Spruce and a station garage on Brentwood Blvd. Together, these two locations sped up repairs for buses in St. Louis County.[125]

In December 1983, McNary vowed not "to use any transportation sales tax money to support a light-rail commuter transit system being studied by the East-West Gateway Coordinating Council."[126] Yet citizens kept calling for one. In March 1984, the East-West Gateway Coordinating Council endorsed a plan to build an 18-mile light-rail system that would connect East St. Louis with Lambert Airport via downtown but declined to add a line from University City to Clayton.[127]

With this victory, and $36 million in initial federal funds, the project gained momentum, but funding remained a make-or-break issue for the project for the next several years, with many questioning whether it would get off the ground and opponents saying it would threaten, if not outright hurt, Bi-State's bus service.[128]

In March 1988, the St. Louis League testified in favor of a light-rail system (MetroLink) at a public hearing at the downtown Convention Center. Representatives urged decision makers to remember the bus system's need for an upgrade and to allocate funds for that along with MetroLink construction funding.[129] Construction was due to begin later that year with an anticipated opening in 1992, but a year of delays forced the schedule to shift to a groundbreaking in 1990 and opening on July 31, 1993.[130]

ZOO-MUSUEM DISTRICT

In 1971, St. Louis voters approved the creation of a cultural district for St. Louis City and County. Originally comprised of the Zoo, Science Center and Art Museum, over time, other cultural attractions asked to become part of the Zoo-Museum District and were added with legislative and then voter approval.

In January 1981, after a comprehensive study of the Zoo-Museum taxing district and member discussion of the issues pertinent to the future of the district,[131] the City and County Leagues backed a proposal to allow Shaw's Garden (now called the Missouri Botanical Garden) to become part of the Zoo-Museum tax district so that the garden could receive funding from property tax.[132] The House passed the bill in May 1981,[133] and Governor Bond signed it shortly thereafter.

The following year, the League "analyzed proposed state legislation for a 5/8 cent sales tax for economic development and cultural institutions in St. Louis City and County." While they took no official stance, they did offer recommendations for improvement on the bill that sought to change funding for the district from property tax to a sales tax. On April 3, 1982, voters in St. Louis City and County defeated the measure.

In 1983, four different issues relating to the Zoo-Museum District were in front of voters, all of which had League support. Three were property tax increases for the original three subdistricts and the fourth added a 4-cent local tax subsidy for the Missouri Botanical Garden (Shaw's Garden). All were passed.[134]

Four years later, the Missouri History Museum asked to become part of the district and voters said yes on Nov. 3, 1987.[135]

Finally, in 1989, the League supported property tax increases for the Missouri Botanical Garden and the St. Louis Science Center, but voters declined both at the polls.[136]

LEAGUE ACTIVITIES

In the 1984-1985 Annual Report of the President, President Debby Waite boldly stated the problems facing the League: "The state of the League is in a holding pattern right now. We can either take off and rebuild our organization into a strong influential local League or we can let it land and turn everything over to National."[137]

She went on to list the challenges facing them— ongoing decreases in membership, the same people volunteering all the time while most of the membership remained uninvolved, financing issues, the need to change to accommodate working members, including male members and younger members, competition from other groups for members' time and attention—in short, "breaking out of the traditional patterns to bring the League into the 21st century; anticipating change rather than just reacting to change."[138]

As an attentive president, Waite hit the nail on the head when analyzing the League's situation. As the following pages will show, the organization was dealing with member losses early in the decade and still trying to find its footing after merging into a single entity in St. Louis County for the first time in its history.

65TH ANNIVERSARY

"65 and Not Retiring" was the tongue-in-cheek theme of the League's 65th anniversary year—1983. The main celebration was a cocktail buffet held at Shaw's Garden Ridgeway Center on April 30. Ten League members were honored for longstanding service, and a commemorative program was created highlighting the honorees and milestones in the League's history.[139]

In addition, a mobile exhibit of the League's

accomplishments over the past 65 years, titled "LWV: 65 Years of Civic Accomplishment—1919-1984," was created by the Metropolitan League Committee to educate the public on the League's origins right here in St. Louis, as well as their civic and legislative activities. The exhibit rotated through area libraries, shopping centers, museums, and historical buildings throughout the year.[140]

70TH ANNIVERSARY

Five years later it was time for another party, the 70th anniversary of the League. It was marked by a celebration in Clayton at the "Top of the 230" honoring Rep. Sue Shear on Feb. 18, 1989.[141] Following is a profile of Sue's amazing life and career.

SUE SHEAR
• •
MARCH 17, 1918-NOV. 15, 1998

S. Sue Hirsch attended University City High School and Washington University,[142] where she studied political science[143] before marrying lawyer Harry D. Shear.

Shear joined the League in 1960.[144] She dipped a toe into politics during campaigns for U.S. Rep. James W. Symington and his father, U.S. Senator Stuart Symington, and working for U.S. Senator Thomas Eagleton.[145]

The newly formed National Women's Political Caucus noticed the outspoken Democrat and asked her to run for a vacant seat in the 83rd district of the Missouri House. "They needed a candidate who didn't have a job or young children tying her to St. Louis, had an interest in state government and was still alive! I fit all four qualifications," Sue quipped to the *St. Louis Post-Dispatch* in 1973.[146] She became one of only 10 women serving in the General Assembly[147] and the state's first female Jewish legislator.[148]

Sue's very first bill was HJR 41, the Equal Rights Amendment (ERA). "The fact is, if women don't push for women's rights, men, for the most part, aren't going to break their necks doing it," she told the *Post* in 1974.[149] Sue believed in the ERA so much that she reintroduced it every year until the 1982 deadline.

Though diagnosed with colon cancer in 1997, Sue continued to travel to Jefferson City to cast votes in support of her major concerns, including funding for higher education, handgun safety, mental illness, protections for children and the elderly, and women's reproductive rights.[150] The House Critical Issues Committee held a special hearing on April 28, 1998, and overwhelmingly passed the ERA. The full House held debate with Sue participating by phone, but no vote was taken.[151]

Sue retired from political life in May 1998, having mentored countless women in politics. She holds the distinction of having served for 26 years, longer than any other woman in the legislature,[152] a record that, thanks to 1993 term limits, will never be broken.[153] Over the course of her career, the number of female legislators in Missouri quadrupled, growing from 10 to 40.[154]

That month, the House passed a resolution creating the Sue Shear Institute for Women in Public Life at the University of Missouri – St. Louis, "the first public university-based public policy program in the country named for a woman elected official."[155] It included the Sue Shear Leadership Academy, "an intensive six-day leadership development program designed to inspire women's civic engagement and leadership through political and community involvement." The program is now run through UMSL's College of Education's Center for Character and Citizenship.[156]

In spring 1997, Sue was awarded an honorary doctorate from UMSL,[157] one of hundreds of awards bestowed upon her in her lifetime.

Although she was frail, Sue was at the polls in November 1998, just two weeks before her death,[158] to vote for her successor, Democrat Barbara Fraser of University City.[159]

REPRODUCTIVE RIGHTS

Some local and state Leagues started experimenting with ways to shorten the time for study of a new position in the 1970s. Concurrence was adopted as a method of adopting positions other Leagues had studied.

In 1982, the St. Louis League came to concurrence[160] and put out a statement in favor of a public policy on reproductive choices. A year later, the LWVUS adopted its position in support of the right of privacy in reproductive choices. LWVUS President Dorothy Ridings said the controversial subject was handled with "sensitivity and strength," helping to "remove blind stridency from the issue."

"This stance was neither controversial nor partisan because it was long after both *Griswold vs. Connecticut* and *Eisenstadt vs. Baird* had been rendered," said K Wentzien. These cases, in 1965 and 1972 respectively, made it legal for both married couples and single people to use contraception.

Abortion was discussed at the 1982 national convention with a position announced by LWVUS in January 1983: "public policy in a pluralistic society must affirm the constitutional right of privacy of the individual to make reproductive choices." The League deliberately used the term reproductive rights rather than abortion because it believes this was not a procedural position but a philosophical one.

League members are free not to advocate for a position they

do not agree with but may not express an opposing position in the name of the League. The reproductive choice issue is unique in that two members in St. Louis Leagues were so upset with the position that they resigned from the League citing religious grounds. Debby Waite recalls a group of Catholic nuns who chose to maintain their membership and support the League's position on "a women's right to choose" since the word "abortion" was not explicitly used in the position.

The League continues to join with other nonpartisan pro-choice groups to oppose legislative proposals that would restrict the right of privacy in reproductive choices.

ONE ST. LOUIS COUNTY LEAGUE

Over the years, the Leagues in St. Louis County had been slowly merging to form fewer groups that covered a wider geographic area than those originally formed in the early decades of the 20th century. First asked in 1977 and defeated in 1980, the question was raised again, "Should we combine our Leagues into one Metropolitan League?" The City League asked not to be included because members felt like its larger Black population had different concerns and feared being lost in the shuffle.[161]

Each League took a vote at its March unit meeting after listening to a presentation and discussing the issue. Because there was no clear answer, a special committee was appointed to represent all the Leagues and study the issue. Further education was provided at the annual meeting in April, and members had the opportunity to ask questions and voice their concerns. The factors in favor that were mentioned included efficiency, saving money, positive public image, and more effective use of womanpower. Member fears included distance involved in attending meetings, size of portfolio board members would have to handle, structural problems, and decision-making being put in the hands of a few rather than the whole membership.[162]

Despite these concerns, the consensus was for the Leagues to merge and so the Leagues of Central County, North County, South West County, and University City dissolved as LWV of St. Louis County was officially formed on May 2, 1980. LWV of Metropolitan St. Louis (Inter-League Organization-ILO) continued to coordinate activities of the entire area and local units met as before, working on issues in their areas.[163]

"Twenty years ago, most Leagues were established under municipal basis, but we have realized more and more that our goals are best met through working with a larger area," said Roseanne Newcomb, first president of the new County League.[164]

Also, on May 22, 1989, the League's Citizens Information/Resource Center (CIRC) changed its name to the LWV Information Service (LWVIS) so that both the public and members could understand better what they did.[165]

Publications

The League's CIRC offered a variety of resources to voters, including a Citizen's Handbook, "What's It All About: Local Government in the St. Louis Metropolitan Area," Know Your County, and a Voters Guide.

The Citizen's Handbook, made possible by funding from Pet, Inc. and Citicorp Person-to-Person, was an 18-page book containing practical information for citizens such as voter registration, government organization and responsibilities, utility rate structures, contact information for government and private agencies, and answers to other frequently asked questions. It was distributed at libraries and public offices.[166]

For the Presidential election years of 1980, 1984 and 1988,

the League produced a special publication called "How to Get Involved." This free booklet explained how voters could become involved in the delegate selection process in Missouri, as well as the structure of political parties in St. Louis City and St. Louis County and included a list of party officials and organizations.[167] It also explained why each person should be involved in politics: "the men and women who make and execute our laws obtain their office with the backing of the active participants in a political party. To influence who will get on the ballot and who will win the election, one must get involved long before Election Day."[168] In 1980, 5,000 copies were distributed; in 1984, that number grew to 7,500; and by 1988, more than 10,000 copies were printed.

In addition, the League regularly produced and updated publications for area residents called "Know Your County" and "Know Your City." These were guides to county/city government for all residents but were especially useful to students and new residents who may not be familiar with the area. By the end of the decade, thousands of copies of the guide were distributed.[169]

Theatre Parties

In order to produce these types of materials, the CIRC needed monetary backing. In 1988, Sydell Shayer had the idea to hold a theater party to raise money. The first was held on Dec. 18, 1988, and featured a St. Louis Black Repertory Theater production of "Black Nativity" at the Center for Contemporary Arts. The event sold out all 244 tickets, had 37 sponsors (thanks to dogged phone calls by Sydell) and netted $5,628, "the most raised by any single fundraising event for CIRC in its 12 years of existence."[170]

Sponsorship grew the following year, with a Theater Party

on Nov. 19, 1989. A reception was held in the Loretto-Hilton Theater after Webster University's production of "Holiday" by Phillip Barry. The League continued to hold annual Theater Parties from 1990 to 2018 with a virtual event in 2021 due to the COVID-19 pandemic. In 2022, an in-person Theatre Party to see "The 25th Annual Putnam County Spelling Bee" at the Stray Dog Theatre quickly sold out.

Asked why she thought the response was so positive, Sydell said, "Members want to support the League's activities; they enjoy socializing with one another; the spouses and friends are supportive of the League; and they found the party a painless—in fact fun—way to contribute to the organization."[171]

METROPOLITAN FINANCE COMMITTEE

The recession of the 1980s did not spare the League. Board meeting minutes from March 1980 declared, "The budget period news is grim."[172] But the women and men of the League were never ones to give up easily.

So, in 1981, they launched a redoubled effort at fundraising through the MFC. St. Louis "is the only area where Leagues work together to raise support money from the community. This cooperative effort includes the finance chair from each League and an overall chairman who is director of the Metro board."[173]

Falling a bit short of the $30,000 goal, the League adjusted the campaign structure to place more emphasis on direct solicitation of major contributions, mass mailings, and following up on general solicitation with a spring phone-a-thon.[174] Some years the League surpassed their goal and others they fell just short. Regardless of the outcome, the money raised was much appreciated and well used. The annual MFC campaign accounted for about half of the League's total income each year.[175]

Conclusion

The 1980s saw a shift toward greater equality in the League, both within the organization through uniting of the county Leagues, and in the community with a focus on fair voting practices through redistricting, the Freeholders Plan, advocacy for affordable transit, and a study of pay equity for women. This set the League up to take on even more issues in the 1990s and navigate an increasingly changing world with the nimbleness and unity of purpose required to be successful in such a fluid environment.

WOMEN WHO MADE AN IMPACT IN THE 1980S

Harriett Woods

June 2, 1927- Feb. 8, 2007

Ruth Harriett Friedman was born in Cleveland, Ohio, to Hungarian immigrant parents. She received her bachelor's in philosophy from the University of Michigan.[176] While working at a St. Louis newspaper, she met a reporter named Jim Woods, whom she married on Jan. 2, 1953.

Harriett got involved in local politics after a rattling manhole cover in front of her house in University City made it difficult to keep her three sons down for naps. She successfully fought city hall, spurring a whole new career.

Harriett served on the University City Council for seven years. When she was criticized for not staying at home with her children, she responded, "Of course, no one said, 'Well, men on the council have full-time jobs and busy children and spouses.'"[177] She took controversial positions on several subjects, including voting in favor of giving a liquor license to St. Louis landmark Blueberry Hill.

A League member since 1970, Harriett was appointed as the first female State Transportation and Highway Commissioner in 1974. Two years later, she was elected to the Missouri State Senate, becoming the second woman ever elected to that office. She campaigned hard for the doomed Equal Rights Amendment, as well as for tax reform to increase state spending for education and services for the elderly.

In 1982, Harriett ran for the U.S. Senate, beating out 10 opponents to garner the Democratic nomination to challenge Republican incumbent John Danforth.[178] Although a newcomer to national politics, she had a strong grassroots base that rallied under the slogan "Give them hell, Harriett!" (a purposeful play on the slogan of fellow Missouri politician and former U.S. President Harry Truman).[179] Harriett lost by only 27,500 votes out of 1.5 million cast, a margin of less than 2 percent.[180]

In 1984, Harriett ran for Lieutenant Governor and won, becoming the first woman (and first Jewish woman) elected to statewide office in Missouri.[181] She held the office through 1989, despite a failed 1986 run for U.S. Senate against former Governor Bond for the seat being vacated by retiring Democratic Senator Tom Eagleton. She lost by only three points.[182]

Harriett was president of the National Women's Political Caucus (NWPC) from 1991 to 1995, leading the multi-partisan organization in recruiting, training, and supporting hundreds of women candidates for elected and appointed office. She also headed the Coalition for Women's Appointments, which worked to place a record number of women in senior policy positions.[183] She was in that role in 1992, when a record number of women were elected to Congress, causing the media to call it "The Year of the Woman."[184] "Although I'm seen as advocating more women being elected to office, actually I'm for changing those systems that are barriers to making our democracy really work for everyone," Harriett said.[185]

In 1999, she was inducted into the St. Louis Walk of Fame.[186] In 2001, she published *Stepping Up to Power: The Political Journey of American Women,* a combination of memoir, political history and biography of the women who went before her.[187] In 1995, the LWVMO honored her at its annual convention by unveiling the Harriett Woods Award for Exemplary Public and Service.[188]

One of her final acts after being diagnosed with leukemia was to attend the swearing in of U.S. Senator Claire McCaskill (D-MO) and the first woman speaker in the U.S. House, Rep. Nancy Pelosi (D-CA). Harriett died in 2007, at the age of 79.[189] Later that year, a U.S. Postal Service facility in University City was designated as the "Harriett F. Woods Post Office Building."[190]

SYDELL SHAYER

DECEMBER 1930- PRESENT

A 1951 graduate of the College of the City of New York with a degree in Elementary Education, Sydell Feinman graduated from the College of the City of New York with a degree in Elementary Education. After marrying Larry Shayer, she began her married life in Wilmington, Delaware, moving to Springfield, Massachusetts, a few years later.[191] At age 27, mother of two children, she took the advice of a friend and joined the League in 1957.[192] Sydell said, "At that time we did not own a TV. I was happy to meet League members whose sole discussion was not what they saw on television the previous night. It didn't take long to get into the swing of things."

"I joined the international relations committee where I met

women like myself who had kids the same age as mine. We brought our children to the study group. Whoever thought I could learn about China at the same time my kids were playing in the next room."

She credits the League for introducing her to strong and intelligent women and learning about subjects she never thought she'd find interesting like taxes and the environment. After a couple of years, she became local League President. "There was so much to learn: how to be non-partisan, how to listen, how to be fair," she recalls. "There was a myriad of subjects to learn like redistricting, the merit system and whether aldermen should be elected by districts or at-large."

Sydell chose to further her interest in foreign policy. When the family moved to St. Louis and she transferred to the Central County League, the state board was looking for an international relations policy chair. She accepted the job. "I was like a fish out of water," Sydell said. "The members of the board were older. Their names were listed with their marital status. Their husbands were executives in large corporations, they smoked, and they all were very smart."

Sydell stuck with international relations, studying the United Nations, recognition of communist China, developing countries, trade, and more. These issues stimulated Sydell to go back to school and earn a master's in political science from the UMSL in 1976. In 1981, she was elected state League president and served two terms.

In 1985, Sydell agreed to fill a one-year spot as President of the League's Citizens Information Resource Center. A year later, she was elected to the national League board of directors which met monthly in Washington D.C. She became chair of a new two-year study titled "Meeting Basic Human Needs." The goal of the study was to "evaluate public and private responsibilities for providing food, shelter, a basic income level and access to health care." Sydell relied on the St. Louis League's social policy committee for input.

Over time, Sydell became a member of the board of ACLU, Confluence St Louis, Missourians Against the Death Penalty as well as President of the local chapter of the American Jewish Congress and advocacy chair for the Jewish Community Relations Council. The mission of these organizations coincided with the League's. It opened more opportunities for collaboration on important state and local objectives.

While on the national board, Sydell represented the League at a conference sponsored by the Consumers Union in Washington, D.C. She found a skill she never thought she possessed: "I learned that I could speak in public even if it meant I had to read from a script," she recalls. "The most enduring benefit the League has given me are the lifelong friendships I have made. Not only have they enhanced my League life, but they have also made my personal life as wonderful as it is."

Reflecting on her 64 years as a League member, Sydell says the four years she served as LWVMO president were the most memorable. "I can say it has been a wonderful journey, one where I discovered that giving is receiving and where one person can make a difference." But she's not done yet. Sydell still attends board meetings on Zoom and writes monthly newsletter articles on the death penalty for LWVMO.[193]

Agnes Garino

August 1944 – present

"Being a member of the LWV is a part of being a citizen, it is part of who you are," Agnes told Anna Reynolds when being interviewed for this book. It may as well also be her personal motto.

Agnes Mohr grew up surrounded by politics. Her stepmother was an election judge, and her uncle was an alderman, so her family "always took one's political responsibilities very seriously." Accordingly, Agnes studied history and political science at Marycrest College in Davenport, Iowa, and was a proud Youth for Kennedy from 1959-1960. After graduation, she conducted political research at Marquette University in Milwaukee, Wisconsin, and worked as a political pollster for the *Chicago Sun Times*.[194]

Agnes joined the League in 1971 when she moved from Chicago to south county. She was a member of the Webster Groves League for two years before moving to the nearby suburb of Kirkwood. In 1975, she joined Kirkwood's rapid transit committee and became newsletter editor and a spokesperson for the Kirkwood League.

In 1973, Agnes researched and wrote the Kirkwood town study: an updated "Know Kirkwood" guide. To be recognized by LWVMO, local Leagues at the time had to produce Know Your City or School District guides." She wrote many other League publications, including the informative "Citizens Handbook."

Agnes served as Kirkwood League president in 1975-1977.[195] "I recall meetings of the LWV in the late 70s as we struggled to define what changes we thought would improve our local government, make it more accessible to the average citizen and more professionally administered as we headed into the ever increasingly technical and complex 1980s," she said of the time.[196]

County LWV Chairman from 1977 to 1978, ILO Vice President from 1979-1981, and ILO President from 1981 to 1985, Agnes is particularly proud of the work to pass the revised St. Louis County charter in 1979. She was also instrumental in the League's work on the Metropolitan Sewer District, the voluntary desegregation program, the Zoo-Museum district, Metro transit improvements, and attempted passage of the ERA.

In the early 1980s, the League encouraged people to join the effort for a Kirkwood charter. This would replace the commission form of government, which many people thought was inefficient, with a mayor-council and city administrator.

"What followed was a most exciting effort, a truly citizen effort to explore the need to look at our form of government," Agnes recalled. "People Interested in a Charter for Kirkwood (PICK), a diverse group of individuals from their 30s-70s, banded together, dedicated to convincing voters of Kirkwood that yes, we did need to take a look at our form of government."[197]

PICK's goal was to persuade voters to approve a Charter Commission and elect 13 members to develop a charter that would be submitted for voter approval within one year of the first election. The new Kirkwood charter was approved in April 1983. Agnes called the victory "the most satisfying moment in my years of citizen effort."[198] She earned the title of "Mother of the Kirkwood Charter," bestowed by Kirkwood Mayor Herb Jones in 1985.[199]

Agnes was president of the LWV of Metro St. Louis ILO from 1981-1985. She led efforts to have a Presidential Debate in St. Louis in 1984. Unsuccessful in securing a location, she was invited to and attended the debate between Ronald Reagan and Walter Mondale in Kansas City. From 1985 to 1989, she served as the League's development staff.

Outside of the League, Agnes was a founding board member of Confluence, a volunteer citizens' organization dedicated to tackling area-wide problems. She also served on the board of the Metro Saint Louis Forum, the Kirkwood City Council (1990-1994), the St. Louis County Boundary Commission (1995-2002) and served as board member and president of the national

Acoustic Neuroma Association (2001-2012).

"Agnes is a shining example of a fast-disappearing breed—the full-time community volunteer," League member Brenda Banjak, told the *West County Journal* in 1985.

Agnes continues that role in a number of ways such as a board member (2010-2015) of the Women's Foundation of Greater St. Louis and now a member of its Advisory Council. Her diverse not-for-profit and government-related involvement includes: board member of the Frank Lloyd Wright House in Ebsworth Park in Kirkwood (2001-present), founding commissioner of the Kirkwood Arts Commission (2013-2020), and member of the Kirkwood Arts Foundation (present).

Primarily because of her long-time interest in government and architecture, Agnes took on "50x60: The Successful Quest to Visit all of America's 50 State Capitols." Trips with husband Dave, son Tony, daughter-in-law Adele, and sisters Katy and Rosie enabled her to complete the challenge in 2004.

Agnes is still highly active in the League, having served in recent years on committees dedicated to marking the St. Louis League's 100th anniversary, the centennial of the 19th amendment and commemorating the efforts of historical St. Louis suffragists. Her birthday is celebrated as Women's Equality Day (Aug. 26). She and husband Dave have been generous donors.

Deborah Waite Howard

November 1945– present

Debby Waite was born to Richard and Eleanor Wexsmith Waite of St. Louis. She attended Lawrence University in Appleton, Wisconsin—the same school that her mother (class of 1933) and grandmother (class of 1909) had attended—earning her bachelor's degree in 1967.

The League was a family affair for Debby; her mother had been a League member for as long as she could remember and served in every leadership role except president, an office her daughter often held.

Seven years after joining the League in 1970, Debby co-chaired the League's Urban Crisis Committee and championed housing access for low-income St. Louisans, as well as a total revision of the St. Louis City Charter. Her first term as president of the St. Louis City League began in 1979, while her mother served on the board as treasurer. Debby would go on to hold the role of president in 1984 and again in 1998-1999. President of the League's Information Service in the early 1990s, she served as president of the Missouri League for four years (1999-2003). She continues to serve as the LWVMO parliamentarian.

In addition, Debby has chaired the Metro St. Louis City/County Governance Committee, served as Vice President, International Relations Director and Finance Chair in the City League, and LWVMO Voter Services Chair.

Outside of the League, Debby worked for Women's Crusade Against Crime, the Census Bureau, the St. Louis City library, Council on World Affairs, the Lieutenant Governor, the St. Louis YWCA and the Department of Revenue.[200]

In 2004, she married Jack H. Howard, a widower with three children. Jack passed away just before she served as a delegate to the LWVUS Convention in Chicago in June 2018.[201]

Debby is still an active League member, championing the passage of the Equal Rights Amendment. She served as a member of the U.S. Coast Guard Auxiliary for 25 years and continues to volunteer with Biome School—a STEAM school teaching underserved children in the St. Louis community.[202]

BARBARA BAIR SHULL

1923- Nov. 16, 1996

Barbara Rose Bair was born in Colorado Springs, Colorado, in 1923. She graduated from Swarthmore College in Swarthmore, Pennsylvania. During World War II, she served as a WAVE (Women Accepted for Volunteer Emergency Service) in the Navy.

Barbara moved to St. Louis in 1947 and married Franklin B. Shull, a physics professor at Washington University, the following year. They had four daughters: Margaret, Cathy, Sarah, and Dorothy.

Barbara joined the League in 1955, serving anywhere she was needed, but especially in roles related to taxes, finance, development, and education. She was a very active League member, with several longtime members calling her indispensable. "Barbara was a wealth of information," administrative assistant Carol Pugh said in 1996. "She knew the answer to practically everything."

As Missouri League president from 1979-1981, Barbara often contacted legislators about state taxes and education. She publicly challenged U.S. Rep. Mel Hancock as he led voters to approve a controversial amendment to the Missouri Constitution in 1980 that limited state tax collections to a percentage of the growth in the personal income of state residents.

Barbara served as president of the League's CIRC in the mid-1980s and then as Revenue Study chair in 1990.[203] In 1989, she was a member of the League's Local Government Committee that opposed St. Louis County's 1/2 cent sales tax increase proposal. She was one of four former presidents honored by the League as a "Distinguished Member" in 1991.

Barbara developed strong public speaking skills and

moderated several candidate forums, including a U.S. Senate debate at UMSL. She was active with the Conference on Education and represented the League with Missourians for Tax Justice.[204]

Barbara was known for her writing and editing skills. She edited the *Metro News* from 1986-1996. She used the House Weekly Journal to get the State Legislative Bulletin out every Friday during the legislative session. Sydell Shayer recalls that her bulletins were brimming with news on legislation of League interest and hints on what members should do.

Barbara passed away on Nov. 16, 1996, at St. Luke's Hospital at the age of 73, after a battle with cancer.[205]

Main Sources Chapter 3 – The 1980s

Annual Reports of the President, League of Women Voters of St. Louis, 1980-1989
Minutes of the 1980 Annual Meeting, League of Women Voters of Central St. Louis County
Board and Council Meeting Minutes, 1980-1989
Newsletters
- *The Bulletin,* February 1980
- *Central County Scene,* October 1974
- *Metro News,* Spring 1980-Spring 1989

League documents regarding
- Election Laws
- Environmental Issues
- Death Penalty
- MSD
- Pay Equity
- Redistricting
- Transit
- Zoo-Museum District

Periodicals
- *Como Magazine*
- *The Atlantic*
- *The Riverfront Times*
- *St. Louis Jewish Light*
- *St. Louis Magazine*
- *St. Louis Post-Dispatch*
- *Webster-Kirkwood Times*
- *West County Journal*

Websites
- Ballotpedia
- City of Kirkwood
- Economic Policy Institute

- Metro Transit St. Louis
- St. Louis Public Radio/NPR
- United States Environmental Protection Agency

For a complete list of sources, please see the endnotes at
https://my.lwv.org/missouri/metro-st-louis/about/our-history.

1980s

Carolyn Clark answering voter questions in 1982.

Brenda Banjak stacking the League's "Big Vote" ballot boxes in 1983.

Leaguers marching downtown in the Veiled Prophet Parade in 1984.

LWVUS board member Virginia Schwartz (left) and Sydell Shayer (right) with 65th Anniversary honorees Terry Fischer, Ginny Deutch, Betty Wilson, Ellen Walters, Mary Greensfelder (back row), Dorothy Moore, Ella Stinson, Avis Carlson, Eleanor Waite and Evelyn Schreiber (front row).

SLPS student Sheila Blair designed this 1984 League billboard. Shown with Agnes Garino, Ida West and representatives of Gannett and St. Louis Public Schools.

Barbara Shull was President of LWV of Missouri from 1979-1981 and President of the League's Information Service from 1986-1991.

CHAPTER 4

The 1990s

THE 1990s WERE a relatively peaceful and prosperous time. The decade began with the fall of the Soviet Union and the release of Nelson Mandela and ended with the Lewinsky scandal and the introduction of the Euro. Congress passed both the Family & Medical Leave Act and the Violence Against Women Act. In 1997, Madeleine Albright became the first woman appointed Secretary of State. The decade was marked by rapid technological advances, from the rise of the internet and personal computing to the launch of the International Space Station.

Within the League, there was less upheaval and more unity than ever before. The decade saw the City and County Leagues merge so that there was now truly one LWV of Metro St. Louis. City presidents Cay Thompson, Zoe Shipman, Judith Arnold, Clarene Royston, Judith O'Briant, Donna Brooks and Marjorie Jokerst; county presidents Mary K. Brown, Susan Trice, Gail Heyne-Hafer, Jean Dean; and the first president of the combined city and county Leagues, K Wentzien, enabled the League to make great gains. Among these were:

- Focus on gun control, reproductive rights and health care reform early in the decade.

- Expanded voter registration and education
- Shifted priorities mid-decade to campaign finance reform and successfully got it on the ballot in 2000.
- A successful Amicus Brief in the Blue Cross Blue Shield case resulting in a multi-million-dollar foundation to assist uninsured and underinsured Missourians.
- A successful joint Amicus Brief with LWVUS to remove term limit language from the Missouri congressional ballot.

As always, voting and election rights were at the fore, followed by St. Louis' continuing efforts to desegregate its schools, reform campaign financing, improve transit, and save the environment. But the 1990s also saw new efforts toward ending homelessness, bringing about gun control, and reforming health care.

VOTER SERVICES

League Wins Right to Register Voters in St. Louis City

One of the greatest victories in this area during the 1990s came in 1993 when the League finally won a 20-year struggle to be officially approved to conduct voter registration during special registration drives in St. Louis City. (St. Louis County had allowed this for years.)

Back in the mid-1970s, the St. Louis City Board of Election commissioners revoked the League's ability to register voters, instituting a policy that only board employees could do so—ostensibly to reduce the risk of voter fraud. The League had been seeking to become deputized since then, not only to be able to fulfil its mission, but also because St. Louis City had seen a steep decline in the number of registered voters in the last several years—a 23% drop between 1980 and 1992, with only 59% of eligible city voters registered, the lowest level in the state.[1]

The League went back to the board again in spring 1992, but the board split 2-2, with Democrats favoring the League registering voters and Republicans opposed. The board did approve expanding "voter registration sites to include nursing homes, fire stations, banks, welfare and driver's license offices and large businesses," adding salt to the wound.[2]

"The League was organized to ensure full voter participation through registration and education programs," wrote Judith Arnold, City League President. "It is extremely important that our League emphasizes to the community that voter registration practices in St. Louis City are restrictive and that expanded voter registration services should include the appointment of League members as voter registrars."[3]

Never ones to give up, the League kept petitioning. In July 1993, members presented the board with information about how other areas use League members as deputy registrars.[4] On October 11, the board finally relented and appointed City League members as deputy registrars. The League wasted no time, immediately setting up a special project to get voters registered in time to vote for the history-making election of two public housing residents to the St. Louis Housing Authority Board of Commissioners on November 13.[5]

Kids' Voting Program

In 1996, Ritenour School District became the first St. Louis-area district to participate in Kids Voting USA, "a national program for elementary and secondary school students to study a 10-week curriculum and go to the polls on Election Day to cast ballots on the same candidates and issues on which adults are voting."[6] The program began in Arizona in 1987.[7]

In 1998, school districts in Clayton, Ferguson-Florissant, and University City joined, bringing the total number of students in the program to about 25,000. In 1999, the St. Louis League received a Citizenship Education Clearinghouse grant from the Deer Creek Foundation to expand the program for children in St. Louis over the next two years.[8]

By 2003, more than 203,000 students were participating, over half of them in the St. Louis area.[9] The program lasted through 2012, with The Magic House in Kirkwood and other St. Louis area-attractions acting as official voting precincts for the kids.[10]

VOTER EDUCATION ON CABLE

While it was not the League's first foray into televised voter education, its cable TV program, "Let the People Know," was one of the most successful. Starting in 1994, the 30-minute show was produced and hosted by St. Louis County League members and featured interviews with guests on a variety of topics of interest to the League and to the public. It was broadcast on Charter Communications' and Continental Cable's local origination channels at least eight times per month. "This cable show enables the League to take action on issues the League is either studying or issues upon which the League reached consensus," wrote coordinator Chris Milligan-Ciha. "These programs reached the public, enabling the League to 'let the people know, make the people care, help the people act.'"[11]

During its first five years, topics included health care reform, Missouri health care legislation, campaign finance reform, how to pick a candidate, Metropolitan Sewer District, floodplain development, juvenile justice issues, the Hancock II Amendment, children at risk, dioxin waste incineration, voter registration, safe drinking water, volunteerism, women's rights, air quality, tax justice, ballot issues, immigration, naturalization, national economics, children's health insurance, the concealed weapons bill, domestic violence, and current legislative issues.

The show kept going into the 2000s with tapes available on VHS for borrowing or on-site viewing at the League office.[12]

"MOTOR VOTER" LAW

In 1990, a provision of the National Voter Registration Reform Act proposed to allow eligible citizens to register to vote when they apply for, renew, or change the address on their driver's license. The so-called "Motor Voter" law was passed by the U.S. House of Representatives but stalled during debate in the Senate for three years.

The League supported the bill because it would make registering to vote much easier for many groups and hoped it would help reverse trends of lower registration across St. Louis. "Studies have shown that, when citizens are registered, they vote in significant numbers," wrote League Presidents Mary K. Brown (St. Louis County) and Cay Thompson (St. Louis City) in a 1990 letter to the *St. Louis Post-Dispatch*. "We need a voter registration system that makes it easier for people to register to vote, which we consider a basic right."[13]

In 1991, the League of Women Voters of Missouri warned that even if its petition drive was successful and the bill passed both houses of Congress, "individual states [could] still determine whether or not voters would be eligible to cast ballots on state and local candidates and issues." In other words, depending on the laws of their state, voters who registered under the Motor Voter law could be eligible to vote for president, vice president, and members of Congress, but not for governor or local city/county officials. This meant that some states would have to keep separate voter rolls for local and national elections.[14]

Finally, on May 11, 1993, the Motor Voter bill passed the U.S. Senate[15] 62-36 after lawmakers ended a GOP filibuster aimed at killing the bill, which they believed could lead to people being coerced to join certain parties at the time of registration. The final bill added a mail-in method of registration, as well as allowing voters to apply at the time of getting their driver's license, applying for public assistance, or at military recruitment centers.[16] President Bill Clinton signed the bill into law on May 20.[17]

However, that was far from the end of the story. States across the country filed lawsuits against the Motor Voter bill, forcing U.S. Attorney General Janet Reno to urge compliance under threat of her own lawsuit against recalcitrant states.[18] For a while it looked like Missouri would be one of these states; in early 1994, the Missouri House rejected the bill, claiming it would cause confusion and protests because government workers weren't trained to register voters— but they reversed course a few months later.[19]

When the law went into effect on Jan. 1, 1995, it was hailed as a great success, registering half a million new voters across the country in just its first month. Missouri registered 11,675 in January through the Department of Revenue, a number the *St. Louis Post-Dispatch* called "one of the highest figures in the nation."[20] By June, the national number had jumped to around 5 million and Missouri's had gone up by 150,000, or about 5% of the state's total number of registered voters.[21]

However, just over a year later, another serious threat loomed. U.S. Senator Alan Simpson (R-WY) introduced an amendment to the Immigration Reform Act of 1996 "that would virtually kill the National Voter Registration Act, the federal Motor Voter law." The bill would have required everyone who registered to vote under the act to provide proof of citizenship (U.S. passport, certificate of citizenship, certificate of naturalization, birth certificate plus driver's license with a picture ID, or similar official state identification). The League explained that this would put an end to registration by mail and that "agency-based registration programs...would be rendered completely ineffective." Members contacted their representatives to voice their opposition. [22] Fortunately, their fears were not realized. While the Immigration Reform Act did pass, Simpson's amendment was nowhere to be found.

REDISTRICTING

In 1991, Missouri once again faced the redistricting process with the release of the 1990 census results. This information was used to redraw the boundaries of the state's congressional nine districts. As League member Sydell Shayer explained, the purpose of apportionment (redistricting) "is to guarantee fair and equal access to the political process for all citizens. The probability of political participation increases if citizens believe that they have equal opportunity to influence government."

The process was easier in the 1990s than in other decades because Missouri didn't lose any Congressional seats.[23] In March, Governor John Ashcroft appointed 28 people to House and Senate redistricting/reapportionment panels who had until September 26 to redraw their respective maps.[24] The General Assembly approved those maps in May 1991 [25] [26] with little of the usual controversy or fanfare. It was the first time in more than 30 years that the Governor approved the House's own plan[27] and avoided having a panel of judges do it for them.[28] The Senate, however, was not so fortunate. They gave up in July, allowing a redistricting panel appointed by the Missouri Supreme Court to draw the lines for Missouri's 34 Senate districts.[29]

CAMPAIGN FINANCE REFORM

In its ongoing quest for campaign finance reform, the League reemphasized the need in 1992, stating "too much money in politics leads to the perception that members of Congress are subject to undue influence from special interest groups. It also reduces competitiveness in elections." They found that the growing influence of Political Action Committees (PACs), special interests, and soft money—"money raised and spent outside the scope of federal campaign finance laws"—were the biggest threats to campaign finance reform because they were loopholes that needed to be closed.

To solve this problem, the League advocated public financing of congressional elections, limiting the amount that candidates can receive from PACS, further limiting large contributions from individuals, and imposing spending limits on campaigns. Members also urged curbing the advantages incumbents have over new challengers, especially in the areas of special interest contributions, and re-establishing tax credits for small, individual contributions.[30]

In 1993, several bills related to campaign finance reform in the Missouri legislature were combined into a single bill, which the League supported. Lawmakers claimed that the people were not demanding such reform, so the League launched a campaign to show them just how wrong they were.[31] In addition to the usual phone calls and letters, members hosted a forum on campaign finance reform at UMSL. The event, held on Nov. 15, 1993, included Senator Wayne Goode (D-13) and Rep. May Scheve (D-98). They co-chaired the joint committee conducting "discussions with citizens around the state with an eye toward introducing campaign finance reform legislation in the 1994 session."[32]

"This is an important opportunity," said LWVMO President

and event coordinator Linda McDaniel, who had been working on campaign finance reform since the 1970s. "The...meeting is our chance to participate in the debate...Lawmakers [need] to know where [voters] stand on public funding of campaigns, limits on contributions to candidates, limits on contributions to and from political parties, and disclosure requirements."[33]

The November 1994 ballot included Proposition A, which limited campaign finance contributions to $300 for statewide offices, $200 for districts with more than 100,000 people, and $100 for those with less. It was supported by the League[34] and passed by a ratio of 3-1 on Election Day.[35]

The passage of Proposition A also created a nine-member, bipartisan Commission on Fair Elections, appointed by the governor and including representatives of public interest groups. The Commission was charged to "hold public hearings, develop a proposal for fair funding of public elections, and submit its report findings and recommendations to the governor and legislature by the end of September 1995.[36]

The League's own Linda McDaniel was elected chairman of that commission after the Missouri Alliance for Campaign Reform, a collection of public interest groups including the League, submitted a list of names. With McDaniel at the helm, the Commission held a series of public meetings to hear from voters on whether campaigns should be publicly financed.[37] After being granted an extension for deliberations, the Commission voted 6-3 in favor of public financing and submitted its recommendation to Governor Mel Carnahan.[38]

Little to no action resulted, so in 1998 Missouri Voters for Clean Elections, which included the League, launched a petition drive to get taxpayer-funded campaigns on the November ballot. While they had more than enough signatures—115,000 even though they were only legally required to gather

72,000—they fell short on money and had to scrap their plans, raising only $250,000 compared to the $1.5 million opponents planned to spend.[39]

But there was still quite a fight over the subject. The League endorsed a discharge position, which "takes responsibility for particular legislation away from the committees to which it has been referred and sends it directly to the House floor." On Aug. 6, 1998, the U.S. House Representatives passed the Shays-Meehan campaign finance reform legislation by 252-179. However, it failed in the Senate when supporters were eight votes short of the 60 needed to "invoke cloture to overcome the filibuster blocking the McCain-Feingold legislation, the Senate companion to Shays-Meehan."[40]

The following year, the League issued an Action Alert to members, making them aware of a new threat to campaign finance reform in the House from U.S. Rep. Dennis Hastert (R-IL), who "made it clear he does not think that campaign finance reform is an important issue, and is in no hurry to bring it to the floor."[41] The League predicted that "opponents of reform will try to derail it by offering a wide variety of amendments designed to split the bipartisan coalition that supports the Shays-Meehan Bill...Substitute bills will also be offered in attempts to defeat the legislation."[42]

On the other side of the fight were the "blue dogs," a caucus of conservative Democrats, who filed a discharge petition, H. RES. 122, that would "force the House to consider campaign finance reform quickly."[43] League members were urged to help "force early action in the house, to ensure that the Senate has adequate time to consider this important legislation in this session... and to look for opportunities during August and the first week of September when your representatives will be out in the community, at town hall meetings and other public events. It is also important to write your representatives urging support for the Shays-Meehan Bill without amendments."[44] On Sept. 14, 1999, the House passed the Shays-Meehan Bill, also called the Bipartisan Campaign Finance Reform Act of 1999, with amendments, 252-177.

During this time, Doris Haddock, also known as "Granny D," an 89-year-old activist from New Hampshire was making her way across the country on foot as part of a campaign to advocate for finance reform. She visited St. Louis on October 1 and met with more than 20 League leaders including the state board. The following day she attended the kickoff for Missouri's petition drive for campaign finance reform.[45]

Later that month, the Senate revised McCain-Feingold, its companion measure, and added amendments and disclosure requirements.[46] It wasn't until 2002, however, that the legislation, significantly changed from its original versions, would be signed into law.

TERM LIMITS

Also in 1992, the League advocated against term limits for elected officials. Contrary to those who pushed for them on the grounds that term limits made it easier to remove bad politicians from office, the League believed that "in a democracy, elections are the voter's tool for limiting the terms of ineffective legislators. Term limits take away that tool." They also argued that term limits bar good politicians from being reelected and are useless in stopping lobbyists and special interest groups from exerting power over elected officials and warned limits could have unexpected consequences for the balance of power in the executive and judicial branches of government.[47]

The November 1992 ballot in Missouri contained two constitutional amendments that would limit how long legislators could stay in office. Amendment 12 would limit state legislators to eight years—four two-year terms in the House and two four-year terms in the Senate. Amendment 13 attempted to place a limit of eight years for the U.S. House (four two-year terms) and 12 years for the U.S. Senate (two six-year terms). Both needed a simple majority to pass and only applied to those elected after the measure went into effect.[48] Unlike other states where term limits specify a break period after which the lawmaker can run for that office again, Missouri's proposals barred the politician from ever running for the seat again, a stipulation the League called "unduly harsh."[49]

Voters did not agree with the League and passed both term limit amendments on Nov. 3, with nearly three out of every four voting in favor. This was a trend across the country, with term limit measures considered in 24 states and approved in 14.[50] In 1995, the U.S. Supreme Court ruled in *U.S. Term Limits, Inc. vs. Thornton* that states cannot impose qualifications for prospective members of the U.S. Congress stricter than those specified in the Constitution.[51]

BLUE CROSS BLUE SHIELD LAWSUIT

A major advocacy project the League took on in the mid- to-late 1990s was Blue Cross Blue Shield of Missouri's (BCBS) desire to change from being a not-for-profit to a for-profit company. The controversy came about because the company was, according to its own historical documents,

> created with the intention of providing affordable health care coverage in the nonprofit context with a community focus. The plans were established to fill significant holes in the health care system. They were created and promoted by the community,

acting in the public benefit. Their history and involvement in creating an alternative health care coverage source—the voluntary, nonprofit prepaid health plan—and their subsequent participation in the development of the Medicare and Medicaid programs have helped ensure that more Americans obtain access to health care coverage.[52]

But now, suddenly, BCBS wanted to abandon that mission and take the money it saved through its non-profit status and other protections into its life as a for-profit company. Led on the state level by St. Louis City League member Rachel Farr Fitch[53] and locally by St. Louis County member Linda McDaniel, the League sought to protect the public's interest because BCBS falsely claimed they did not have a public debt obligation—even though they had been a not-for-profit for more than 60 years.

In 1994, the Missouri Department of Insurance approved BCBS's request to create a for-profit company, RightChoice Managed Care Incorporated, without a charitable asset set aside.[54] BCBS transferred approximately 90% of its assets to RightChoice and then a few months later, publicly traded 19.5% of RightChoice stock and kept 81.5%.[55] This initial public offering made $38 million for BCBS.[56]

The League and other consumer groups were concerned that BCBS was allowed to do business in that manner. One anonymous editorial in the *St. Louis Post-Dispatch* stated that BCBS was "literally walk[ing] away from its public benefit obligations as it moves into the for-profit health insurance business...State officials have put no dollar value on the company's obligations, but consumer groups place them at $200 million or more."⁵⁷ The League argued that the company should be required to "transfer their not-for-profit assets to a nonprofit foundation dedicated to charitable health purposes."⁵⁸ Because of this public outcry, the Missouri Department of Insurance reviewed the case and found that BCBS "disclosed false and incomplete information, thereby illegally transferring assets from its non-profit parent corporation to its for-profit, publicly traded subsidiary, RightChoice Managed Care, Inc."⁵⁹

BCBS responded by saying that their tax-exempt status ended a long time ago and they only moved part of their assets, so they didn't owe anyone anything. Governor Mel Carnahan attempted to negotiate with BCBS, but talks quickly fell through, so the Missouri League penned a bill (SB 997) asking the legislature to require BCBS to honor its public benefit obligation. The bill was introduced by Senator Jet Banks and it was voted out of committee.⁶⁰ But before it could go any further, BCBS sued the Missouri Department of Insurance and the attorney general, alleging misconduct and essentially asking the government to leave them alone. This lawsuit was the first in the country to deal with the process of non-profit companies becoming for-profit.⁶¹

A coalition of 65 Missouri groups representing health care consumers was quickly formed under the name Missouri Consumer Health Care WATCH, with Rachel Farr Fitch, LWVMO's director for health issues, named as chairman. They filed a petition with the Missouri Department of Insurance, "signed statements of concern urging the state to aggressively collect the debt that Blue Cross owed the public and to dedicate those funds to charitable health purposes." The coalition eventually grew to include more than 90 organizations representing over a million Missourians.⁶²

The League and other consumer groups attempted to join

the lawsuit, but when a judge ruled they could not,[63] they chose to participate as amici curiae (friends of the court). On Dec. 30, 1996, the St. Louis Circuit Court ruled against BCBS, saying it "abused or exceeded its authority as a nonprofit by transferring its assets to a for-profit subsidiary, which was organized to benefit private shareholders."[64] BCBS appealed, and on Aug. 4, 1998, the Missouri Court of Appeals Western District affirmed the Circuit Court's ruling that BSCS violated state law. BCBS appealed again, this time to the Missouri Supreme Court.

On Sept. 20, 1998, while the case was pending, the parties negotiated a settlement agreement. On November 4, a Circuit Court judge appointed Robert G. Russell "Special Master" to review the settlement agreement. He, in turn, invited amici curiae, including the League, to "participate extensively in all hearings on the proposed settlement agreement which did not have the endorsement of the Missouri Consumer Health Care WATCH coalition."[65] The parties and consumers reached an amended settlement on March 12, 1999. It was further amended a few days later and filed by the Special Master in October. On December 9, the Missouri Supreme Court ruled that court approval of the settlement agreement was not required because it was considered a private business agreement.

The result was the creation of the Missouri Foundation for Health (MFH), which inherited all the money from BCBS as a profit-making entity. The foundation also received over $1 billion from the sale of RightChoice shares.[66]

EDUCATION

St. Louis's voluntary desegregation and busing program, conducted through the Voluntary Interdistrict Choice Corporation (VICC), continued into the 1990s and by all accounts was doing what it was intended to do. According to the Missouri

Department of Elementary and Secondary Education, in 1991, 11 county school districts had an average Black enrollment of 20%.[67]

In October 1993, the City and County Leagues held an event where they invited members of the public to tell them "the good, bad, and ugly concerning the desegregation program." It went well, but afterwards, in a startling break with tradition, Mayor Freeman Bosley, Jr., "made a statement which was not in conformance with [the] League position," i.e. that he was in favor of ending the area's school desegregation program in favor of a focus on "school equity," because he believed busing had not been good for Black neighborhoods or schools.

The League responded by publicly and emphatically reiterating that "The League of Women Voters support equal access to quality education for all persons regardless of their race, color, gender, religion, or national origin," a position they have held since the late 1970s through legislative threats and other challenges and are "committed to racial integration of schools as a necessary condition for equal access to education."[68]

However, City League president Judith Arnold emphasized, "the kind of housing desegregation that would make school desegregation natural and easy does not exist in many neighborhoods and communities including the City of St. Louis." She urged members to "write the Board of Education and the mayor's office and let them know...busing is not only a means to an end. Let the mayor know he needs to concentrate on the business of rebuilding strong economically mixed neighborhoods and instituting a strong neighborhood marketing strategy which will change the complexion of future housing patterns."[69]

After that disagreement, things went back to normal until the end of the decade. The VICC program continued to grow, reaching peak enrollment of 14,626 students in 1999, when participating districts saw an average student population of 20% Black students, as opposed to a projected 4% without the program.

On Jan. 6, 1999, a judge agreed that the St. Louis City schools could continue the VICC program without court involvement for three years, the first time the city was allowed to operate it on its own since the program was implemented in 1980. The agreement was contingent on voters approving a 2/3 of a cent tax increase to make up for the loss of court-ordered state funding that came with the program being independent. The vote was set for February 2.[70]

Ahead of that important vote, the League published *Focus on Desegregation: Questions and Answers*, a booklet outlining the case and its outcome. At the same time, the League's units discussed materials on the St. Louis desegregation plan produced by FOCUS St. Louis, a regional catalyst for positive community change that was created in July 1996 by the merger of the Leadership Center of Greater St. Louis and Confluence St. Louis.[71] The League had worked with Confluence and quickly formed a close partnership with FOCUS.[72]

City voters passed the tax by 63%. Exit polls showed that of those who voted in favor, 45.6% did so because they believed the tax "would strengthen neighborhood schools," which they viewed was more important than school integration. Concern for their schools was by far the most often cited answer,[73] showing that voters were more likely to agree with the former mayor's way of thinking than the League's.

Six months later, a monitoring committee that was a requirement of the settlement had still not been set up. The League voiced concern that this was an important form of accountability for St. Louis Public Schools. The League said they "support a communication process involving all segments of the community within each school district. Since the monitoring committee is to include representation from parent groups, businesses, higher education, teacher organizations and the parties in the case, it would meet that basic requirement."[74]

As the year wound down and still nothing was done, St. Louis City Schools faced a possible loss of accreditation for failing to comply with the terms of the settlement.[75] Indeed, the future of the whole program was in question. The VICC was constructed to slow down each year until it finally phased out; it had to be this way because of a 1991 U.S. Supreme Court decision[76] that said "race-based education programs cannot run into perpetuity."[77] What was more, several of the original school districts had left the program: Hazelwood had enough natural diversity that it no longer had to participate as of 1998, and Ladue and Ritenour pulled out in 1999. That meant fewer choices for students, and potentially fewer volunteers.[78]

HOUSING

Housing for St. Louisans, especially in the most economically disadvantaged areas, has long been a focus of the League. In the 1980s, the League attended a conference on housing needs in St. Louis County that revealed "the number of residential units were increasing at a decreasing rate...the need for housing overall was increasing even with a static population... [and] the cost of housing relative to income was growing."[79] Out of this conference a St. Louis County Housing Coalition was created, which included the League.

In 1990, Proposition 1 was placed on the ballot in St. Louis County, asking voters to approve a measure that would:

> establish a fund to help provide services for homeless families by adopting a $3 increase

in certain recording and filing fees of such instruments such as deeds, lease agreements, certified copies of wills, etc. The money collected will be used to provide financial assistance to agencies supplying housing related services to homeless families in shelters and aid homeless individuals to develop self-sufficiency and independence. Passage of Proposition 1 would enable the community in partnership and other agencies to expand their services to the homeless population of St. Louis County.[80]

The League was firmly in support of Proposition 1 and wrote a letter to the *St. Louis Post-Dispatch* urging voters to vote for it. They shared the sobering statistic that "an increasing number of the estimated 5,000 homeless in St. Louis County are families with children. The total bed capacity of all county shelter facilities numbered fewer than 100."[81] On Nov. 6, voters passed Proposition 1 by 177,748 to 61,378.[82]

The following year, the League co-sponsored a statewide conference on homelessness called "A Place to Call Home: Homelessness and Affordable Housing Issues in Missouri." During the keynote speech on April 13, it was announced that Missouri had set a goal of ending homelessness by the year 2000.[83]

In September, the St. Louis Housing Resource Commission heard stories from five homeless mothers who were residents of the Salvation Army Community in Partnership Family Center talk about the low availability of shelter rooms for people who call the homeless hotline—in July, of 388 calls, fewer than 10 people could be placed in existing emergency shelters—and a new program called Room at the Inn. This St. Louis County program worked closely to match hotline callers with churches and synagogues that could provide nighttime facilities, services and volunteers for emergency shelter for up to one week.

1993 kicked off with the second annual Housing Conference sponsored by the Low-Income Housing and Homelessness Task Force of the Missouri Association for Social Welfare and the League. The event, held in the Capitol Rotunda in Jefferson City on April 1, focused on the Housing Trust Fund bill, SB298, which was introduced by Senator Phil Curls of Kansas City. Even though similar bills were vetoed in the past, hope was high for successful passage under newly elected Democratic Governor Mel Carnahan, who had been a housing advocate prior to election. During the event, attendees learned how to lobby and were set loose to talk with legislators. Workshops were also held, where speakers included keynote Mary Brooks, director of the National Housing Trust Fund Project, Governor Carnahan, State Treasurer Bob Holden and Attorney General Jay Nixon.[84]

The bill was passed in 1994, creating The Missouri Housing Trust Fund. According to the fund's website, it "is supported by a $3 recording fee on all real estate documents filed in the state of Missouri...The Missouri Housing Development Commission administers the Trust Fund, which provides funding for a variety of housing needs, such as homeless prevention, rehab or new construction of rental housing, rental assistance, and home repair."[85] When passed, it was projected to generate $6 million a year to combat housing issues and homelessness.[86] The Fund is still helping "meet the housing needs of very low-income families and individuals" today.

Also in 1993, St. Louis made history by holding the first-ever election in the United States to "elect residents of public housing to its policy making board." Conducted by the St. Louis City League, this election was held at polling places set up throughout the city where 455 residents voted in the election for two resident commissioners of the St. Louis Housing Authority. Voter Services Chair Clarene Royston was appointed a member of the credentials committee with responsibility for the entire monitoring process, which was manned by League volunteers who counted ballots. The winners were Bertha Gilkey with 499 votes, and Loretta Hall, with 440 votes.[87]

ENVIRONMENT

Though the League had been leading the environmental bandwagon since the 1960s, it was finally in the 1990s that they began to see some serious interest from members of the public, as the country grew ever more aware of the looming environmental crisis.

On June 28-29, 1991, the League co-sponsored an "Earth Summit" with the United Nations Association of St. Louis and the Midwest Citizens Network at the St. Louis Zoo in the Living World. Attendees included residents and representatives of non-governmental organizations who participated in a seminar on "action for a sustainable future."

Also on the agenda was a public hearing with testimony from organizations, individuals and government representatives from six Midwestern states on a variety of environmental topics ranging from quality of life and concern for the poor to air, land, and water resources, toxic materials and environmental emergencies. The League was represented by LWVMO President Elaine Blodgett, who spoke on water issues. Michael Deland, chairman of the White House Council on Environmental Quality, was charged with writing the United States' reports for the Conference on the Environment and Development to be held the following year in Brazil. Deland said the hearing was a chance for local citizens to have input into the White House's report.[88]

AIR POLLUTION

Much to the joy of the League and environmentalists across the country, on Nov. 15, 1990, Congress passed, and President George H.W. Bush signed into law the Clean Air Act amendments of 1990, which established new requirements and deadlines for meeting national clean air standards. According to the Environmental Protection Agency, "the amendments were designed to curb four major threats to the environment and to the health of millions of Americans: acid rain, urban air pollution, toxic air emissions, and stratospheric ozone depletion."[89]

Under these revisions, the states of Missouri and Illinois were required to develop new state implementation plans for ozone control, both of which would affect air quality in the St. Louis area. In addition, the East-West Gateway Coordinating Council established an Air Quality Advisory Committee (AQAC). It consisted of members of the advisory committee as well as representatives from local civic and business groups, environmental and health organizations, state and local transportation agencies, government agencies and citizens.

The purpose of the AQAC was to advise on air quality matters, particularly those related to transportation, conduct public information activities, and assist the East-West Gateway Coordinating Council in analyzing transportation control measures to reduce ozone emissions. Marina Cofer-Wildsmith represented the League on the Council.[90]

WATER POLLUTION

As mentioned in the last chapter, the League was one of the sponsors of the Partners in Protecting the Environment (PIPE) project aimed at educating middle-grade students about clean water. PIPE started as a pilot project presented to approximately

20 fifth graders from four city and four county schools. In 1991, students at Lexington Elementary School in the city joined students from the Pattonville School Districts and Carrollton Oaks Elementary School for the kickoff of the full-scale education program.[91] In 1992, the number of students reached was more than 630,[92] about 700 in 1994,[93] and was estimated to be close to 1,000 by 1998.[94]

Also on the subject of water, on March 19, 1997, the St. Louis League sponsored a national video conference on drinking water protection. The video call included a panel of environmental experts on drinking water from across the country, who were interviewed and answered questions submitted by viewers by phone or fax. After that, a local panel discussion with experts from the Missouri Department of National Resources, Continental Water Company, the St. Louis City Water Division and the Weldon Springs Department of Energy explored issues in the St. Louis Metro area.[95]

Metropolitan Sewer District

MSD started off the 1990s by submitting a proposal for the February 6 election that would determine the fate of a rate increase to fund needed repairs. The League supported this increase, but it was defeated at the polls.[96]

In February 1992, MSD's executive director announced a proposed 31% rate increase for single family homes to begin July 1, possibly without being put to a vote,[97] a right he believed MSD had thanks to a recent Missouri Supreme Court decision "exempting public bodies from certain obligations of the Hancock amendment."[98] The court ruled the Hancock amendment applied only to taxes, not user charges and laid out five criteria for determining what is and is not a tax.[99]

League members spoke in opposition to the increase at a

February 26 public hearing. They feared that rearranging charges was "almost certain to be misunderstood as a violation of an earlier promise that the surcharge would be discontinued."[100] But MSD made the increase anyway. These two moves were early indications of what no one, especially MSD, wanted to admit: the organization was in dire financial straits.

One year later, in July 1993, MSD again adjusted sewer bills, changing its billing cycle to monthly instead of quarterly, increasing charges, and changing billing for single family customers from a flat amount to basing on winter water usage for metered customers and a formula based on housing characteristics for non-metered customers.

In December 1993, MSD's worst nightmares came true when the Missouri Supreme Court ruled that a 1992 rate increase was invalid—it only passed two of the five criteria for being a charge rather than a tax. This also threw into doubt the legitimacy of the 1993 rate, which was calculated based on that increase. As a result, MSD was facing the possibility of having to refund $40 million to users for 1992 and $83 million for 1993, which would bankrupt the company because the money had already been spent on operational and maintenance costs as well as sanitary sewer replacement projects. Making matters worse, MSD's board of trustees was unable to enact legislation to resolve their financial problems because they were short two trustees and City Circuit Court judges would not confirm the mayoral appointments who could appoint those trustees.[101]

The League began working with Confluence St. Louis on a report regarding how the coalition could help MSD with members testifying at public forums on the matter. After nine months of study, the task force concluded that "A structural alternative must be found to address issues of finance and governance... MSD is the only major metropolitan sewer agency in the country that must obtain voter approval for rate increases and is so severely restricted in its access to long term financing."[102]

After considering many alternatives, the task force recommended that voters in St. Louis City and County approve an amendment to MSD's charter to enable it to take care of its emergent financial needs. The nature of that amendment changed many times before it was finally presented to voters as a series of four amendments in November 2000. Voters approved all four amendments by more than double the number opposing them.[103] Passage of MSD Amendment 1 allowed MSD to use property taxes to help repair aging sewers. MSD Amendments 2-4 helped solve the board problems that prevented MSD from getting any new funding and made sure it didn't get into a situation like this again.[104]

TRANSIT

On July 31, 1993, after decades of advocating for transit reform and three years of construction, the League saw the fulfillment of a long-awaited dream: the grand opening of MetroLink, St. Louis' first light-rail system. The initial route carried passengers from St. Louis County to St. Clare County in Illinois. It was much appreciated by the public, with more than 180,000 people riding it during its first three days and more than 1 million in its first month.[105]

In 1994, MetroLink expanded to Lambert Airport in the west and East St. Louis in the east. Around the same time, St. Louis City and County voters were asked to approve a ¼ cent sales tax increase for public transportation for the next five years, after which it would have to be reauthorized by the government every two years. If passed, the monies would be used not only to cover MetroLink and bus operations, but also to replace old buses and for planning new MetroLink routes. It would also supplement money meant for public transportation that the government was using to fund road construction and repair instead.[106] The League supported the tax and voters enthusiastically approved it on Aug. 2, 1994, with nearly twice as many people voting for it than against in both the city and county.

At the time, it was said that "a substantial portion will be used to extend MetroLink lines to the north, south, and west portions of the county."[107] Alas, that was a plan never to be fulfilled, or at least not as of this writing. In 1998, MetroLink did add a second station at Lambert Airport's Terminal 2[108] and expanded in 2006 from Forest Park to Shrewsbury,[109] but despite multiple attempts, that is as far as expansion went. Between 1995 and 2022, several new routes were discussed including ones connecting Clayton and University City; Clayton and Westport Plaza; North Hanley to I-270 in Hazelwood; Shrewsbury to I-44/Butler Hill Road.[110]

The strongest reason for this situation has always been lack of funds. In 1999, the federal government severely cut funding for transit, forcing Bi-State, Metro and other transit systems across the country to go into cost-savings mode.[111] The League emphasized that MetroLink was just one part of St. Louis' overall transportation plan that also included buses and will continue to support it as "a system that causes the least damage to the environment with as little disruption to communities and use of existing rights of way as possible."[112]

HEALTH CARE

The League took the lead in the 1990s when the subject of health care reform came to the fore. A small study of health care had begun in the 1980s. In 1988, the Missouri League tried and failed to get legislation passed that would have created a Missouri Health Care Trust, "a state government-owned insurance company which would have had the powers of a private-sector insurance company and would have made insurance available to families who could not afford a private insurance plan or who were not covered by health insurance through employment."[113] Opponents had painted the measure as monstrous to seniors and played on fears of AIDS and big government.

The failed effort did help demonstrate that League members in Missouri were experts on health care. As the State League noted in 2019, each health care bill the League has supported since 1990 has passed and each bill the League opposed has failed.[114]

In April 1993, the National League adopted its national health care position, which became that of the St. Louis League as well:

> The League of Women Voters of the United States believes that a basic level of quality health care at an affordable cost should be available to all U.S. residents. Other U.S. health care policy goals should include the equitable distribution of services, efficient and economical delivery of care, advancement of medical research and technology and a reasonable total national expenditure level for health care.[115]

This position was just in time for the national debate on health care reform, which the St. Louis League supported whole-heartedly, insisting on an employer mandate that would allow all employees to receive coverage through their employers and universal guaranteed coverage for preventive, primary, and acute care.[116]

There was also a major health care debate going on in Missouri. That year, two competing bills emerged as the top contenders for much-needed health care reform in the state. HB 191, sponsored by Rep. Gail Chatfield (D-St. Louis) proposed universal health care for all Missourians, modeled after the Canadian Health System. It was a single-payer plan that was strongly opposed by insurance companies, physicians, and hospitals as too expensive.

The other bill, HB 564, was sponsored by House Speaker Bob Griffin and promoted increased access to health care for 600,000 Missourians, mostly children. It was very similar to the doomed 1988 legislation in that it "targeted underserved populations by expanding the state's Medicaid program, creating school health clinics, adopting collaborative practice arrangements, offering financial incentives to lure physicians into underserved areas, and extending liability protection for health providers serving the poor...Most notably, the bill expanded Medicaid eligibility for uninsured children up to age nineteen [and] made additional Medicaid funding available for school health clinics that were to serve as a source of primary care for students."[117]

That it was to be funded through increased taxes on alcohol and tobacco and greater matching federal funds available through Medicaid isn't why the bill was sharply criticized; it came under scrutiny because it "allowed school nurses to refer students for additional health services," which conservatives read as abortion and contraceptive services.[118]

However, as the Missouri League pointed out, "there was general agreement that this was important legislation and individual agendas must be set aside temporarily. The state League took the lead in demonstrating that there could be negotiation between the issues of reproductive choice and health care."[119]

And that compromise was very successful. The General Assembly approved the bill on May 11, 1993.[120] Governor Mel Carnahan signed the bill on July 1, in a high-tech event that involved remarks from First Lady Hillary Clinton delivered via satellite. She congratulated the state of Missouri for its innovation, saying, "The country will be able to look to you as a state that is coming to terms with the shortcomings [of our health care system.]"[121]

In December 1993, the St. Louis City League partnered with its counterparts in St. Louis and Jefferson Counties to educate the public through a program called Campaign for Public Voice on Health Care Reform. It was led by Rachel Fitch, City League member and Missouri League Health Care Director.

During January and February, the League studied the health care proposals that were set to be introduced to Congress[122] and held town hall meetings on health care reform that were also broadcast on KMOX radio. Special guests included Senator Kit Bond (R-MO), Congressman Richard Gephardt (D-MO), Congressman Richard Durbin (D-IL), Dr. James Kimmey from St. Louis University, Sherman McCoy of the St. Louis Regional Medical Center, and Father Kevin O'Rourke of the Center for Health Care Ethics at Saint Louis University. LWVMO President Linda McDaniel said, "Citizen involvement in the health care debate is critical if Congress is to design a comprehensive plan that will meet the health needs of every American. These town meetings will give people access to their elected officials in a balanced and open environment."[123]

GUN CONTROL

The Second Amendment's right to bear arms has been a treasured part of the Bill of Rights since it was first penned in 1791. Over the years, interpretation of it has changed, and in many instances, become very controversial. As gun violence proliferated into the 1990s, the LWVUS took a stand, stating they believe that

> The proliferation of handguns and semiautomatic assault weapons in the United States is a major health and safety threat to its citizens. The League supports strong federal measures to limit the accessibility and regulate the ownership of these weapons by private citizens.
>
> The League supports licensing procedures for gun ownership by private citizens to include a waiting period for background checks, personal identity verification, gun safety education and annual license renewal. The license fee should be adequate to bear the cost of education and verification.
>
> The League supports a ban on "Saturday night specials," enforcement of strict penalties for the improper possession of and crimes committed with handguns and assault weapons, and allocation of resources to better regulate and monitor gun dealers.[124]

While that was a noble position, many in Missouri, especially in rural areas, did not agree. They wanted more firearms freedom, not less. Missouri's first concealed weapons bill was introduced into the legislature in 1992 by gun advocate Joe Driskill. He argued that 35 other states allowed concealed carry, so Missouri should as well. If this occurred, it would put an end to an 1874 law that made hidden weapons illegal.[125] The House

Civil and Criminal Laws Committee, led by chairman Ronnie White of St. Louis, disagreed, killing the bill, which many believed was really sponsored by the National Rifle Association (NRA) and its 100,000+ Missouri members, though all involved denied such accusations.[126]

Despite this early loss, the door was now open to such legislation and it didn't take long for pro-gun advocates to start calling for a change in Missouri's laws. One of the loudest voices was John Ross of St. Louis, founder of Missouri Citizens for Civil Liberties, who said that Missouri's gun laws favored criminals and left average citizens without a way to defend themselves and that the tight laws were leftovers from discrimination and racism of the past that aimed to keep Black citizens under police control.

Opponents of concealed weapons included Attorney General John Ashcroft, St. Louis Police Chief Clarence Harmon, Law Enforcement Officers of Greater St. Louis, a group representing 52 local law enforcement agencies, and Coalition Against Concealed Guns, which was made up of 10 local groups, including the League of Women Voters.

The Driskill bill was amended in March 1992 after strong outcry from supporters at its defeat to allow all people age 21+ the right to apply to their local sheriff for a concealed carry permit. In just those few months, support for such legislation blossomed and it was adopted 124-24. In order to get it through the House, it was attached to a larger crime bill, which passed 110-40. This was, coincidently, right around the time of a tragic shooting at the St. Louis County Courthouse in Clayton on May 5, 1992, that killed six people. In the aftermath, Driskill's amendment was withdrawn.[127]

Around the same time, League units were discussing the subject of gun control[128] and Rep. Sue Shear, a League member, introduced her own bill into the Missouri legislature, one that required gun owners with children to either lock up their guns or use trigger locks.[129] It also established a 1,000 foot "safe zone" around schools in which guns were not permitted.[130] The measure passed the House in late April, but Shear had to pull the bill when a concealed carry amendment was added to it.[131]

True to their word, concealed carry advocates were back in the next legislative session. "The concealed weapons bill SB295 has been introduced again and is well organized; supporters are out in force," St. Louis County League president Susan Trice warned League members in a March 1993 newsletter before urging them to contact their representatives to ask them to oppose the bill.[132] The legislative session ended without passage of the bill, to which the League responded, "Hurray for Missouri and our legislators."[133]

In May 1993, Jim Brady—former assistant to President Ronald Reagan who was shot and permanently disabled protecting the president from an assassination attempt in 1981—and his wife, Sarah, visited St. Louis to urge support for the Brady Bill—formally named the Brady Handgun Violence Prevention Act—which required federal background checks on all gun purchasers and a five-day waiting period before weapons could be obtained. They met with the League and "were...very supportive of our efforts to prevent concealed weapons."[134]

Ironically, even as gun violence increased throughout the 1990s and mass school shootings became a regular occurrence, the issue of gun control quieted in the Missouri legislature. That is until 1998, when the NRA formed the group Missourians Against Crime as a focal point for those who supported concealed carry laws.[135]

In January 1999, the NRA donated $75,000—the largest

contribution to date in the campaign—to help pass Proposition B at a special referendum on April 6, 1999. Proposition B would allow sheriffs "to issue concealed weapons permits to those who are at least 21 years old, who have not been convicted of a felony and who have passed a hand-gun safety course."[136]

Missouri was the first state to put the issue of concealed weapons to a vote in a binding referendum. The League, of course, was against the proposition, but former opponent John Ashcroft, who was up for reelection as Attorney General, had changed his tune, saying "safeguards in the measure were 'plenty tough.'"

Voters didn't seem to know what to think. Just days before the referendum, a *St. Louis Post-Dispatch* poll showed 42% against, 37% in favor and 21% undecided.[137] The results were nearly as close on voting day; the measure failed 52% to 48%.[138] It was certainly not the last word on the issue of gun control in Missouri, but it was for the decade.

LEAGUE ACTIVITIES

Within the League, two major activities took place in the 1990s. The first was that the St. Louis City and St. Louis County Leagues agreed to merge, creating a single League of Women Voters of Metro St. Louis.

While the County Leagues went through many mergers in the past, the City of St. Louis League always preferred to remain its own entity, arguing that because its population and issues were different, it should be separate from the County. But by 1999, things had changed. City president Marjorie Jokerst wrote that a merger was "a chance to make the League a stronger, more formidable organization" where the two Leagues could "work together more freely" and more "efficiently."[139]

However, when the issue came up for a vote in April 1999 after two months of work by a joint committee, not all members were thrilled to be asked to give an opinion so quickly. Esther N. Young, a member of the St. Louis County League, believed the League was moving too fast, forgoing its usual methods of study and discussion. She wrote, "The proposed merger of the City of St. Louis League and the St. Louis County League needs study and deliberation. ... Should members desire, the plan proposed could then be part of materials considered in study of the issue over the next two or three years.[140]

Time proved her to be in the minority. When the two Leagues met at the St. Louis Women's Club on April 18, the consensus was that the two Leagues should merge. K Wentzien, first president of the single League, wrote that being one "will enable the organization to speak with one voice in the region, as well as to consolidate its efforts to increase grassroots citizen participation in government...The League has changed from 10 years ago."[141]

75th Anniversary

League members celebrated their 75th anniversary from 1994-1995. Activities began in December 1994 with a holiday luncheon where Catherine Allen of the Columbia League reminded members "of the origins and purposes of the League and of the efforts of those who worked so hard to bring us to where we are today" with a presentation on the women of the suffrage movement.

In March, the City and County Leagues celebrated together at a series of events, including brunch with Congresswoman Patricia Schroeder (D-CO) which was held in conjunction with the opening of the national touring exhibit Women in Action: Rebels and Reformers; a special performance by the Historyonics

Theatre Group about the suffrage movement, based on the speeches and writings of suffrage leaders; and a dinner honoring Harriett Woods and past LWVMO presidents.[142]

Celebrations continued in August with the Webster University "Women in Cinema Film Series." On August 19, they held a special reception for League members and half of that evening's box office proceeds went to the League. On August 26, the anniversary of the ratification of the 19th Amendment, the St. Louis League joined 14 other organizations in sponsoring Shoulder to Shoulder, a march and other events honoring the historic day.[143]

In addition, over the course of the anniversary year, the Higher Education Center of St. Louis, presented videos from the St. Louis County League's *Let the People Know* series, including episodes on the history of the League and the suffrage movement, on its CCTV cable station. Special episodes included two showings of The Women's Movement Now and two of a special production commemorating the League's 75th anniversary. The station also scheduled 13 showings of the St. Louis City League's show *Impact on Issues*.[144]

Conclusion

The 1990s saw the League expand into new areas of advocacy such as gun control and health care, while maintaining activities related to voting access/rights, as well as redistricting and campaign finance reform to ensure elections were fair. The explosion of technology toward the end of the decade was a preview of what lay ahead in the new millennium, when the League would have to adapt to an increasingly electronic and cyber-connected world.

WOMEN WHO MADE AN IMPACT IN THE 1990S

K WENTZIEN

● ●

FEBRUARY 1940 – PRESENT

K Elaine Armstrong grew up on a farm in rural Iowa. She attended the University of Iowa and earned her bachelor's in journalism in 1961. A highlight of her college career was meeting Dr. Rev. Martin Luther King, Jr. when he spoke on her campus.

After graduation, she lived in Phoenix, Arizona, while working for a weekly newspaper. She was particularly drawn to stories of racial issues among the Native American, Hispanic, Black and white populations of the area.

The Dean of Women at the University of Iowa instructed her to join the League, which K did in 1966 when she was living in Oak Park, an inner-ring Chicago suburb.

One of K's main memories from that time was the League embracing the mission of implementing the Voting Rights Act of 1965. While in Illinois, she was also part of the Oak Park Congress created by that League's first Black member, Sherlynn Reid, to address housing equity on a national level.

K, her husband, Paul, and their four children moved to Webster Groves in 1979. She immediately joined the local League, and it wasn't long before she was taking on leadership positions. K served as president of the Webster Groves League from 1985-1987 and of the League's Information Service from 1999-2001. One of her biggest challenges as president was her work to promote environmental safety and health while the League fought against the building of a domed football stadium in the Riverport area. Other highlights of her work in St.

Louis include voluntary redistricting, school vouchers, abortion rights, fair housing, and anti-flood plain development. K also led a "monumental" voter registration drive in 1992.[145]

In 2019, K reflected upon the many opportunities to serve she has found in the League.

"We appreciated the agony and the ecstasy of planning, conducting, and living with the aftermath of interminable board meetings," she said. "We appreciated the ups and downs of getting smart, strong-minded people to work together to build consensus without destroying each other."

K continues to head the Kirkwood/Webster Groves Unit on Zoom or in person at the First Congregational Church of Webster Groves. In 2020, the League had a display celebrating the centennial of suffrage in front of her home for a "reverse parade" before the 4th of July.

Outside of the League, K has volunteered with the American Friends Service Committee, Focus St. Louis, Care & Counseling, the Deaconess Foundation, Webster-Rock Hill Ministries, Webster Arts, the Center for Women in Transition and the Webster Groves Juvenile Conference Committee.

She is well known for her work in the local community. After unsuccessfully running for Webster Groves City Council in 1988, she served on the city's planning commission. She also served as treasurer of the Conference on Education and as part of its valuing diversity project, which reflects her lifelong concern for issues of racial harmony.

In January 1993, K was chosen as citizen of the year by the Webster Groves Chamber of Commerce as a person who "provides a level of service to the community that goes beyond good ordinary citizenship."[146] On May 15, 2015, K was awarded an honorary Doctor of Humane Letters from Eden Theological Seminary in honor of her service to the community of Webster Groves.[147]

Besides social justice, K's other big passion in life is horses. She is a part or full owner of thoroughbreds that run at Fairmount Park in Illinois and other tracks around the United States and Canada. She loves the thrill of racing.[148]

LINDA CLAIRE MCDANIEL

MARCH 1942 – PRESENT

Linda McPearson was first introduced to the League as a senior in high school in 1960[149] while she was doing political party work for her precinct with a neighbor who invited her to a League luncheon. While she loved the League from that moment on, she was only 18 and the League had a minimum age requirement of 21 years (now 16). She moved to Kansas to attend college and while there, went to a few League meetings.

After marrying John, Linda moved to Poughkeepsie, New York, then Boulder, Colorado, and finally settled in St. Louis in 1967. She was a League member in every city where she lived. Linda served as president of the North County League from 1973-1975. She was particularly passionate about gun control, serving on the Missouri Council to Control Handguns in the 1980s.[150] the same period when she held the role of the League's Government Chairwoman.[151]

Linda was influential in multiple battles for fair redistricting. In 1982, Linda and Sydell Shayer were two of the defendants in a lawsuit. Twenty years later, she stressed in another case that "broad communities of interests should be kept intact. Minority representation should be protected."

McDaniel took on state service in the mid-1980s, as First Vice President of the Missouri League, Tax Director in 1991, and as President from 1993-1997.[152] "As president, the greatest challenge I faced was always speaking on behalf of the

League, even when my personal beliefs differed," she said. "I never wavered in my belief in the League and what it stands for, however."

After her term, McDaniel served as chairwoman of the Commission on Fair Elections.[153] In the late 1990s and early 2000s, she worked for campaign finance reform, often speaking throughout St. Louis on the subject, both on behalf of the League and as a member of the Steering Committee of Missouri Voters for Fair Elections.[154]

Issues she was particularly proud of working on during her career include integration of the Florissant and Berkeley school districts; successful state and federal redistricting lawsuits; a constitutional amendment on redistricting that passed; campaign finance; and health care. She also served as chair of a study on consensus issues.[155] McDaniel served as the League's Advocacy Committee Chair from 2000 to 2004, as well as Chair of the Missouri First Vote Foundation and as Research/Data Director of the United Way of Greater St. Louis.

In 2004, McDaniel took on her first National League Board role as First Vice President of LWVUS and the LWV Education Fund.[156] The following year, she was appointed by Secretary of State Robin Carnahan as the only lay member to the Missouri Automated Voting Equipment Qualification Committee; the other 10 members represented county election authorities, the disabled community and academia. The committee was charged with reviewing automated voting equipment and advising the Secretary of State on machines which could be sold in Missouri.[157]

McDaniel was elected co-president of the St. Louis League in 2009, working side-by-side with Kathleen Farrell until 2017. The pair reached an agreement with the *St. Louis Post-Dispatch* to publish a Voters Guide before each election. They also built new relationships with the African American Community. Linda was key to the success of the "Celebrate the Vote" event in 2016 to honor the early suffragists who held a "walkless-talkless" demonstration at the 1916 Democratic Convention.

NANCY BOWSER

JUNE 1937 – PRESENT

Nancy Bowser was born in 1937 in Pittsburgh, Pennsylvania. She had two sisters, Linda and Dorothy, the latter of whom has since passed on. Nancy became interested in government and politics in high school when she took a required course on civics that put a strong emphasis on the Constitution. "This is the kind of course that I think should be required of all students before they graduate," she said. Nancy went on to study political science at Chatham College, where she graduated with a bachelor's degree in 1959.

She met her husband, Ralph, in 1960 and they married three years later. They had three children, David, Susan and Paul.

Though she isn't sure precisely *when* she joined the League of Women Voters—it was when her youngest child started school, sometime in the mid-1970s—Nancy remembers exactly *why* she joined. "It gave me the opportunity to continue my interest in government," she recalled. "I was impressed with what I had heard about the League's role in the development of the St. Louis County Charter and because of the reputation of the organization. I was attracted to it because it was non-partisan and studied and acted on a variety of public issues."

Nancy was President of the University City League from 1977 to 1979. She was a member of the education coalition for information on school desegregation that operated from summer 1981-February 1982 and sat on the University City Citizen

Panel that studied a school tax hike in 1984. The following year, she coordinated candidate forums prior to November elections.

By 1999, she was on the League board of directors. She fought for gun control in the late 1990s and charter amendments in the 2000s. In 2002, Nancy was named to the New Citizens Advisory Committee of the Metropolitan Parks and Recreation District, which was created as a result of the passage of proposition C in November 2000. The League was one of the organizations appointed to the Commission and Nancy was the League representative from 2003 to 2016.

Her strongest passion is environmental issues; she served as Environmental Quality Chair 2000- 2014. Beginning in 2003, she was part of the MSD Rate Commission, becoming secretary in 2007. Nancy was president of the St. Louis League from 2004-2005. In 2006-2007, she stepped forward to assume the role of acting development coordinator and first vice president when no one was elected. She received a special award from the League in 2007 for her many years of dedicated service.

Main Sources Chapter 4 – The 1990s

Annual Reports of the President, League of Women Voters of St. Louis, 1995-2011

Minutes of the Meetings of the Board of Directors of LWVSTL, July 20, 1999 and Nov. 16, 1999

Books
- Horner, William T. *Showdown in the Show-Me State: The Fight Over Conceal-and-carry Gun Laws in Missouri.*

Newsletters
- *In League Reporter,* February 1992- March 1999
- *Metro News,* Summer 1991-Fall 1999

League documents regarding
- Blue Cross and Blue Shield Lawsuit
- Campaign Finance Reform
- Education
- Guide to State Action 2017-2019
- Motor Voter Legislation
- MSD
- Redistricting
- Term Limits

Periodicals
- *Consumer Reports Advocacy*
- *The Riverfront Times*
- *St. Louis Business Journal*
- *St. Louis University Law Journal*
- *St. Louis Post-Dispatch*
- *Webster-Kirkwood Times*

Websites
- Metro St. Louis
- Next City: The Works
- The Trace
- United States Environmental Protection Agency

For a complete list of sources, please see the endnotes at https://my.lwv.org/missouri/metro-st-louis/about/our-history.

1990s

Agnes Garino, Barbara Shull, Becky Minogue, Gail Heyne-Hafer and K Wentzien, honored as Distinguished Members in 1991, are pictured with speaker Kathryn Nelson (far right).

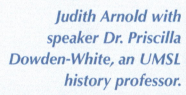

Judith Arnold with speaker Dr. Priscilla Dowden-White, an UMSL history professor.

LWVMO honored former Lt. Gov. Harriett Woods in 1995 by creating the Harriett Woods Award for Exemplary Public Service. She's pictured with Linda McDaniel (left) wearing "Votes for Women" sashes similar to those worn by the suffragists.

Gail Heyne-Hafer taping a broadcast for the League.

Carol Portman at a March 1998 Lobby Day.

CHAPTER 5

The 2000s

THE NEW MILLENNIUM was highly anticipated as a fresh start and chance at progress. After the September 11 terrorist attacks in 2001, social media and the internet became commonplace. Jean Carnahan briefly served in the U.S. Senate in 2001-2002, with State Auditor Claire McCaskill becoming the first woman from Missouri elected to that position in 2006; Condoleezza Rice became the first Republican woman and first Black woman to serve as U.S. Secretary of State in 2005; Congresswoman Nancy Pelosi became the first woman Speaker of the House in 2007; and Senator Barack Obama was elected as the first Black U.S. President in 2008.

Within the League, change was a constant as well. Volunteers kept busier than ever registering new voters at naturalization ceremonies and special events. New technology changed the way we cast our votes and got our election information. Advocacy work covered some of the same topics as in previous years, such as charter revisions, education, the environment, health care, and the revival of the Equal Rights Amendment. But it also took us into bold new territory with a strong call for election reform after the debacle of 2000 and moratoriums against the death penalty in Missouri. Highlights include:

- Fighting for funding for public education; access to quality, affordable health care; and children's safety.
- Testifying at the state legislature in 2003 about energy efficiency with the Missouri Clean Energy coalition, which the League co-founded.
- Joining the Missouri Sunshine Coalition in favor of the free flow of government information.
- Joining the Pew Center on Global Climate Change to collect information about how Missouri addresses climate change.

As in every other decade, we could not have done all of this ambitious work successfully without the guidance of our presidents: K Wentzien, Arlene Nickels, Elise Joerger, Nancy Ulman (Thompson), Norma Jean Downey, Nancy Bowser, Jeanne Morrel-Franklin, and Doris Buzzell.

VOTER SERVICES

Registration at Naturalization Ceremonies

The League began investigating registering new citizens as voters at naturalization ceremonies in 1965[1] and was doing so on a monthly basis by 1966.[2] Judge Roy Winfield Harper wanted to have a "suitable ceremony" and asked the League to attend in order to add "prestige" to the event. A team of League members attended to handle registration, hand out a copy of the Voters Key and information on laws surrounding registration and voting, plus say a few words about the importance of voting in the lives of U.S. citizens.[3]

Over time, demand for the League to do this dwindled. It was brought back to life in 2001 by League member Carol Portman and her husband Darwin, an immigration lawyer,[4] with permission from Chief District Judge Jean C. Hamilton.[5]

Volunteers started registering newly naturalized citizens at ceremonies twice a month at the Eagleton courthouse, at the Old Courthouse three times a year, and at special ceremonies at Harris-Stowe State College. At first, only about a third to half of the new citizens registered at each ceremony, resulting in about 440 new registered voters in the program's first six months.[6] That number grew to 1,200 new citizens at 25 naturalization ceremonies in 2004 when average registration increased to 50%-60%. In 2008, the League attended 45 ceremonies at 24 different locations and registered 1,700 new citizens. The League has attended almost every ceremony since July 20, 2001[7] declining only rarely when demand was greater than our capacity or COVID restrictions closed ceremonies to the public.[8]

One new citizen stuck in Carol Portman's mind. Before he registered, he asked whether registration would require him to vote every time. When Carol told him it was his choice, he remarked, "That is democracy!"[9]

In these naturalization ceremonies, the League worked closely with the International Institute of Metropolitan St. Louis. The League helped their workers become deputized to register voters. In the 2004 election cycle, the League worked with them to ensure translators were present at primary and general election candidate forums so that new voters and those soon to become citizens could understand the proceedings in their native language in case they weren't proficient in English.[10]

In addition, the League was part of the ElderLink Festival of Citizenship where the elderly were introduced to voting, registered if they desired, and new citizens were honored. League members also served on the 2003 FOCUS St. Louis task force studying educational opportunities for new Americans.[11]

For these efforts, especially those around the naturalization ceremonies, the League received FOCUS St. Louis' 2005 "What's Right with the Region Award" in the "improving racial equality and social justice" category. Portman accepted the award on behalf of the League and her late husband.[12]

Since 2001, the League has helped an estimated 25,000 new citizens register to vote. League volunteers continue to attend these ceremonies several times a month, registering more than half of those who attend. Those who do not register have many reasons. Some are from Illinois, in which the St. Louis League has no jurisdiction; some must get back to work or on to other things because of the length of the ceremony; others simply are not ready.[13]

New Voting Machines

After the "hanging chad" controversy of the 2000 presidential election that left American citizens and election officials without an answer as to who was the next president for more than a month,[14] the race was on to improve voting machines across the country so that a situation like that never occurred again. Thanks to the Help America Vote Act of 2002, touch screen voting and "scantron" machines were poised to take over. The latter was familiar to students who filled in bubbles on tests and had their answers scanned and recorded by an optical scanning machine.[15]

In March 2004, the National League came out in favor of voter verification of each ballot before it was cast. It opposed a more complex system for Direct Recording Electronic (DRE) voting machines that had each voter verify a paper confirmation for her/his ballot, saying this made voting more difficult for those with disabilities and language issues, threatened security, and didn't meet federal certification standards. DRE machines already provided paper records that election officials could use if a recount was needed.[16]

On Dec. 20, 2005, the St. Louis County Election Board, in a unanimous vote, awarded Election Systems and Software the contract to supply high-tech voting machines. In St. Louis County, voters would be primarily using touchscreen voting machines, but at elections where voter turnout was expected to be high, they would also have optical scan ballots on hand. The April 2006 elections were the "farewell to chad." It was the last election in which the punch-card ballots, which had been in place in the County since 1975, were used.[17] St. Louis City voters, on the other hand, got a taste of the new Diebold voting machines during a pilot in April's election. Voters were given a choice to use a touch screen or optical scan machine.[18]

Prior to both the April and August 2006 elections, the League distributed information about the two new voting systems at city halls in the county, at registration fairs, in the Voters Guide, and on the League's website. As they had been doing since the days of the lever-voting system, League members demonstrated the new machines and gave voters the opportunity to practice using them. The "unveiling" of the new systems took place on June 1 at the county government center in Clayton.[19]

Smart Voter Website

The growing popularity of the Internet provided the League with a new way to get ballot and candidate information to the public. In 2008, League member Mickey Croyle brought to the St. Louis League her 10 years of experience with LWV of California, and she built a webpage for St. Louis voters as a subpage of the larger Smart Voter site created by the LWV of California Education Fund (SmartVoter.org/mo/sls).

"Smart Voter" "provide[d] a wealth of election information

in an easy to use, interactive format."[20] It included a list of candidates for elections in St. Louis City and County, as well as all state, county and local issues and races. Also listed were the candidates' responses to League questions for the August 2008 primary election and the November 2008 general election.[21]

More than 50 volunteers formed 12 teams, coordinated to reach out into the community to communicate the amazing new information and materials available for St. Louis area residents through the Smart Voter site. They helped approximately 250,000 citizens through these new community partnerships and a variety of print and electronic tools.[22]

The Smart Voter website was used to promote the primary in August 2008 and general election in November 2008. It had 347,032 page views in the month before the presidential election.[23] In addition, Croyle answered more than 300 questions from potential voters via the Smart Voters email address.[24]

The Smart Voters website was used locally from 2008-2012 and is still online today as VOTE411.org.

YOUNG PEOPLE AND POLITICS

In October 2002, the League agreed to help the Kids Voting Missouri program in St. Louis Public Schools. St. Louis became the first urban school system in the nation in which all schools participated.[25]

In 2004, 11% more Americans under 30 voted than in previous elections—the largest turnout for that age group to date. "Smackdown Your Vote!" helped maintain that momentum. This voting awareness and education program sponsored by World Wrestling Entertainment (WWE) created a "new voter issues paper addressing the key issues facing 18-to-30-year-old Americans." The League joined 34 organizations in the Smackdown Your Vote Network working to get greater numbers of young people to vote.[26]

The League continued to educate young people about the government and interest them in becoming part of the political process when they turn 18. The League partnered with the Missouri Historical Society to put on a special event called Constitution Day for fifth through eighth graders from St. Louis City, County, and Jefferson County. On Sept. 17, 2007, members gathered at the Missouri History Museum to see eighth grade students from Kirkwood's Nipher Middle School perform a play written by Nipher seventh grade teacher Beth Wehling, daughter of League secretary Mary Beth Reynolds. The play centered on James Madison's landlady, who narrated the show by recalling highlights of the summer of 1787, when the Constitution was framed, as well as stories from Madison's life. Students were able to vote on how the Constitutional Congress should proceed and so were actively involved in learning history.

The consensus of the students was that it was "exciting to see history come alive" and the students routinely used the word "fun" in their feedback.[27] The show was so popular it sold out a month early, so a second performance was scheduled. It was also featured on the local news.[28]

ELECTION REFORM

Anyone of voting age in 2000 likely remembers the fiasco that was election night 2000 and the days and weeks following. A margin of only 537 votes separated Democrat Al Gore and Republican George W. Bush. Because some parts of Florida used a punch card system of voting, when voters didn't completely push through the perforated square on the ballot, the little scrap of paper still attached (the infamous "hanging chad") called the validity of the vote into question. Weeks of counting, lawsuits and scrutiny of every aspect of Florida's elections followed. Eventually, the U.S. Supreme Court declared George W. Bush the winner, which gave him the necessary electoral college votes to be declared president, even though Al Gore won the popular vote by 543,894 votes.[29]

Not surprisingly, calls for national reform of the election process promptly followed. LWVUS Legislative Director Lloyd Leonard testified before the House Judiciary Committee on Dec. 5, 2000, laying it all out on the line:

> Mr. Chairman, many Americans were shocked by the problems in election administration that were exposed by the 2000 election. We in the League of Women Voters, however, were not surprised. Unfortunately, the kinds of problems we saw in 2000 are not unusual. They represent the harvest from years of indifference that has been shown toward one of the most fundamental and important elements of our democratic system— our election mechanisms.

To counter "disastrously outdated voting procedures used all across the country," the National League strongly proposed that "Congress should pass, and the new president should sign, legislation to help states implement 'best practices' voting systems. We need a constitutional amendment to abolish the Electoral College and provide for the direct election of the president," they said. "Beyond this we also need meaningful campaign finance reform."[30]

In St. Louis, the League wrote a memo to the St. Louis Board of Election Commissioners detailing the complaints they received on Election Day. These included that registered voters with voter ID cards and other proper identification were not listed on the voter rolls and therefore not allowed to vote; a woman who voted without being asked to present any identification; people being turned away; the length of time it took to take affidavits; people being told spouses couldn't help because of visual impairments; bad attitude among election workers; polling places that were not in service; lack of privacy; and that the city election board and city polling places were kept open later than others.[31]

Ida West, First Vice President of LWV St. Louis and one of the League's strongest and longest-serving voter registration advocates, testified before the Election Reform Commission on Jan. 12, 2001. Her testimony drew a clear picture of the need for reform within the Board. She stated:

> The St. Louis Board of Election Commissioners has 12 supervisors and 16 staff positions. How can 16 staff persons take orders from 12 supervisors? Under the present organizational structure, the system can't possibly work efficiently. It needs to be reviewed and changed.[32]

K Wentzien, St. Louis League President, and Board Members Ida West and Joyce Guard, spoke at the Secretary of State's Hearings on Election Reform, also held January 12. K Wentzien said:

> We commend both the City and County Boards and Directors of Elections for trying to make [voting] easy and for their cooperative efforts with each other. But there are still problems. The disabled aren't always accommodated with the access they deserve. People think they

are registered when they are not. We live in a transient society. Young people and poor people, in particular, move all the time. Changing their voter registration is not uppermost in their minds during those times. But we need to make it so.

The bottom line is we need to take advantage of technology, we need nonstop education of the public at every level, and we need to explore better ways of making the voting booth accessible in our changing society. Above all, we need to be consistent.[33]

DODD-MCCONNELL ELECTION REFORM BILL/HELP AMERICA VOTE ACT

In December 2001, Senators Christopher S. Dodd (D-CT) and Mitch McConnell (R-KY) agreed on a bi-partisan election reform bill that was the culmination of 13 months of negotiations. Unlike the House version passed earlier that year, it allowed the punch card method of voting to remain in place. It required polling places to be accessible to disabled voters and use systems that alert voters if the machine detects they may be trying to vote for more than one candidate when only one vote is needed. Also, by 2004 it required that all states have a computerized statewide voting list in place to prevent fraud through multiple registrations by one person and that all election offices offer provisional voting for people whose names are not on voter lists on Election Day.[34]

LWVUS praised the new bill. "The new Dodd-McConnell bill in the Senate can be the antidote to the flawed election reform bill recently passed by the house," said President Dr.

Carolyn Jefferson-Jenkins. "The League urges the Senate to take up this bill quickly and pass it so that the election administrators can get to work improving our election systems."[35]

The House passed the bill in December 2001, and the Senate passed a similar bill on April 11, 2002. The two versions differed primarily in the amount of federal money provided and how strict federal controls would be.[36] After much discussion and compromise, a final bill was sent to the president for signing.

On Oct. 29, 2002, President George W. Bush signed into law the Help America Vote Act of 2002. It gave $3.9 billion to states to help them replace punch card and lever voting systems with updated equipment in time for the 2006 election and improve training for poll workers and voter education.[37] It also "require[d] every state to develop and administer a 'single, uniform, official centralized interactive computer statewide voter registration list' that contains the 'name and registration information of every legally registered voter in the state'" for use in future elections. States were to be given help in completing these tasks by the newly created U.S. Election Assistance Commission.[38]

MISSOURI VOTER ID LAWS

Missouri had long required voters to show some form of identification in order to vote. It could be any Missouri driver's license, military ID, or other government issued ID, or a college ID, a driver's license from another state, an expired ID, voter identification card, or even a utility bill.[39] But beginning in the 2000s and continuing into today, there was a push from both legislators and citizens to tighten those laws to only allow photo IDs.

In June 2006, a Voter ID law was passed and signed by

Republican Governor Matt Blunt that required voters to show some form of government-issued photo ID.[40] The League argued that restrictive Voter ID laws made voting more difficult, if not impossible for the elderly, disabled and low-income people because of the cost and effort involved in obtaining the official documents (like birth certificates) required to get an acceptable form of ID.[41]

A few months later, the Cole County Circuit Court said the law was unconstitutional because of the cost and that it violated the Hancock Amendment.[42] This was appealed to the Missouri Supreme Court. On October 16, the Court issued a partial agreement with the Cole County Circuit Court, agreeing that the cost made it unconstitutional, but that it did not violate the Hancock Amendment.[43] This was enough for the law to be invalidated.

Supporters of stronger voter ID laws continued introducing legislation. In 2008, they proposed a constitutional amendment, HJR 48, "that would have required all citizens to have photo identification and proof of citizenship as a prerequisite to voting." It was considered one of the most restrictive voter ID bills of its kind in the nation.[44] When it passed the House in early May, it looked like it had plenty of votes to pass the Senate as well, including support from Republican Governor Blunt and Senator Bond.[45]

In response, the League helped create Missourians for Fair Elections, "a coalition of organizations and individuals that worked diligently to educate the legislators and voters of Missouri about the negative ramifications of the proposed constitutional amendment." With the help of AARP, labor organizations, disability advocates, and other community organizations, they contacted lawmakers in the last two weeks of the legislative session to ensure that every citizen's voting rights were protected by making sure this bill did not become law.[46] Thanks to their efforts, other bills taking up more time than anticipated, and pressure by opponents, including Democratic Secretary of State Robin Carnahan, the bill never made it to the Senate floor.[47]

The League estimated the bill would have kept approximately 240,000 Missourians from voting. "The death of this bill is the rebirth of hope that all Missouri voters will have their voices heard this November," said National LWV President Mary G. Wilson.[48] It also meant that the decade would end without a new Voter ID law on the Missouri books.

NATIONAL POPULAR VOTE

Since 1970, LWVUS has been in favor of abolishing the Electoral College and having the president elected by national popular vote. From 1970-2009, the official position stated:

> The League of Women Voters of the United States believes that the direct popular vote method for electing the president and vice president is essential to representative government. The LWV believes, therefore, that the Electoral College should be abolished. The League also supports uniform voting qualifications and procedures for presidential elections.[49]

Each year, members "testified and lobbied for legislation to amend the constitution to replace the Electoral College with direct election of the president, including provisions for a national runoff election in the event that no candidates (president or vice president) received 40% of the vote." In 1971, it passed the House and nearly passed the Senate.

In 2008, the National Popular Vote Compact was gaining popularity. This was a proposed "agreement among the states to...guarantee the Presidency to the candidate who receives the most popular votes across all 50 states and the District of Columbia."[50] This prompted the League to take another look at its position. LWVUS opened the year-long study and consensus process to the 766 local Leagues across the country and the St. Louis League participated[51]—an October 2005 poll had shown 70% of Missouri voters supported the National Popular Vote.[52]

The final consensus showed that "55% of the local Leagues in the country favored the compact, but the remaining 45% were divided between not favoring the compact and not reaching consensus." Within the League, to say there is consensus, "overwhelming support" must be evident, so the League's official position became: LWVUS "affirms its support for the direct election of the president and abolition of the Electoral College, but the LWV of the United States has no position on the National Popular Vote Compact as currently proposed."[53]

From 2006-2009, three separate National Popular Vote bills (HB 2090, HB 289, and HB 974) were introduced in the Missouri House, but none ever progressed. In the 2010s, more than a dozen such bills were introduced in both the House and Senate, but still no real action has been taken. As of August 2022, a National Popular Vote Interstate Compact has never even been heard on the floor of either the Missouri House or Senate.[54]

CHARTER REVISION

In the 1960s and 1970s (and to a lesser extent in the 1980s) the League fought for revisions to charters for St. Louis County and several cities in the county to establish Home Rule, or the right to determine their own type of government and make changes without having to go to the state legislature for approval.

In 2000, Proposition 1 was placed on the April 4 ballot. It sought to revise the charter of St. Louis County. The question on the ballot did not enumerate the 16 changes it would make; those were to be posted nearby in the polling place. In addition, voters did not have the option to indicate which changes they approved; a "yes" vote approved all 16, while a "no" vote also applied to all 16. The League opposed Proposition 1 for many reasons, but the main concern was that two of the changes would "override the process by which salaries [of elected county officials] are determined and fire district business is conducted."[55]

The proposition failed by a large margin (38,894-74,993).[56] It was reintroduced on the November 2000 ballot as Proposition 3, with the only difference being it no longer included the salary increases for county elected officials. The League took the same stance opposing it.[57] It failed by less than 10,000 votes.[58]

In April 2001, Webster Groves had seven possible amendments to its city charter out for voter approval. Members found them to be "sound," that they "would only strengthen [the charter's] purpose," and would "modernize some outdated provisions."[59] All seven passed.[60]

In 2003, the League was against proposed amendments to Kirkwood's charter. This was a bold stance given that the League helped create the original one in 1983. The amendment would change at-large elections to wards/districts. The League said the amendment "does not meet League criteria for good governmental process...Because of the amendment's lack of clarity, the possibility of costly court action and, most importantly, the lack of wide-open citizen input," they urged a "no" vote.[61] Voters agreed with the League on November 4, with 76.43% voting against it.[62]

In November 2002, St. Louis City asked voters for home rule. *The St. Louis Post-Dispatch* explained the city's unusual position: "St. Louis is unique in that it is one of the few cities across the country that is both a city and county. St. Louis residents already have home rule powers to make changes in the city charter. But they lack home rule authority over the city's 'county' functions"—such as circuit clerk, collector of revenue, license collector, public administrator, recorder of deeds, sheriff and treasurer,[63] which were elected positions. If the amendment passed, those positions would be appointed by the mayor.

The League Board voted unanimously to support home rule, saying,

> This issue is a remnant of history when the state governments throughout the country enjoyed substantial control over the charters of municipal and county governments. As recently as 1989, the Board of Aldermen attempted to change and improve the structure of the function of governance in St. Louis but was, once again, denied by the courts. If successfully passed, home rule only authorizes the right to change the structure of St. Louis city government.[64]

Voters passed the constitutional amendment on Nov. 5, 2003.[65]

DEATH PENALTY

Thanks to the dogged efforts of Leaguer Sydell Shayer, opposition to the death penalty in Missouri became a St. Louis League priority in late 2008. On March 1, 2008, the Missouri League issued the following moratorium resolution:

> Fairness and justice demand a moratorium on executions, an irreversible punishment, until the Missouri capital punishment system can be thoroughly evaluated and addressed. Therefore,
>
> Be it resolved that the LWV of Missouri calls on the governor of Missouri and our senators and representatives in the General Assembly to take the necessary steps to initiate a thorough study of various aspects of the death penalty with a moratorium on executions in Missouri while the study takes place, and implement legislation, policies and procedures which:
>
> Ensure that death penalty cases are administered fairly and impartially in accordance with basic constitutional guarantees such as the right to due process of law, guarantee competent legal representation to every capital defendant and eliminate the risks that innocent persons may be executed.[66]

In December 2008, Sydell convinced the board to approve the resolution.[67] She became a one-woman committee, keeping members informed through newsletter articles and working with other groups such as Missourians to Abolish the Death Penalty, the leading anti-death penalty organization in Missouri.[68]

While no legislation passed, an anti-death penalty bill got farther in 2008 in the legislature than ever before.[69] In March 2009, another bill was introduced that called for "formation of a Commission to study the death penalty in Missouri and a three-year moratorium on the use of the death penalty while the Commission is working."[70] In April, the bill made it out of the committee as "do pass." A hearing took place on the Senate floor, but it was moved to the informal calendar when it became clear there were not enough votes for it to pass. "This was the first time a death penalty bill made it to the floor of either legislative body," Shayer noted.[71] The work of this committee continued into the next decade.

EDUCATION

BUSING AND CHARTER SCHOOLS

St. Louis's voluntary busing program continued into the new millennium. It was difficult to believe such a program was still necessary—more than 50 years after desegregation of schools should have been accomplished. The League continued to support the system, but a new solution was quickly taking shape: charter schools.

Charter schools are nonsectarian, non-religious and non-discriminatory public schools funded by taxpayers and operated by parents, educators or community members. They function independently of the local school board[72] and must be approved by their local school district or a four-year public college or university in the same or an adjoining county.[73]

The legislature approved a bill to allow charter schools in St. Louis and Kansas City in 1998.[74] The League failed to come to consensus, and so stated that they do "not support or oppose charter schools. Since Missouri law permits Charter schools, the League supports criteria for governance and operations similar to those of traditional public schools, but accountability and accreditation should be the same as those of traditional public schools."[75]

Mayor Clarence Harmon, on the other hand, welcomed

charter schools with open arms, seeing them as a positive for the city. The first, Lift for Life Academy, opened on Aug. 31, 2000. Two others opened the following week.[76]

Charter schools expanded tremendously beginning in 2001 with the election of Mayor Francis Slay, who would go on to be called "a recruiter of charter schools." The 2002 financial crisis caused by the end of state funding for desegregation gave Slay the opportunity to experiment with the idea of running the school district like a corporation that emphasized efficiency and privacy of operations. This included outsourcing "the district's school lunch program, computer education program, and buildings maintenance to private firms."[77]

That plan did not work well. "By 2004…St. Louis had closed 21 schools and laid off 1,000 employees. The negative effects made national headlines," reported *The Washington Post*.[78] "Student enrollment continues to decline, teachers complain about poor morale and low pay, parents are unhappy about school closures, and voters are up in arms about high salaries paid to top administrators."[79]

As a result, the St. Louis City School District lost its accreditation in 2007.[80] That same year, the Voluntary Interdistrict Choice Corporation (VICC) voted to extend St. Louis's voluntary busing system for another five years,[81] a wise move considering many parents would not want their children attending unaccredited schools.

Around the same time, the Missouri League, led by the St. Louis League's Education Committee, prepared to study charter schools once again. Members visited six St. Louis charter schools, gave a presentation to all League units, hosted speakers and provided background information to members.[82] They did not come to a consensus but issued a set of guidelines that charter schools should ensure:

- Equality of opportunity in education, access to quality education and adequate financing should be available for students in charter schools as these are in traditional public schools.
- Charter school sponsors should have additional documented oversight responsibilities.
- Charter schools should be funded at the same rate per student as those in traditional public schools.
- Charter schools' governance/operations should go through the same process of mediation as in traditional public schools.
- Charter schools should not become Local Educational Agencies.
- Charter schools should not be extended beyond those permitted in Missouri State Statutes as of December 2006.[83]

That last point would become the basis for a change in League position in the next decade when lawmakers decided to extend charter schools across the state. This issue will be discussed in the next chapter.

Education Funding and Teacher Preparation

Despite the fact that Missouri ranked 37th out of 50 states in funding for public education,[84] this funding was the target of many a lawmaker's red pen in the 2000s. It was used as leverage in a nasty budget battle. Early in 2003, Democratic Governor Bob Holden threatened to cut up to $140 million from Missouri's education budget if lawmakers couldn't plug a hole in the budget. In late February, he cut $83 million from education, mostly from elementary and high schools, in addition to $75 million for state agencies.[85] Later in the year, he vetoed the public schools' budget, again because of overall problems with budget balancing.[86]

The League despaired over this, given that "the effects will be more pronounced for the poorer districts who receive a greater portion of their funding from the state of Missouri." Members noted the cuts could be up to 15% of their budget or more, and likely would take place in programs such as fine arts, foreign languages, and drivers' education.[87]

At the same time as the educators were facing these cuts, they were grappling with new standards set by the No Child Left Behind Act, when it was signed into law the previous year. It was a major update to the 1965 Elementary and Secondary Education Act that "place[d] more effort and resources into assuring the educational achievement of all children in public schools." It emphasized accountability, flexibility beyond government opinions of what is best, the choice of parents to transfer students out of failing schools and educator use of research-based strategies.

Opponents voiced displeasure about "unfunded mandates, more stringent teacher qualifications, and, most recently student testing," known as the Missouri Achievement Program or MAP. With the way tests were reported, "the more diverse the school population, the more opportunities there are to fail."[88]

In 2004, the League joined a coalition on public education that held seminars to educate parents and taxpayers on issues affecting public education, including why public schools were getting $91 million less in funding than just two years ago,[89] and explain the No Child Left Behind Act.[90] According to education committee chair Doris Buzzell:

> At the national level, the No Child Left Behind Law has raised issues of funding, student testing

and reporting, district reclassification and teacher certification. At the state level, the legislature is working to find ways of funding schools at a time when the budget is strained and attitudes are polarized. And, at the local level, each school district is facing financial shortfalls and struggling to meet No Child Left Behind mandates.[91]

That same year, the League attended the Kids First Rally in Jefferson City on February 12. There, members stood in the cold with more than 2,000 other Missourians, including teachers, parents and students, to protest Governor Holden's cuts to education funding. According to the *St. Louis Post-Dispatch*, it was the largest education rally in about 12 years.[92]

By 2008, the League's Education Committee turned its attention to "exploration of how nearby universities are preparing regular and/or special education elementary teachers to best serve today's learners."[93] Over the next year, members interviewed representatives from "the Department of Elementary and Secondary Education, school district administrators, principals, mentors, first- and second-year teachers, as well as university personnel and organizations that train mentors" to find out what is expected of new teachers, how teacher preparation has changed over the years, and what the first year of teaching does to prepare new teachers for the second. When the study concluded, the committee gathered their findings and shared best practices with participating schools and the Department of Elementary and Secondary Education as recommendations to be built into new teachers' curriculum.[94]

ENVIRONMENT

Nuclear Waste

Nuclear energy was once again a subject of League scrutiny in 2002, although this time it was not for its production but rather the transportation of its waste. With the rise of domestic terrorism and lingering fears over the September 11 attacks, more people feared what could happen if nuclear waste, transported by truck or train, were to fall into the wrong hands.[95]

While this was not a new subject of protest, it took on a new urgency when the government announced its intention to ship high level nuclear waste to the Yucca Mountain repository in Nevada for storage. A likely Midwestern route would send waste down I-70, right through the heart of St. Louis.

The St. Louis League joined other Leagues across the country and several environmental groups in opposing the government plan. A series of media events were held to "draw attention to the inadequacy of the Yucca Mountain site and the grave dangers inherent in the transportation of thousands of tons of waste by barge, truck and rail to the site."[96] League member Nancy Ulman spoke at a meeting at Webster University, and Nancy Bowser appeared at a press conference at Kiener Plaza.

Despite the dangers of nuclear waste and the fact that "tens of thousands of radioactive waste shipments will go through at least 43 states and more than 100 cities on the way to Yucca Mountain," passing within a half-mile of the homes of more than 50 million people,[97] SJR 34 was passed 60-39 the week of July 12. The bill established Yucca Mountain, just 90 miles northwest of Las Vegas, as a "permanent underground burial for the nation's spent radioactive and nuclear waste."[98]

Metropolitan Sewer District

Two League members were appointed to Metropolitan Sewer District (MSD) groups in early 2001. Nancy Ulman, the League's Legislative Chair, was appointed as its delegate to the MSD rate Commission, a four-year appointment. In the aftermath of the agency's rate increase woes in the 1990s, the Commission was charged with reviewing every rate increase proposal created by MSD and providing a recommendation as to whether it should be placed on the ballot.[99] In November 2002, Ulman was succeeded by Nancy Bowser, Environmental Quality Chairman, who also served on MSD's Stormwater Advisory Committee of MSD.[100]

More Financial Troubles for MSD

By May 2011, MSD was in hot water again over financial matters, this time over "serious concerns" voiced by St. Louis County Executive George R. "Buzz" Westfall to the governor[101] about its operations. Governor Holden asked State Auditor Claire McCaskill to audit the district, the first such audit in 15 years.[102]

The following month, when three trustees went into additional detail about the reasons behind the audit, it was revealed that MSD's legal fees had more than doubled over the past year. It was alleged that MSD's "Executive Director Willie Horton violated the district's charter by awarding a contract for legal services to Charles Polk without board approval."[103]

The audit found a dozen issues that needed to be addressed, including a massive number of uncollected bills and unwise use of funds such as reimbursements for unreasonably expensive business meals and massive payouts for unused paid time off and sick leave.[104]

These findings were yet another reason why it was important that the League maintained its close relationship with MSD and had members sitting on several of its committees. In this way, the League could fulfill its mission as a "watchdog" for the people.

Bond Issues

In April 2003, voters were supposed to vote on a $500 million MSD bond issue, which the League supported. It would have been used for constructing, improving, renovating, preparing, replacing and equipping new and existing MSD sewer facilities. However, the Board of Trustees took it off the ballot. Reasons given for the removal included fear of low voter turnout, a need to restructure after the financial scandal, and that increased time would give trustees more time to explain the issue to the public and demonstrate the changes in governance and fiscal management which they were implementing.[105]

The bond issue was placed back on the February 2004 ballot.[106] It passed with nearly 70% of voters in both St. Louis City and County supporting it.[107]

Four years later, another League-supported bond issue, Proposition Y, was before St. Louis City and County voters. The $275 million would fund necessary Missouri Department of Natural Resources and EPA mandates that are part of the Federal Clean Water Act through a combination of bonds and a pay-as-you-go form of revenue.[108] This form of financing was chosen because "it will enable the district to continue to move forward on the infrastructure replacement program with less of an impact on the customer rates than financing by pay-as-you-go alone."[109] On August 5, it passed by a wide margin.[110]

Renewable Energy

As the finite nature of fossil fuels became more apparent—86% of Missouri's electricity was generated by coal-fired power plants in 2008—the League, along with much of the country, turned its attention to renewable sources.

The League was one of the co-founders of the Missouri Clean Energy Coalition (MCEC), a group dedicated to "grow[ing] our clean and renewable energy economy to reduce fossil fuel pollution, address climate change, and create jobs."[111] In 2003, as part of the MCEC, the League testified at the state legislature about energy efficiency.

In 2007, the Coalition asked the legislature to pass a mandatory Missouri Renewable Energy Standard (RES) to amend Missouri law to "require more of Missouri's investor-owned electric utility companies to supply part of their power from renewable energy sources, such as wind, solar and biomass energy," on a gradually increasing scale over time. Instead, it passed a voluntary standard, which, unsurprisingly, few companies were quick to adopt.[112]

Knowing that a mandatory RES, which 26 states already had, was the only way to get Missouri to take action, in April 2008, members of the Environmental Quality Committee worked with other organizations to form Missourians for Cleaner, Cheaper Energy and collect signatures to get a RES petition on the ballot. They succeeded and Proposition C was placed on the November 2008 ballot.[113] It passed with over 1.2 million votes in favor, double those opposing.[114]

Just a few months later, the League worked with Ameren UE, the area's main electricity provider, to begin bringing "green power" to St. Louis. At a January 2009 League meeting, Ameren committed to "adding the first 100 megawatts of wind power to their system before the end of 2009." However, that wouldn't be easy because the only two wind generating areas in the state are in the northwest and northeast corners and how to get wind power from there to where it was needed hadn't been solved yet. The company revealed it was looking into solar and hydroelectric power, but neither seemed very promising.[115]

CLIMATE CHANGE

While the League had been a part of the fight against climate change since the 1960s, members took a significant public step in February 2008, by joining the U.S. Mayors' Climate Protection Agreement along with national groups like the Sierra Club and local organizations such as Women's Voices Raised for Social Justice.[116]

As part of this, the League participated in the "Cool Cities" campaign, which urged mayors to join more than 700 of their counterparts across the country in signing the mayoral climate protection agreement. The League sent letters and cards from members to many mayors in the St. Louis metro area and received responses that some had already signed it, while others were considering it.

In addition, the Environmental Quality Committee visited an Ecological Expo near Columbia, Missouri. Members learned about global warming and geothermal, solar, wind and other alternative energy methods. Many League members also attended the climate summit meeting held at the Ethical Society in March where state and local leaders presented their accomplishments.[117]

In 2009, the League joined with the Pew Center on Global Climate Change and many other organizations in Missouri to show both lawmakers and the public the advantages of "greening" Missouri's economy. They did this by "collect[ing] information on the activities of individuals, organizations, companies and communities in Missouri that are taking action to address climate change."[118]

Lead Poisoning

The League's study of lead poisoning began in 2005 with the Education Committee, members who were interested in the issue from the perspective of how it affects children's educational achievements. "It has long been known that lead poisoning affects the nervous system causing learning disabilities, lowered IQ, and attention deficit disorders," they wrote in a League newsletter. "As we pondered the problem of failing schools this seems to be one area where the public and legislators should be held accountable. This is fixable." Members worked with Lead Safe St. Louis—pioneers in the issue who already had in place a plan to remove lead paint from old buildings in five local neighborhoods—to learn more.[119]

In February 2006, the Environmental Quality Committee took over the study,[120] beginning a year and a half of research. Among the startling statistics found were that while the national average number of children found to have lead poisoning is 1.2%, in the City of St. Louis it is 7.4%—even going over 20% in some areas, between seven and 16 times the national average.[121]

Members also worked with the Jewish Community Relations Council and gathered resources from Lead Safe St. Louis and St. Louis Lead Safe Coalition before presenting to League units in March.

EQUAL RIGHTS AMENDMENT RATIFICATION

Contrary to popular belief, the push to ratify the Equal Rights Amendment (ERA) never really ended. Even after the 1982 deadline passed, it was reintroduced to Congress each year.

In 1999, the Missouri League was asked to once again become a part of the Coalition for ERA and work in coordination with others in the group to show legislators that their constituents still supported ratification of the ERA.[122]

In 2000, hope was strong that Missouri might be one of the states to push the ERA over the finish line. "The Missouri vote is the cutting edge of the 'three state strategy," columnist Ellen Goodman wrote in May 2000. "This is a long shot plan to bring the amendment back to life by getting it passed in three more state legislatures." The strategy, uncovered by three female law students in 1995, dated back to James Madison and an amendment that languished unpassed for more than 200 years. In 1992, it was ratified after Congress agreed to accept both new ratification votes and the original state votes in the tally.[123]

Legislators in both the Missouri House of Representatives and the Senate sponsored measures to ratify the ERA. Rep. Deleta Williams (D-Warrensburg) sponsored HJR 42 and Senator Mary Groves Bland (D-Kansas City) sponsored SJR 43. Ratification was supported by many Democrats as well as Governor Mel Carnahan, the Coalition for ERA, which included the League, the Missouri Human Rights Commission, AFL-CIO, Missouri NOW, and the American Association of University Women.

But the opposing voices, including Phyllis Schlafly's Eagle Forum, were strong. And many of the arguments were the same—how the ERA would force unisex restrooms, gay marriages, and women in combat upon an unsuspecting public, even though those things were already taking place. One of the loudest voices was Congresswoman Vicky Hartzler (R-4). She called the ERA a "moot issue" and implied that it wasn't needed, saying, "I think we have reached a valuable position in society.... My message would be for women and girls to get an education and to take advantage of all the opportunities we have today."

In the Missouri House, the Critical Issues Committee held a hearing and voted the bill "do pass," so it looked like it may have a chance. However, Rep. Dennis Bonner (D-Springfield) made a privileged motion to table the bill —a response usually reserved for "actions which damage the integrity of the House or to public allegations of improper official conduct by its members."[124] His motion was approved by the House 84 to 57, ending any chance of passage that year.

Hope dimmed after that, but legislators did not give up. In 2001, Rep. Williams sponsored HCR 4 and Senator Groves Bland sponsored SCR 7 and SJR 7. Again, it was the House that showed more willingness to pass ERA legislation. After a public hearing and a "do pass" approval vote by the Critical Issues, Consumer Protection, and Housing Committee, HCR 4 was defeated in the House on April 22, 94 to 57. In 2002, the exact same scenario occurred with HJR 25 and SJR 28.[125]

By 2003 and 2004, it must have felt like the House was playing games with ERA supporters, showing just enough interest to get them excited, but then letting the bills languish in committee. Both years, Rep. Vicky Riback Wilson (D-Columbia) and Senator Groves Bland introduced ERA bills. Each year, the House bill was referred to the Judiciary Committee, where it died.

In 2004, the St. Louis League, frustrated with the lack of real action in the Missouri legislature, turned its sights to its neighbor across the river, Illinois. It was possible that the more progressive state could become the 36th State—and the first in 20 years—to ratify the ERA. In May 2003, the Illinois House voted to ratify the ERA 76-41. The bill went on to the Senate, where it was voted out of committee 8-5. Sponsor Emil Jones

(D-Chicago) decided he didn't have the votes to bring it to the Senate floor but planned to do so in the second legislative session, which ran through May 30, 2004. St. Louis League members urged their friends and families in the Land of Lincoln to contact their representatives.[126]

Meanwhile in Missouri, from 2005-2017, the same pattern kept repeating. Hopeful Representatives and Senators introduced ERA bills that were left to die in committees, sometimes with one hearing.[127] Despite this, the League continued to support all legislation on the outside chance Missouri might take one of the final three remaining spots for states needed to ratify the amendment.

There was a ray of sunshine on the dimming situation in 2014 when the AAUW renewed Missouri's efforts and asked League members to join them.[128] That April 8 was Equal Rights Action Day in Jefferson City. That gathering of supporters included a legislative briefing coordinated by the Missouri Women's Network, a March for Women's Rights, a Women's Equality Rally under the dome and lobbying for the ERA.[129]

But the ERA was not to be ratified in Missouri, despite Missouri lawmakers introducing an ERA ratification bill in every legislative session between 1999 and 2017.[130]

In March 2017, 35 years after the original deadline, Nevada became the 36th state to ratify the Equal Rights Amendment. Illinois quickly followed in 2018, and Virginia on Jan. 27, 2020.[131]

In March 2021, the U.S. House passed legislation eliminating the arbitrary 1982 deadline for the ERA, but the Senate did not act on the bill.[132] Attempts have been made in five states to revoke their ratification.

LEAGUE ACTIVITIES

Major Gift from League Member Janet Becker

In fall 2009, Janet Becker, a 50+ year League member, and her husband, Dr. Bernard Becker, donated a major gift of bonds (valued at approximately $300,000) to the League's Information Service (IS). The Becker legacy gift gave the League stability and began a move to professionalize the organization.

Janet founded the IS, then called the Citizens Information/Resource Center (CIRC), in 1976, with the mission of providing voter information to citizens. Over the course of 35 years, the IS provided "voter hotlines, publications, a year-round telephone information service and citizen participation workshops."

Janet was quoted in an article in the Fall 1980 issue of *Metro News* as saying that while the League had provided her many satisfying experiences, her "greatest pleasure is seeing the success of CIRC."[133] See her profile in Chapter 2.

Mission Statement Change

At the 2008 annual meeting, held on May 10, 2008, the St. Louis League voted to change its mission statement to include the educational work it does. The new mission statement was identical to the old, except for the addition of the phrase in italics:

> The League of Women Voters, a nonpartisan political organization, encourages the informed and active participation in government, *works to increase understanding of major public policy issues*, and influences public policy through education advocacy.[134]

League Awards

The League was honored with two awards during this decade. As mentioned in the Voter Services section of this chapter, it received a 2005 "What's Right with the Region Award" from FOCUS St. Louis. The League was honored in the "improving racial equality and social justice" category for its naturalization registration efforts.[135]

The St. Louis Housing Authority honored the League on Jan. 17, 2007, with a plaque in appreciation of service to the tenant affairs board. The League had monitored the tenant affairs board elections and provided services for candidate forums prior to those elections for the last eight years. The award was accepted on behalf of the League by Ida West and Kathleen Kelly, the League coordinators of those services.[136]

March for Women's Lives

An estimated 2,500 Missourians showed up for the March for Women's Lives in Washington, D.C., on April 25, 2004.[137] More than a million people gathered to show their support for women's reproductive and contraceptive rights. Representing the St. Louis League were Carol Portman; her son Bob and his wife Charla Portman; Cindy Mitchell; Claralyn Bollinger; Joanne and Raleigh Wilson; Dianne Modrell; and mother-daughter Leaguers Mary and Suzanne Kirkpatrick. Carol and Bob Portman carried League banners. Bob and Charla Portman and Cindy Mitchell had the privilege of meeting LWVUS President Kay Maxwell who greeted marchers as they completed the route.[138]

Golden Lane Anniversary

On Sept. 6, 2008, the League commemorated the 92nd anniversary of one of St. Louis' great events in suffrage history, the Golden Lane. Taking place in 1916 during the Democratic National Convention, 7,000 women wearing long white dresses and carrying yellow umbrellas, their mouths taped shut to signify their lack of voice in voting, lined the route to the convention center.[139] Delegates were forced to walk past them to get to and from their meeting. They saw with their own eyes the support for women's suffrage.

The modern-day parade was sponsored by the Ben and Jerry's Foundation and the LWV Information Service and took place at Boileau Hall at Saint Louis University. This time, instead of silently lining the streets, the women "walked to recall the importance of walking to the polls," led by LWVUS President Mary Wilson and St. Louis League President Doris Buzzell. Half and full mile routes were set up to accommodate differing needs.[140] Though the women did not place tape over their mouths this time, "Rumor is rampant that at least one husband has offered to supply the tape," Buzzell joked.[141]

"Our motto is 'remember the past, act in the present, influence the future,' and the parade is the perfect way to represent this idea," Wilson said. "The 'walkless, talkless' parade was a key demonstration in the history of the League which displayed the silenced voices of women. Now, we want to remind Americans that their voices are becoming silent"[142] through repressive voting laws and voter apathy.

The event included voter registration, and rally speakers stressed "the value of having every eligible American vote in every election."[143]

LWVUS President Visits

League members had the opportunity to meet with Dr. Carolyn Jefferson-Jenkins, president of the League of Women Voters of the United States and the League of Women Voters

Education Fund during the third week of October 2000. She was in Missouri to promote the passage of Proposition B to regulate puppy mills.[144]

Conclusion

This was a challenging decade—as a nation, with the terrorist attacks on Sept. 11, 2001; financially, with the Great Recession lasting from 2006-2009; culturally with the rapid adoption of the Internet and web-based technologies; and politically with a highly-contested presidential elections, but also with threats to voting rights. As they have for decades, the League met these challenges head-on, promoting new voting machines, making election information available online, fighting for voter rights through election reform, advocating for the National Popular Vote, and challenging laws that would require photo IDs to vote. Many of these issues would be ongoing battles as the political climate of the nation changed, gradually becoming more conservative and less open to change.

WOMEN WHO MADE AN IMPACT IN THE 2000s

Lois Bliss

December 9, 1936 – June 12, 2019

Lois Wanslow was born Dec. 9, 1936, in Norfolk, Virginia, to Buford and Catherine Wanslow. In high school, Lois showed a talent for theatre, performing both at St. Scholastica Academy and the community theatre.[145]

Lois had been a League member before she and her husband Malcolm A. Bliss II moved from Little Rock, Arkansas, to St. Louis. As she told the *St. Louis Post-Dispatch* in 2011, "I was invited to a League meeting, and I just loved it. We were transferred a number of times [because of Malcolm's work], and the League was an immediate way to get involved in the community."

Lois joined the Kirkwood League in 1968 and served as president of the Kirkwood League from 1971-1973. She was active in both the Metropolitan League and the Citizens Information/Resource Center (CIRC), both Inter-League organizations comprising the city and county Leagues.[146] She fought for the ERA in the 1970s and served on the education coalition created after the courts created voluntary school desegregation in the early 1980s.

Lois had a particular affinity for education and library issues. "I love books and reading and libraries. They are one of the few institutions supported by the community but totally open and free and accessible to all," she told the *Post*.[147] It's not surprising, then, that Lois was a charter member of the Friends of the Kirkwood Library in 1978.

Lois was the perfect fit to chair the Missouri League Public Library study from 2003 to 2007. In retirement, Lois arranged for League members to purchase donated Kirkwood Library children's books at the annual Holiday Luncheon to be distributed to select charitable organizations.

Lois served as vice-chair of Kirkwood's Charter Commission in the early 1980s. "It became clear about the great advantages in moving to a charter form of government," she recalled.[148] The Kirkwood charter was approved in 1983.

Lois also served in a critical role as a volunteer on the U.S. Department of Justice City/Community Mediation Team, created in 2008, following the Kirkwood City Hall shooting on February 8 that killed seven people, including the gunman.[149]

The team was created to help ease racial tensions after the event and improve race relations in the city." That was an opportunity to learn how people really felt and what their perceptions were, to build relationships, trust and new avenues of communication," Bliss said.

Lois was also a well-known community speaker and a valued member of the former Conference on Education, Confluence St. Louis (now FOCUS St. Louis) and a graduate of the Leadership St. Louis program. In addition, Lois served as an elected member of the St. Louis Community College Board of Trustees.

In 2011, she was honored by the West County Journal Awards for her community service.[150]

Lois passed away in her sleep on June 12, 2019, at the age of 82.[151] She donated her body to St. Louis University School of Medicine.[152]

Carol Portman

January 1934 – present

Carol Michles was born in Fremont, Ohio, and studied at The Ohio State University. She married Darwin Portman in 1962 and had two sons, Alan and Bobby. She first attended a University City Unit meeting on education in 1968 to learn more about local schools as one of her two sons started kindergarten. She quickly discovered she had a passion for juvenile justice and reproductive rights. Carol joined the board and served as president of the University City League from 1975 to 1977.[153]

Carol began working at the state level shortly thereafter, serving as LWVMO Juvenile Justice Chair from 1986-1993; vice president from 1993-1997;[154] and president from 1997-1999. She fought for campaign finance reform[155] and gun control,[156] among other issues. She presented more than 20 speeches for the League.

In 1995, Carol helped found the Harriett Woods Award for Exemplary Community Service, bestowed by the LWV of Missouri. Carol herself was a recipient of this award in 2007.[157]

Carol was instrumental in uniting all the local Leagues in the area. She served as CIRC treasurer, committee member for many special events and projects, including the League's 65th and 70th anniversary celebrations, unit leader for University City from 2004-2007, and Voter Registration Chair beginning in 2008.[158]

She is perhaps best known for coordinating voter registration at naturalization ceremonies for the St. Louis League, a project she founded in 2001 with her husband Darwin, an immigration lawyer.

Carol contributed one of the blocks for a historic quilt representing the League's first 90 years. She promoted a DVD with "Buttons, Banners and Ballots: Memories of the Suffrage Movement," a 15-minute video by TV journalist and League member Betsey Bruce about suffrage items collected by U.I. "Chick" and Cecilia Harris of St. Louis.

Carol worked in juvenile justice for St. Louis County for decades. She served as treasurer of the Missouri Women's Network, and a member of the local ACLU, Mentor St. Louis, a tutor for students grades K-3 with OASIS, volunteer with Habitat for Humanity and a roving election judge for the St. Louis County Election Board.[159] She was also active with the Jewish Community Center Association, showing artwork back in 1967 and campaigning for the Equal Rights Amendment in 1977.[160]

State Treasurer and Merchandise Chair Mary Merritt often stayed in Carol's home when she traveled to St. Louis. On July

2, 2021, Carol joined several other Metro members in Sedalia for Mary's memorial service.

MICKEY CROYLE

SEPTEMBER 1953- PRESENT

Mickey Croyle was born in Brooksville, Pennsylvania, and moved to Seneca Falls, New York, in 1964. Steeped in women's rights history, she was a perfect candidate for the League, which she first found out about as a student at Keuka College when she worked with the League to hold candidate forums for her Political Parties and Special Interest Groups class project. Not long after, she graduated with a bachelor's degree in biology. She went on to complete a Med Tech program and get a master's in physiology and biophysics from the University of Iowa.[161] Over the next 20 years, Mickey worked as a molecular biologist and then in health physics and radiation safety.

Mickey and her husband Chris Erwin moved to Cincinnati in 1986. There, the League president contacted her, and Mickey joined. When the Internet Age began in the mid-1990s, she used her knowledge to help the League of Women Voters of the United States get a nuclear waste discussion grant. From 1994-1995, she focused on nuclear waste, serving as the League of Women Voters Cincinnati representative on the National Dialogue Pilot Field. In 1994, she created the League of Women Voters of Cincinnati Election Central, an early website providing election information on the Internet.

Likewise, she established the League of Women Voters of Cincinnati website in 1996 and worked closely with both LWVUS and the Ohio League. Mickey was also on the Campaign Finance Committee, worked on issues of county and city government, served as Natural Resources Chair (2004-2007), and on the Voter Services and Program Development committees. She served on the Cincinnati League's board from 1997-2005, as a trustee of the education fund from 2002-2007, as their webmaster from 1996-2007, and as a Smart Voter coordinator from 1998-2007. In 2004, Mickey received the Martha B. Taft award from the Ohio League as a member who "contributed extensively to fulfill League purposes and whose leadership has carried over to the community at large."

In July 2007 Mickey and Chris moved to St. Louis, where she took a job as a health physicist at Washington University. When choosing her home, Mickey specifically looked for one near the League office so she could continue her volunteer work.

Mickey served on the local League board from 2008 to 2014 and was the Smart Voter coordinator from 2008-2010. As a dedicated environmentalist, Mickey has served on and now chairs the League's Environmental Quality Committee. She is the League representative on the MSD Rate Commission and on the Missouri Clean Energy Coalition.

Main Sources Chapter 5 – The 2000s

Annual Reports of the President, League of Women Voters of St. Louis, 2002-2013

Minutes of the Meeting of the Board of Directors of LWVSTL, June 4 2008 - March 4, 2009

Newsletters
- *In League Reporter*, March 2002-April 2009
- *Metro News*, Spring 2001-Summer 2011

League documents regarding
- Campaign Finance
- Charter Revision
- Election Day/Voting
- Election Reform
- Guide to State Action 2017-2019
- Home Rule
- Smart Voter Website
- Voter Photo ID

Oral Histories: Linda McDaniel

Periodicals
- *Kansas City Business Journal*
- *The Riverfront Times*
- *St. Louis Jewish Light*
- *St. Louis Business Journal*
- *St. Louis Magazine*
- *St. Louis Post-Dispatch*
- *The New York Times*
- *The Washington Post*

Websites
- Ballotpedia
- Historical Context of the ERA in Missouri
- History.com
- Missouri Clean Energy Coalition

- Missourinet
- National Popular Vote
- St. Louis Public Radio

For a complete list of sources, please see the endnotes at https://my.lwv.org/missouri/metro-st-louis/about/our-history.

2000s

LWVUS President Kay Maxwell with Esther Clark on Sept. 6, 2008.

Kirkwood Leaguers and long-time friends Brenda Banjak, Lois Bliss, Carol Sipes, Pat Soraghan, Maxine Gilner (back row), Eleanor Barnes, Patricia Schark, Sydell Shayer and Agnes Garino (front row).

Elaine Blodgett (right front) and other Leaguers at a 2009 advocacy march.

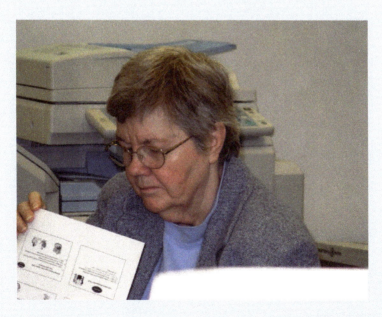

Nancy Bowser served as the League's representative to MSD committees and carefully studied environmental issues.

CHAPTER 6

The 2010s

THE 2010s WERE a decade unlike any other, with a global financial crisis and the Black Lives Matter movement moving racial issues to the forefront of public consciousness. Hillary Rodham Clinton became the first woman to be a major party›s presumptive nominee for president. Despite receiving almost 3 million more popular votes, Clinton conceded the 2016 election to Donald J. Trump who won the most Electoral College votes.[1]

"The 2016 election catapulted people's participation in politics, and the League's numbers grew, our partnerships grew, and an activist sentiment intensified.," says Kathleen Farrell.

Amid all of the upheaval, the St. Louis League focused on its mission and continued to do what it has done for the last 100 years: educate voters and advocate for the people and the causes they hold dear. Some of the highlights included:

- Co-sponsored candidate forums at the Missouri Black Expo in 2012 ahead of the election.
- Defeated a strict voter ID law in 2014, as well as a court appeal in 2018.
- Commemorated the 100th anniversary of the 1916 Golden Lane walkless-talkless parade with a 2016

Celebrate the Vote event.
- Fought for the future of our planet as part of the Missouri Clean Energy Coalition
- Supported CLEAN Missouri election reforms and Raise Up Missouri's campaign to increase the minimum wage.
- Sponsored the January 2017 Women's March in downtown St. Louis.
- Commemorated our 100th Anniversary in 2019 and joined the nation in the centennial celebrations of the 19th Amendment in 2020.

Since many women worked full-time and the continued expansion of League activities made it difficult for one person to lead the organization. Several teams of co-presidents led the St. Louis League during this decade: Becky Clausen and Linda McDaniel; Linda McDaniel and Kathleen Farrell; and Louise Wilkerson and Nancy Miller.[2]

VOTER SERVICES

Voter Registration

Volunteers continued to register voters in St. Louis City and County. In 2018, the League expanded into high schools to register students who were at least 17-and-a-half and eligible to vote when they turned 18. The League was asked to register voters at marches and community events in more diverse areas. LWV of Metro St. Louis received grants from LWVUS to expand both youth and new citizen voter registration.[3] At the time, naturalization ceremonies accounted for 80 percent of new registrants, with high school students coming in second.[4]

Voter Education

As in previous years, many community groups asked to partner with the League to help educate citizens and future voters. Some of this work was funded through a $9,950 grant from the Roblee Foundation to increase participation in state and local politics by new citizens and young adults through the Your Voice is Your Vote program. It taught them about state and local government, trained and encouraged them to attend public meetings, communicate with public officials, and vote in local elections. These workshops were held in partnership with the International Institute and local student government organizations, beginning in March 2015.

Another enthusiastic partner was Kids Voting. In 2011-2012, they worked together to provide students and teachers with candidate and ballot information to complement their voting programs. In addition to holding mock elections, they used the League website and online Voters Guide in the classroom to help educate students on the candidates and issues on the ballot. Kids Voting took place in the St. Louis City, Jennings and Valley Park school districts.[5]

But kids weren't the only ones using the League's website to learn about what they were voting on. The League linked its information to many media and organization websites to reach as many voting adults as possible.[6] In 2012, LWVUS and the LWVSTL Information Service debuted a new website called VOTE411.org. It contained the same candidate and ballot measure information that Smart Voter did in previous years, but also enabled voters to find their polling places and contained absentee ballot information, early voting options and ID requirements in their areas.[7]

Also in 2012, the League started a new monthly 30-minute cable television show on Charter channel 992 and AT&T

channel 99. Called *Impact on the Issues,* it covered topics on the ballot as well as information about legislation and issues affecting the St. Louis area. It was also available on YouTube.[8] For those who preferred to get their information in person, the League continued to hold candidate forums before each election across the St. Louis area. One of the best attended was at the Missouri Black Expo August 4-5, 2012. League members visited the KMOV TV Channel 4 studios for their first Election Day Hotline on Nov. 6, 2012. Starting at 6 a.m. until the polls closed, three teams of five League experts answered calls to help prepare voters to cast their ballots.[9]

The League shared input with the St. Louis County Election Board on new voting machines in 2019. The county converted electronic voting to paper ballots. Unlike previous systems, these machines used more secure paper ballots with a sophisticated scanning system. Voters hand-marked their choices on the ballots with blue or black ink. When completed, they fed them into a Verity Scan machine.[10] Because the new system printed ballots on site, voters were able to go to any polling place in the county to cast their ballots.

Voters Guide

While the League had been producing Voters Guides for decades, it gained powerful allies in 2010 with a partnership with the *St. Louis Post-Dispatch* and the *Suburban Journals.* The papers would publish the guide as a special insert and on their websites before each election.[11] The League office would receive thousands of extra copies of the print guide for volunteers to distribute. Guides were also available at Schnucks grocery stores. This allowed the League to reach tens of thousands of additional voters in the St. Louis area with valuable election information.

The guides ranged in size from "the March 2011 St. Louis City primary of fewer than 30 candidates to the whopping 36-page guide in April 2011 that covered more than 900 candidates and 56 ballot initiatives and propositions." The guides were so popular they routinely ran out of the first print run of 10,000 available at libraries, YMCAs, coffee shops, union halls, senior centers, recreation buildings, churches, beauty shops and grocery stores, and had to have more printed.[12]

Thanks to this partnership, the League reached approximately 300,000 *Post* subscribers with their first insert. This number skyrocketed to over 1 million combined for the 2010 and 2011 elections.[13] By 2012, the number of *Post* subscribers reached was up to 500,000[14] and in 2014, the printed inserts were also available at popular locations like Starbucks.[15] In 2015, the League received special requests from Black churches to distribute guides to more than 4,000 members.[16]

Candidate Forums

Throughout the decade, the League hosted hundreds of candidate forums, bringing voters and politicians together in person to get to know those running for office and their stance on the issues. The April 2015 elections saw record attendance at 15 forums including candidates running for the University City School Board, Ferguson City Council, mayor of Jennings and St. Louis City Elected School Board.[17]

By 2017, both incumbents and challengers for office were in a race to reserve their spots at League forums, viewing League members as experts at facilitation of these events. That year was particularly important because for the first time in 16 years, the mayoral election and aldermanic races had numerous candidates. The mayoral forum was broadcast on KSDK Channel 5 and iHeart Radio, while smaller races such as school boards, fire districts, and city councils were staffed by League members at in-person only events that set attendance records for the time.[18]

The following year, the League again moderated candidate forums in the run-up to the April 3 municipal election and the August 7 primary.[19]

VOTER ID LAWS

While the League recognizes the need for voters to show identification, members believe there should be multiple options, including a student ID or voter registration card. Since the 2000 election, Missouri lawmakers have been trying to pass a Voter ID law that restricted acceptable forms of identification to non-expired state or federal photo IDs. An estimated 250,000 Missourians still do not have this type of government-issued ID.

The League always opposed strict photo ID requirements, calling it "a modern-day poll tax."[20] Members recognized the "significant barriers to the poor and the elderly" produced by the cost and difficulty for many of them to get the documentation required to obtain such identification.[21] Those who have been adversely affected by natural disasters or fire, those born at home, and those whose birth state couldn't locate their records wouldn't be able to access the necessary documentation. What's more, the League stressed that "no cases of voter impersonation fraud have ever been documented in Missouri. Every national study conducted has found that such allegations are not supported by empirical evidence."[22]

In the summer of 2011, LWVMO won a victory in this area when members urged Governor Jay Nixon to veto SB3, "which imposed stringent identification requirements for voting." Governor Nixon vetoed that bill[23] and two similar bills, HB1104 and SB442, the following year.[24] In 2014, a strict photo

ID provision was dropped at the last minute from an early voting bill.[25]

However, 2016 was a different story. HJR53 made it to the November ballot as Amendment 6. The measure would amend article VIII of the Constitution of Missouri and adopt one new section relating to elections. Working with the Missouri Voter Protection Coalition, led by Leaguer Denise Lieberman, the League coordinated a statewide campaign against Amendment 6 that included radio ads and media events.[26]

In September 2019, the League and NAACP sued in Cole County to stop the Secretary of State's implementation of the photo ID law, saying it caused great confusion among voters that lingered even three years later despite massive public education campaigns.[27] While this case was making its way through the court system, Priorities USA, a progressive policy advocacy organization, and two St. Louis-area residents[28] filed a similar suit that was heard in the lower courts and sent to the Missouri Supreme Court before the League case. On Jan. 14, 2020, the Supreme Court ruled that most of the law was unconstitutional, specifically regarding affidavit requirements, but left in place the photo ID requirement and provisional ballot option for those who don't have ID but return with one within 72 hours.[29]

"Because this case was ruled on first and the injunctions were essentially the same, our claims were declared moot in an April 20 ruling by Circuit Court Judge Jon E. Beetem," said League co-president Nancy J. Miller.[30]

VOTING RIGHTS ACT

In 2013, the U.S. Supreme Court ruled in *Shelby County vs. Holder* that using the coverage formula in Section 4(b) of the 1965 Voting Rights Act to determine which locations have to get permission from the Justice Department before making voting-related changes, as outlined in Section 5, was unconstitutional. These sections applied to certain states and counties with a history of discrimination against minority voters.[31] According to the Justice Department, from 2003-2013, the Attorney General received between 4,500 and 5,500 Section 5 submissions, and reviewed between 14,000 and 20,000 related petitions to change voting laws per year.[32]

On October 10, members of the League and Women's Voices Raised for Social Justice gathered to discuss what this meant for Missouri, and St. Louis in particular. While Missouri wasn't specifically covered by the affected sections, the ruling still significantly weakened the Voting Rights Act and shifted the burden of proof of discrimination from the states to voters who are discriminated against. In addition, the ruling meant that states could close polling places, enact strict Voter ID laws—something Missouri had been trying to do for nearly a decade[33]—require proof of citizenship in order to vote and make other changes without federal oversight.[34] As a result, the two organizations continue to work together, especially regarding voting-related issues.[35]

The League continued to work to restore the voting rights of Missourians. In June 2019, LWVUS gave the first pass-through grants to the Missouri League to support federal voting rights legislation. These bills sought to restore the Voting Rights Act, improve election security and transparency, modernize the redistricting process, and make election systems fairer and more accessible to all eligible Americans. The League opposed efforts to remove voters from rolls and supported restoration of voting rights to people convicted of felonies once they completed their sentences.

The League used the 2019 grant to encourage U.S. Senators Roy Blunt and Josh Hawley to request a hearing on these reforms. In addition to sending postcards to the two Republican senators, the St. Louis and Kansas City Leagues wrote letters to the editors of their biggest newspapers. LWVMO President Evelyn Maddox met personally with staff for both Senators.[36] Unfortunately, Senate Majority Leader Mitch McConnell (R-KY) blocked the measure from being heard.[37]

"MOTOR VOTER" VIOLATIONS

When the Motor Voter Act passed in 1993, it was supposed to provide the opportunity to register to vote when a person applied for, changed, or renewed a driver's license, and automatically update any change in address in the state voter registration records. However, in 2017, it became clear that the Missouri Department of Revenue (DOR) was not fully complying with the law when renewals took place online or by mail because they were not updating address changes to keep voter registrations current.[38]

In 2018, the LWV of Missouri sought a preliminary injunction to require the DOR to contact the 40,000 registered voters who changed their addresses online or by mail in time for the Nov. 6 election. Judge Brian Wimes requested mediation from Magistrate Judge William Knox in Jefferson City on August 28. St. Louis League co-presidents Linda McDaniel and Kathleen Farrell participated in the mediation process, along with the League's lawyers. No agreement was reached, so the case was sent back to Judge Wimes.[39] On Sept. 21, 2018, the Judge ordered the DOR to comply before the midterm elections.[40] A little over a year later, this decision was made official when the State League accepted an agreement with the state of Missouri on Nov. 1 to settle the League's lawsuit against the Missouri Secretary of State and the DOR.[41] The agreement also included changes to in-person and mail change-of-address processes, as well as requiring the DOR to conduct regular audits, publish the results publicly, and "designate a National Voter Registration Act coordinator to ensure compliance with the settlement."[42]

REDISTRICTING

"Missouri's redistricting commissions don't have a very successful track record," an Associated Press story said in December 2021.[43] Commissioners failed to reach an agreement on Senate maps every decade since the 1980s, so the process moved to judicial panels. After a court battle in 2011, Senate redistricting had to go to a second bipartisan commission and wasn't completed until 2012. Judges also had to take over when House redistricting commissioners failed to reach agreement in 2001 and 2010.

For decades, LWVMO had fought for fair maps. Linda McDaniel stressed the League position: "Districts should be apportioned substantially on population with compact and contiguous districts, recognizing that there are diverse interests within them and that broad communities of interests should be kept intact. Minority representation should be protected."[44]

In 2017, the St. Louis League joined a coalition endorsing the Clean Missouri ballot initiative, which changed the model for drawing districts to prevent partisan or racial gerrymandering. The proposal focused on legislative reforms,[45] "imposing gift limits for legislators, lowering campaign contribution limits, [and] changing the length of time required before becoming lobbyists."[46] During the last week of the 2018 legislative session, co-president Nancy J. Miller testified in Jefferson City against HJR100. She stressed the LWV position that political and racial gerrymandering distorts and undermines representative democracy by allowing politicians to select their voters rather than voters being able to pick their elected officials.

League members in St. Louis and across the state gathered signatures to get Clean Missouri reforms on the November 2018 ballot. The coalition submitted 346,956 signatures to the Secretary of State's office in Jefferson City. The initiative was on the Nov. 6 ballot[47] as Amendment 1. "More competition and transparency in the redistricting process will mean that more officials, of any party, will be more responsive to the needs of their entire districts," Miller said. "Amendment 1 ensures we're able to hold legislators accountable when they fail to act in the public interest. This constitutional amendment will take power away from special interests and give it back to the people," added board member Angie Dunlap.[48] The Amendment passed with 62% of the vote, winning in every state Senate district. Nearly 570,000 more people voted for Clean Missouri than against it.[49]

However, that was not the end of the story. Opponents immediately set to work trying to get the amendment reversed. Republican leaders in the General Assembly proposed another constitutional amendment to repeal Clean Missouri. Amendment 3 would eliminate most lobbyist gifts, but Clean Missouri had already capped these gifts at $5. It lowered campaign contributions, but only to State Senate candidates and by just $100 ($2,400 instead of $2,500). It allowed the government to operate with more secrecy and partisanship, created new loopholes and weakened protections for minority communities. Most importantly, it eliminated the Clean Missouri provision that required a "non-partisan demographer to draft legislative district maps with a high priority on districts being fair and competitive." It replaced that person with a bi-partisan commission, appointed by the Governor, just like it was before Clean Missouri.

"Hidden in Amendment 3 is language that could make Missouri the only state not using the total population count when drawing legislative districts," the League warned. "Instead, maps could be based on the number of eligible voters. That would leave out 1.5 million Missouri children and non-citizens."[50]

The League sued in Cole County over the ballot language and Cole County Circuit Court Judge Pat Joyce agreed. When the decision was appealed, the Western District Court of Appeals found "major problems" with the ballot language and ordered it to be re-written so as not to mislead voters. They also agreed that the amendment, as written, "would permit a level of gerrymandering at twice the level typically described as 'severe.'"[51]

Amendment 3 passed on Nov. 3, 2020, by just 59,000 votes. Opponents believe that it passed because of the way the measure was written, with the redistricting language buried after the lobbyist and campaign contribution provisions so that voters thought they were voting for those provisions and didn't realize the full ramifications.[52]

In 2019-2021, the League worked closely with Show Me Integrity, "a cross-partisan movement for more effective, ethical government of, by, and for the people of Missouri and beyond."[53] The League worked with two of its teams, the St. Louis Clean Defense Coalition and the Show Me Integrity Coalition, to attend hearings on legislation, meet with legislators, distribute postcards for voters to send to their representatives, and conduct advocacy in favor of Clean Missouri.[54] They also helped gather signatures and educate voters on related measures supporting the League position on election reforms.[55]

EARLY VOTING

Beginning in 2009, the St. Louis League undertook a study of early voting and procedures in place across the country in preparation for coming to a consensus and issuing an official position. They found that the rationale for Election Day being set on the first Tuesday after the first Monday was established in 1845 to allow farmers enough time to travel to their county seat without interfering with the Sabbath (Sunday) or market day (Wednesday).[56]

Today, less than 1% of the population are farmers, and modern life holds very different work and family demands. Thirty-seven states allow no-excuse absentee voting by mail and or no-excuse in-person early voting. Residents of Colorado, Hawaii, Oregon, Utah and Washington vote entirely by mail, resulting in 43-46% of votes being cast before Election Day.[57] The consensus the Missouri League adopted was that it "support[ed] absentee voting, advanced voting and measures that facilitate participation in the election process."[58]

In 2019, the League made a concerted effort to advocate for no-excuse absentee voting, specifically HJR5, sponsored by Rep. Peter Merideth (D-80), which would create an early voting period and add satellite voting sites.[59] The bill was referred to the Elections and Elected Officials Commission, where it died.[60]

Amber McReynolds spoke at the LWVMO State Convention in St. Louis on May 4, 2019. A former Director of Elections for Denver and the executive director of the National Vote at Home Institute, she is a strong advocate for innovative practices to increase the security, convenience and efficiency of elections. She told delegates, "Let's make the voting experience something everyone can celebrate."[61] At the same convention, city treasurer and now Mayor Tishaura Jones spoke in favor of election reforms "to ensure an effective government of, by and for the people." She shared her support for alternative voting systems such as ranked choice or approval voting.

After that, the St. Louis League partnered with the Gamma Omega Chapter of Alpha Kappa Alpha Sorority, Inc., and testified before the St. Louis Board of Aldermen and the St. Louis County Council. Members asked each group to adopt a resolution in support of early voting and same-day registration and direct the Missouri General Assembly to enact the appropriate legislation.[62]

MISSOURI PRIMARY CHANGES

As previous chapters have shown, Missouri has an inconsistent history of how and when it conducts primaries. The St. Louis League has been advocating for open primaries since the 1970s.

In 2019, the St. Louis League approved "advocacy for alternative voting systems as part of Making Democracy Work," a St. Louis-based effort to implement Proposition D, which "calls for an open and nonpartisan system to elect the offices of mayor, comptroller, president of the Board of Aldermen and Aldermen" in the City of St. Louis. Under that system, in the primary, voters would be able to vote for as many candidates as they wanted and then the top two candidates would be part of a run-off election in April. This is also known as "approval voting" and was favored for its potential to "decrease the influence of big money by allowing voters to support grassroots candidates who have less money."[63]

The League noted that "in several elections, less than 40% of St. Louis City residents voted for the winner and approximately 65% voted for someone who did not become the winner," so reform is necessary to increase voter turnout and show voters that their votes matter.[64] Proposition D was a hit with voters, who approved it by 68% on Nov. 3, 2020.[65]

In 2021, the League, Show Me Integrity and the Center for Election Science worked to educate candidates and voters about the new system before the March 2 primary and April 6 runoff, the first under the new system.

EDUCATION

BUSING

The 2010s saw the winding down of a 60-year-old tradition of desegregation in St. Louis, the Voluntary Interdistrict Choice Corporation (VICC) student transfer program, or as it was previously known, busing. Desegregation had taken place in St. Louis since the 1960s, but VICC was mandated by law in 1982. "It was designed to offer students better academic options and also to present underperforming school districts with something akin to a nuclear option: do better at educating the students you have or pay the hefty price of educating them elsewhere," MSNBC reported.[66]

Since St. Louis Public Schools were no longer accredited due to severe financial and academic underperformance,[67] more families signed up to have their students enrolled in other districts through the VICC program. A quarter of Normandy students left after that district lost its accreditation in 2013,[68] with an estimated 2,200 students leaving those three unaccredited districts (St. Louis Public Schools, Riverview Gardens and Normandy).

Questions arose about the legality of so many students seeking to be transferred from failing schools to schools in better standing. A lawsuit followed which made its way to the Missouri Supreme Court and in October 2013, the court "[upheld] the current law allowing students in an unaccredited school district to transfer to another school district in the county or adjoining counties."[69]

While the League chose not to take a position on the ruling itself,[70] it worked to educate parents, teachers, students and members about the law.

In February 2014, the State Board of Education devised a

plan to help intervene in failing schools before they lost their accreditation. The plan included five tiers related to performance.[71] It went on to be combined with other bills to become SB 493, which allowed individual schools within a district to be accredited rather than the district as a whole, as well as requiring charter schools to be accredited. It allowed students from unaccredited schools to transfer to private, non-sectarian schools within the school district.[72] The bill passed both the Senate and the House, but Democratic Governor Jay Nixon vetoed it on July 24, 2014. The Senate adopted a motion to override the veto two months later, but no further action took place.[73]

The beginning of the end for VICC started in 2016, when its board voted to extend the program for its final five years. There were many reasons the board decided it was time to end the program, including low application numbers. A total of 2,488 Black students applied to VICC for the 2017-2018 school year, but only 413 were accepted, as opposed to more than 13,000 in the early 1990s. VICC's program will end after 2023-2024 school year.[74]

Expansion of Charter Schools

Though the League could not come to a consensus on charter schools, one thing members agreed upon was they were not in favor of them expanding beyond St. Louis and Kansas City, the areas specified in the original law allowing them to operate.[75]

Governor Jay Nixon signed a bill on June 27, 2012,[76] allowing the expansion of charter schools into unaccredited and provisionally accredited districts in the state, as well as allowing local school districts' boards of education to establish charter schools within their district.[77]

In 2019, the League strongly opposed SB 51 which would "allow charter schools to open in any charter county or city of 30,000 or more, even if no school in the district is underperforming." The League felt that this bill didn't provide for enough input from voters as to where the schools might be located, so they favored other bills instead.[78] SB 51 was referred to the Senate Education Committee, where it died.[79] Legislators continue to try to expand charter schools into every district in the state; the League continues to oppose any expansion of charter schools in Missouri.[80]

OTHER EDUCATION-RELATED CONCERNS

In 2011, the Education Committee participated in a national consensus study on the role of the federal government in public education, which included equity and funding, and the Common Core standards.[81] The short version of the League's consensus read: "The League of Women Voters believes that the federal government shares with other levels of government the responsibility to provide an equitable, quality public education for all children pre-K through grade 12. A quality public education is essential for a strong, viable and sustainable democratic society and is a civil right."[82]

Toward the end of the decade, funding for traditional public schools was a concern for the League because of state and federal tax cuts that reduced the revenue given to education and programs/policies that "redirect money from public school districts to charter schools, online schools and home schooling."[83]

In 2018, the League issued a statement against Empowerment Scholarship Accounts (ESAs) because they would "provide a 100% tax credit for funds placed into such an account, which would be used to fund private and parochial school tuition. This would reduce Missouri general revenue, making it harder to fully fund the public school system."[84] Instead, the League believed that the government should focus on fully funding the Foundation Formula, Missouri's primary method of distributing money to public schools that established "the least amount of spending necessary to provide students with a basic education."[85]

Despite League opposition, on July 14, 2021, Republican Governor Mike Parson signed an ESA bill making Missouri one of the first two states in the country with an ESA funded through tax credits. The Missouri Empowerment Scholarship Accounts Program "allow[ed] taxpayers to claim a tax credit of up to 50 percent of their liability for contributions to educational assistance programs." The resulting money was then "pooled in ESAs for students to use on tuition, textbooks, tutoring services, and other costs."[86]

HEALTH CARE

In 2004, the League supported a bill sponsored by Senator Michael Gibbons (R-Kirkwood) pertaining to children's mental health. It passed, creating a comprehensive children's mental health service system. It was the first bill signed by Democratic Governor Bob Holden in the legislature's spring session.[87]

Around the same time, League member Rep. Barbara Fraser (D-University City) introduced legislation in the House (HB1495) for single-payer health insurance.[88] It was read twice and referred to the Financial Services Committee, but no further action was taken.[89]

The League's Health Care Committee took a break from 2005-2008 and was reformed in summer 2008 under the leadership of chairman Joanne Simpson and then Katherine Kilpatrick.[90] In 2009, the committee undertook a study of issues concerning the financing of escalating costs in the health care system[91] and how the U.S. health system compares with programs in the rest of the world.[92]

PATIENT PROTECTION AND AFFORDABLE CARE ACT

Health care really took off for the League when the Patient Protection and Affordable Care Act (ACA) was passed on March 23, 2010. While the League ideally wanted a National Health Insurance plan financed through general taxes that provides a basic level of quality health care including primary, acute, long-term, mental, dental, hearing, and vision care, members felt the ACA was "a step in the right direction."[93] The League supported it and opposed all attempts at repeal or defunding.[94]

The League made extensive efforts to educate its members and the public on the intricacies of the ACA including positive changes regarding pre-existing conditions, young adults on parent policies, preventive care costs, lifetime limits, cancellation of policies and appeals.[95]

In 2013, the League joined the Cover Missouri Coalition, more than 70 groups "seeking to help Missourians—including individuals, families and small business owners—find quality affordable health coverage." The coalition was a project of the Missouri Foundation for Health and aimed to reduce the rate of uninsured in the state to less than 5% by 2018.[96]

MEDICAID UNDER THE ACA

The Supreme Court upheld the ACA in June 2012 but left Medicaid expansion in the hands of the states.[97] The League joined the Medicaid Expansion Coalition,[98] Missouri Health Advocacy Alliance, Cover Missouri Coalition, Missouri Health Care for All and Missouri Medicaid Coalition[99] in order to make more progress in convincing lawmakers to take advantage of the Medicaid expansion option under the ACA.

On Aug. 14, 2013, Health Care Committee Chair Dianne Modrell testified before a House committee, urging legislators to support full Medicaid expansion that meets the 138% federal poverty level for full federal reimbursement up to three years—something the Missouri Chamber of Commerce and the Missouri Hospital Association supported as well. Such a step would insure 250,000-300,000 Missourians, reduce emergency room use and result in a healthier population.[100] By doing so, she said, "Missouri would receive 100% of federal monies available through the ACA. Missouri leaves money on the table by not choosing immediate, full expansion,"[101] an estimated $8.2 billion through 2020.[102]

Over the next seven years, dozens of bills attempted to do exactly that. Missouri refused to consider such legislation "due to budgetary concerns," even though a 2019 analysis by the Center for Health Economics and Policy at Washington University in St. Louis found that MO HealthNet (Medicaid) expansion would be budget neutral.[103] Moreover, "between January 2018 and March 2019, Missouri dropped 85,000 people, including 67,000 children, from Medicaid. In April 2019 alone, more than 11,000 individuals were dropped from Medicaid, including 9,000 more children." The League participated in a campaign calling for Governor Parson to end this purging and promptly re-enroll those who had been dropped. The state tried, but its new system wasn't very effective.[104]

In August 2019, the League supported proposed changes to Missouri health care law by MO HealthNet to expand Medicaid coverage to individuals ages 19-64 who qualify under the required federal poverty level and cover birth control and family planning for all Missourians over the age of 13.[105] This was the basis for a Medicaid Expansion amendment to the Missouri

Constitution that would be placed on the Aug. 4, 2020, ballot as Amendment 2—but without the birth control and family planning provision.

The League worked with the Missouri Organizing and Voter Engagement Collaborative (MOVE) and Missouri Health Care for All to educate voters and motivate them to go to the polls to vote on Amendment 2. Health Care for Missouri set their sights on undecided voters who might be persuaded. It used a Medical Ambulance Response Vehicle (MARV) to tour Missouri and raise awareness. League volunteers helped staff a Missouri Health Care for All phone bank available five days a week from Jun. 22 through Aug. 4. [106] On Aug. 4, Missouri became the 38th state to enact Medicaid Expansion when voters approved Amendment 2 by a vote of 622,036 to 580,969. Cost savings estimates for Missouri range from $39 million to $1 billion per year by 2026.[107]

In addition, on Oct. 4, 2021, just over a year later, President Joe Biden signed the American Rescue Plan, which further expanded Medicaid coverage to approximately 275,000 more Missourians under the ACA. This Act also made Missouri eligible for an additional $968 million in federal funding for MO HealthNet through 2023.[108]

DEATH PENALTY

The League firmly opposes the death penalty and has been working for decades to get it abolished in Missouri. The two main reasons for this stance are that innocent people may be killed and that death penalty trials are around $2 million more expensive for states than non-death penalty trials.[109] Although no death penalty legislation has passed in Missouri, several positive steps occurred during the decade.

The American Law Institute is an organization comprised

of around 4,000 judges, lawyers and law professors that created the 1962 model Penal Code, including a framework for the death penalty. In 2010, the institute conducted a study of the death penalty and concluded it had many problems including "racial disparities, underpaid and incompetent defense lawyers, and plain unfairness." As a result, they revoked their approval of the death penalty and removed it from the model Penal Code.[110]

The American Bar Association also decided in 2010 to review how the death penalty is administered in Missouri, making it the 9th state in a 50-state project to undergo study.[111] A special independent committee analyzed a dozen aspects of Missouri's death penalty process from arrest to execution, including the handling of DNA evidence, police interrogation procedures, and prosecutor and defense services.[112]

The same year, Rep. Bill Deeken (R-Jefferson City) introduced HB 1683 that proposed establishing a study commission on the death penalty and a three-year moratorium on executions while this took place.[113] In addition, SB 930 proposed the same for four years. Due to budget issues commandeering lawmakers' time, neither bill made it out of committee, but they were the basis of future legislation and nearly identical bills were introduced for the next three years.[114]

In 2013, Senator Joseph Keaveny (D-4) called for a state audit of the cost of first-degree murder cases where the death penalty is sought versus ones in which it is not. The League initially supported his bill (SB61) but pulled back when the Senate changed it to be funded with private money.[115] It was sent to the informal calendar for perfection and never progressed. By April of the following year, Missouri was becoming one of the national leaders in executions, having carried out the death penalty seven times in seven months.[116]

But two years can make a big difference. In April 2016, state death penalty chair Sydell Shayer reported, "There has been a significant change in the climate surrounding the death penalty. Many prosecutors, wardens and judges have been convinced that the death penalty serves no positive purpose...The Innocence Project has brought flaws of the death penalty to light...The percentage of people opposing the death penalty has grown."[117]

Despite this trend, the federal death penalty was reinstated in 2019 after a 16-year lapse in executions.[118] Opponents of the death penalty feared some states would reverse their prohibitions.[119] Following 13 executions in the last six months of Trump's presidency, it seemed likely that the subject would be put to rest. President Joe Biden campaigned against the death penalty and Attorney General Merritt Garland declared a moratorium in July on the federal death penalty until a review on the Department of Justice execution policies and procedures could take place.[120]

ENVIRONMENT

Member Representation on Councils and Committees

Thanks to the League's reputation for nonpartisanship and expertise in environmental matters, members continued to sit on the Air Quality Advisory Committee and Water Resources Council of the East-West Gateway Council on Governments, as well as the Rate Commission of the Metropolitan Sewer District (MSD).[121] The League also joined the Greater St. Louis Transit Alliance (2011),[122] St. Louis County Phase Two Stormwater Management Plan (2013),[123] and Clean Energy Coalition (2015).[124]

Energy Efficiency

Energy-efficient homes and businesses had become all the rage by the 2010s due to advances in technology and increased environmental awareness. They were also a part of the country's goal to significantly reduce greenhouse gas emissions. League Environmental Quality Committee Chair Mickey Croyle continues to provide tips in each newsletter to give members ideas on how to make their homes more energy efficient. Tips included everything from changing the type of lightbulbs they use and unplugging household appliances and electronics when not in use to adding sensor lights and smart power strips to each room.[125]

At a public hearing on the future of St. Louis County's energy efficiency standards for residential buildings in February 2017, League members spoke in favor of the County adopting the 2015 International Energy Conservation Code (IECC). IECC was the most up-to-date energy efficiency building code for new residential buildings—but with "commonsense, cost-effective measures" like programmable thermostats, blower door testing and duct testing that were removed from the code added back in.[126] Supporters were successful; the IECC 2015 code was adopted with minor amendments.[127] A few months later, the League joined the Clean Energy of Missouri Coalition.[128]

Air Pollution

In January 2013, the St. Louis League board voted to support the Sierra Club's plan for action on clean air and protection from coal pollution.[129] Because of this, members were prepared when Ameren later proposed creating two new landfills for coal ash, which is "the waste product from burning coal [that] contains toxins such as mercury, lead and arsenic." They opposed a landfill at Ameren's Meramec coal plant in South County, which is in a floodplain.

The League opposed the repeal of several environmental measures adopted by the Obama Administration. Members were concerned that a proposed coal ash disposal rule by the Missouri Department of Natural Resources (DNR) would weaken existing requirements for coal ash landfills, allow new landfills to be built on unstable terrain, reduce the number of contaminants tested for and throw out requirements for utilities to publicly report results.

The EPA spoke out against the plan, as did neighbors and other environmental groups. In April 2019, the League was one of the signatories of a letter to the DNR that pushed the agency to pull the proposed rule, citing lack of "clear guidance on enforcing cleanup."[130] In July, the EPA announced a proposal to roll back coal ash regulations.[131]

Land, Agriculture, and Landfills

In May 2010, the Missouri Gaming Commission was eyeing the Columbia Bottoms at the confluence of the Missouri and Mississippi Rivers as the location of a new casino. The League joined the Save the Confluence Coalition,[132] and members attended meetings and wrote letters opposing locating the casino in such an environmentally important area. The casino was later given to Cape Girardeau.[133]

In a first for the League, from 2013-2014, the Environmental Quality Committee studied food, specifically genetically modified organisms, antibiotics in food and agriculture. This was in preparation for helping the National League update its agriculture consensus.[134]

From 2017 to 2019, the committee focused on the Westlake Landfill, an unlined landfill known to contain radioactive waste and be prone to underground fires. In September 2017, they sent a letter to the EPA urging action to clean up the landfill and another in 2018 regarding a proposed EPA action to remove approximately 70% of the radioactive waste from the landfill.[135]

The League acknowledged that this new plan was better than the original 2008 decision which called for the EPA to cap the waste and leave it there.[136] However, members continued working with coalition partners Just Moms STL, activist Kay Drey, the Sierra Club, and Missouri Coalition for the Environment to urge the EPA to remove *all* of the radioactive material.

METROPOLITAN SEWER DISTRICT

In 2001, Metropolitan Sewer District (MSD) examined the problem of stormwater runoff, rainwater not absorbed into the ground that runs off over the land, causing storm sewers to overflow and basement backups. They completed a high-tech mapping project that showed, in great detail, every bit of land in the city and county of St. Louis that was vulnerable to runoff, what MSD termed an "impervious surface."

This was done in preparation for the day that MSD asked voters to approve a rate increase based on how much impervious surface each customer had on their property in order to fund half a billion dollars' worth of stormwater upgrades.[137] That day came on April 5, 2016, in the form of Proposition S, which sought to create a uniform stormwater tax rate of $0.10 per $100 assessed valuation for MSD's service area.[138] The League supported this plan.[139] It needed a simple majority to pass, and it did, 104,008 to 62,875.[140]

The League also supported Proposition Y on the April 5, 2016, ballot. It authorized MSD to issue $900 million in revenue bonds for the $1.5 billion capital improvement and replacement wastewater plan. This would help MSD eliminate sewer overflows, prevent backups into buildings, and increase the capacity of the treatment plants—all without increasing rates.[141] The proposition passed in a landslide, 127,211 to 39,716.[142]

GUN SAFETY

On Feb. 21, 2013, the LWVUS sent a letter to federal lawmakers asking them to pass "common sense solutions" to gun violence. "It is time for Congress to adopt legislation that will close the gun show loophole, increase penalties for straw purchase of guns, ban assault weapons, place limits on high-capacity ammunition magazine size, and fund research and reporting on gun violence in America," the letter stressed. "Curbing gun violence is a critical matter of public safety, public health and public confidence."

Over the next year, the St. Louis League held community meetings to try to help both sides of the debate understand one another. Members also worked closely with a new St. Louis chapter of Moms Demand Action, a national gun safety group.[143]

In 2014, the Missouri Right to Bear Arms, or SJR36, was placed on the August 5 ballot as Amendment 5. It "established the unalienable right of citizens to keep and bear arms, ammunition and accessories associated with the normal functioning of such arms, for the purpose of defense of one's person, family, home and property."[144]

The Missouri League opposed the amendment, saying, "The League believes that state and local authorities will be hampered in their ability to regulate firearms (with this amendment). It will be more difficult to enforce local, state and federal common-sense laws to reduce gun violence, [because] the amendment makes the relationship between federal and state firearm regulation ambiguous."[145] However, the amendment passed by

64%, 602,076 to 385,422.[146]

The biggest change came in 2016, when lawmakers passed SB 656, allowing anyone age 19+ to carry a concealed weapon without a permit, if the gun was legally owned. Governor Jay Nixon vetoed the bill on June 27, 2016, but after the legislature reconvened on Sept. 14, 2016, both houses voted to override the veto, 24-6 in the Senate and 112-41 in the House,[147] angering opponents like Moms Demand Action and the League.[148]

The law went into effect Jan. 1, 2017. Off-limit locations included police stations, courthouses, correctional facilities, government meetings, certain locations within airports, within 25 feet of a polling place on Election Day and without permission of the owner/administrator of any school, childcare facility, casino, amusement park, hospital, church, sports venue seating 5,000+ or location selling alcohol.[149]

Still firmly for gun safety, on Sept. 19, 2019,[150] the St. Louis League adopted a new gun policy based on the National League's position: "Protect the health and safety of citizens through limiting the accessibility and regulating the ownership of handguns and semiautomatic weapons. Support regulation of firearms for consumer safety." This policy made gun safety an advocacy priority for the League and "allowed members to advocate for changes in local gun laws to address recent gun violence.[151]

MINIMUM WAGE

In 2018, Proposition B, a proposal to raise Missouri's minimum wage over the next four years so that it reached $12/hour in 2023,[152] was gaining in popularity fast. To better understand it, the St. Louis League formed a study group.

Members began by researching how much money it takes to live in different areas across the state—urban, suburban and rural—for families of different sizes. To calculate this, they added up expenses such as food, childcare, medical, housing, transportation, and taxes and then input the information into the MIT Living Wage Calculator. They then compared this living wage to the state minimum wage of $7.85/hour and the proposed new minimum of $12/hour, while also keeping in mind the concerns of those opposed to such a raise.

They presented their findings in favor of the proposed $12/hour minimum wage and held open discussions at all area unit meetings.[153] The St. Louis and Missouri boards accepted the proposed position. The League's official position stated: "A minimum wage of at least $12/hour in Missouri is necessary to advance self-sufficiency for individuals and families."[154] Proposition B passed on Nov. 2, 2018, with 62% of voters in favor.

LEAGUE ACTIVITIES

UNITING THE LOCAL LEAGUES

Linda McDaniel and Becky Clausen saw benefits in restructuring to present a clear, unified image of the League as a nonprofit organization. On Oct. 29, 2014, the board proposed "To move all current LWV money, budgets, obligations and governance into what is currently LWVIS which is designated as a 501(c)(3) entity by the government."[155] By combining assets, the majority of donations would be tax deductible.[156] Members approved this change at a special member meeting on Feb. 19, 2015.[157]

By 2018, LWV of Metro St. Louis had units in the City of St. Louis, Webster/Kirkwood; Chesterfield/West County; Clayton/University City; North County; South County and St. Charles County.[158]

90TH ANNIVERSARY

The St. Louis League celebrated its 90th birthday on April 24, 2011, with a luncheon for members and friends from across the state including special honors for 50-year members and one outstanding member from each local League. The theme "Women: Then, Now and Tomorrow," was the subject of presentations by Vivian Eveloff, executive director of the Sue Shear Institute, and Jo Mannies, a political reporter. Both spoke about how women have often held political roles long before expected, like the two women who were elected to school boards in the late 1800s, long before women got the right to vote.

In addition, St. Louis League member Carolyn Nolan won a historic quilt, in which each block represented a famous woman in the suffrage movement and the continued fight for women's rights.[159]

LWVUS PRESIDENT VISITS ST. LOUIS

LWVUS President Elisabeth MacNamara visited St. Louis on August 30-31, 2011, at the invitation of the Missouri Bar Association, who wished to speak with her about the merit system of electing judges. During her time in town, she met with the editorial board of the *St. Louis Post-Dispatch* to discuss the League's position on certain issues and tell them about our voter service efforts. She also met with Diane Carlin, national chairman of Kids Voting about their work and collaboration with the League, and Dr. William Kincaid, chair of the St. Louis Asthma Consortium about the importance of enforcing the Clean Air Act.

Then it was the St. Louis League's turn to talk with her. More than 30 leaders gathered to hear her speak about the importance of all Leagues working together on the issues so that they presented a united front in the face of opposition. Elisabeth also attended a local leader meeting where continued collaboration in providing Voters Guides to St. Louis was the main topic. After this, Elizabeth headed to Springfield to meet with leaders there.

The Women's March

On Jan. 20, 2017, a group of St. Louis League members, family, and friends gathered at the League office to hold a sign/poster-making session for a special event the following morning. Even the media showed up to film the women, men, and children carefully craft the signs they would hold at the Women's March the next morning.

What made the January 21 march special? It's not often anymore that a group of people unite for a common cause, especially one focused on hope for the future. But, unlike some others attending the march, that is what the League chose to focus on.[160] "We feel if we carry signs with language and hate aimed at [politicians], we would be taking away from this powerful moment…[and] removing the focus off of important issues of marginalized people," said League co-presidents, Linda McDaniel and Kathleen Farrell.[161]

The next day, these same members, others carrying the yellow umbrellas of the League, and 15,000 other St. Louisans gathered at Union Station for the march that winded its way down Market Street to Luther Ely Smith Park. "Many of the participants carried signs and many wore pink hats, constructed in a variety of styles," the co-presidents later reported. "The march was originally supposed to stay on the sidewalk, but as the numbers grew, the St. Louis Police decided to allow marchers on the street. The mood of the marchers was energized, focused and they were happy to be there."[162]

The march was followed by a rally and then an action/

volunteer fair at the YWCA Phyllis Wheatley Center that provided information on a variety of social justice and women's issues. "We march[ed] for women, but not just women. We also march[ed] for immigrants, minorities, those with diverse religious convictions, LGBTQIA individuals, those with disabilities, the economically disadvantaged, and survivors of sexual assault," McDaniel and Farrell wrote in a piece reflecting upon the event. "We march[ed] for anyone who has felt marginalized by the results of the latest election. We are not defining this march as a protest. It is a powerful movement of millions of people from almost 200 locations around the world."[163]

The event was such a success, the League participated in marches held the following three Januarys. "The message that citizens around the country are sending is clear: If we want better government, we must be engaged in it. That means voting, providing citizens with accurate and non-partisan information, and registering new voters," the co-presidents wrote.[164]

100TH ANNIVERSARY CELEBRATIONS

The Missouri League was founded during a convention October 16-18, 1919, with the St. Louis League forming a month later. The St. Louis League formed a Centennial Committee in 2018 to begin organizing and planning commemorations.[165] The League invited members to join a special 100th Anniversary Hundred Dollar Club to "celebrate this milestone in our history and kick off the next century."

The special year kicked off on January 19, with League members participating in the third Women's March in downtown St. Louis. This was followed by the League's annual trivia night fundraiser. In April, the League held a Centennial Tea at the historic St. Louis Women's Club. The lovely event featured League member and historical impersonator Rebecca Now portraying suffragist Elizabeth Cady Stanton and CHARIS, the St. Louis Women's Chorus.

May was a busy month, with a special suffrage tour of Bellefontaine Cemetery, visiting the graves of local suffrage greats such as Edna Gellhorn, first president of the Missouri League; Virginia Minor, founder of the Woman Suffrage Association of Missouri; and Phoebe Couzins, noted suffragist, speaker, and the first female graduate of Washington University Law School. The Missouri League held its state convention in St. Louis. Special events included a costume parade featuring period fashion through the years.

In July, dozens of League members dressed in white marched and rode in the Webster Groves parade. The League won an award for "Outstanding Civic Entry." In September, the League had a booth at the Kirkwood Greentree Festival where members registered voters and provided education. St. Louis League intern Lexi White designed a suffrage coloring book. The League also distributed bookmarks profiling 11 suffragists to all branches of St. Louis County Library.

The celebrations were capped off on Nov. 13—100 years to the day the League was founded in Missouri—with a gala banquet at the Sheldon Concert Hall, the original meeting place of the St. Louis League. All attendees received a souvenir wine glass. Television personality Betsey Bruce served as emcee. A special guest was Gay Gellhorn, granddaughter of past president Edna Fischel Gellhorn. The program included special honors for past St. Louis League presidents and a video on local League history and women's suffrage.

A Suffragist in the Hall of Famous Missourians

In 2012, for the very first time, the Speaker of the Missouri House, Tim Jones (R-110) announced he would let the Missouri people vote for two of the next three people to be inducted into the Hall of Famous Missourians in the Capitol Building in Jefferson City. He specifically said he was seeking the names of those who had previously been overlooked.[166]

The St. Louis League, as part of the Missouri Women's Network, joined with the American Association of University Women (AAUW) and other women's groups to nominate a woman. At the time, only seven out of the 38 inductees were female.[167]

They nominated Virginia Minor, the woman who brought women's suffrage to Missouri, and asked all the women's organizations in the state to vote for her.[168] In the end, the female vote was split because other women were nominated – including beloved former League member and State Rep. Sue Shear. Virginia only received 3,000 votes, far less than the men who were nominated. Thankfully, the Speaker recognized the value of having a woman included in the Hall of Famous Missourians. Breaking with previous tradition, Speaker Jones decided not to raise funds for the bust but instead to have them all privately funded.[169] By February 2013, donors had come forward to fund the busts of the men, but no one was willing to pay for Virginia's.[170] The League put out a call to members in their May 2014 newsletters and, with help from the other women's organizations, eventually the bust was funded.

Virginia was inducted into the Hall of Famous Missourians on Sept. 10, 2013.

COMMUNICATION

The League has adapted to changing technology over the decades. A new website at lwvstl.org would be launched in 2020. Bulk mail is still used to send a print version of the *In League Reporter* newsletters to more than 200 members, but a PDF version is emailed to members at the beginning of each month. Social media posts are made regularly on Facebook, Instagram and Twitter.

Office Staff Changes

On Feb. 28, 2019, office assistant Julie Behrens retired after almost 35 years of working for the League. Chantal Hoffsten was hired to serve as part-time bookkeeper.

Jean Dugan was hired as administrative manager in March 2018 and now serves as executive director for LWV of Missouri and Metro St. Louis. Earlier staff members included Carol Pugh, Joyce Guard, Miki Huffman, Anna Mennerick, Jan Scheurer, and Elizabeth McDonald. League leaders Brenda Banjak, Mary K. Brown, Agnes Garino, Mickey Hall and Peggy Vickroy also served as office staff through the years.

The state and local League have shared space at 8706 Manchester Road in Brentwood since 1995. Other office locations included 4910 West Pine in the 1950s, the YWCA on Locust downtown, the Forest Park Hotel, and 6665 Delmar in University City.

Conclusion

This was a decade of both looking back and forward for the League. They celebrated the centennials of the suffragists' Golden Lane demonstration and the founding of the local and state Leagues with pride and gratitude to all who came before. But they also looked ahead as they advocated for health care reform and gun safety in an increasingly violent world, and fought efforts to restrict voting rights through strict laws and gerrymandering. As they have from the beginning, Leaguers supported St. Louis voters, fighting misinformation with non-partisan facts, and suppression and oppression with openness and access. Little did they know that the beginning of the next decade would usher in their greatest challenges yet: a politically charged election amid a global pandemic.

WOMEN WHO MADE AN IMPACT IN THE 2010S

KATHLEEN FARRELL

APRIL 1951- PRESENT

Kathleen Farrell joined the League of Women Voters in Iowa City, Iowa, in 1991, serving in a variety of positions including as membership chair. That same year, she was selected as one of 35 college and university professors to attend a special seminar in Washington D.C. on how educators can use C-SPAN in the classroom.[171]

Kathleen married Julian Long, moved to St. Louis and joined the League in 2002. Since then, she has served on the board, as first vice president, as co-leader of the St. Louis City Unit with Betty Ann Gilbert, coordinated the Voters Guide, registered voters and moderated candidate forums. She served as co-president with Linda McDaniel from 2010-2017.[172] In that role, she fought against restrictive Voter ID laws and for the earnings tax, fair redistricting, education of the public on ballot issues and candidate stances. She continues to moderate candidate forums and write issue summaries for the Voters Guide.

As a professor of communication at Saint Louis University, Kathleen taught public argument and political communication. "The League's presence in our communities is needed now more than ever," she said. "We face great challenges at the national, state, and local level. Citizens need good information about candidates and issues. Local government needs our input on boards and commissions."

As head of the St. Louis City Unit, Kathleen was a strong advocate for Prop D for Democracy, which passed in the November 2020 election with over 68% approval. It established a non-partisan approval voting system for city officials that ensures winners have a mandate to govern.

More recently, Kathleen and Joan Hubbard led more than 58 city members in supporting Prop R for redistricting and ethics reform in the city. Prop R won with 69% of the vote on April 5, 2022. Many at the victory party said that it could not have been done without the League's support. Several members of the Board of Aldermen tried and failed to repeal Prop R. Its reforms include conflict of interest provisions and protection for Prop D and other measures approved by city voters.

Louise Wilkerson

April 1945 – present

Louise Wilkerson was born at Homer Phillips Hospital in St. Louis, the eldest of three children. After her parents divorced when she was four years old, she and her siblings spent time with both parents, including two years in New York City.

Extremely bright, Louise started high school at age 12 at Soldan High for the first semester and then transferred to Sumner High, where she graduated at age 16. She graduated from Harris Stowe Teachers College with a bachelor's degree in elementary education and a minor in biology. She went on to earn a master's degree and master's plus 30 with a concentration in special education. She nearly completed her Ph.D. (all but dissertation) in education at Southern Illinois University at Edwardsville.

In 1968, she married John F. Wilkerson, III, with whom she had one child, Kirsten Louise. They divorced in 1994, and her long-time companion in recent years has been Ronald G. Hill.

Louise began her teaching career at age 20 in the St. Louis Public School District, where she taught for 15 years. She was the first female and Black person to be named Executive Director of Special Education for St. Louis Public Schools. Louise was also an Assistant Professor at Fontbonne University in the Special Education/Education Department from August 2001 until May 2011, when she retired.

As president of the St. Louis Alumnae Chapter of the Delta Sigma Theta sorority, the largest Black women's organization in the country, Louise began a project called Project Power to the People to register voters for the 2012 presidential election. Kathleen Farrell and Linda McDaniel recruited her to join the League board after she completed her term as sorority president in 2014.

Louise was eager to join the League. "I was aware they had a long history in the community, supported voter registration, kept up with current state and local legislation, and maintained involvement in advocacy," she said. "I was particularly drawn to the League because of its commitment to protecting every eligible citizen's right to vote, informing voters about what will be on their ballots, and helping voters make their voices heard each election."

Louise served as League co-president with Nancy J. Miller from 2017-2021. Under her leadership, they increased the League's outreach to members in Black sororities and other minority organizations to diversify membership.

Louise stresses the value of the League's policy positions and advocacy on issues, particularly public school funding and fighting for everyone's right to vote. "We take a position on issues and don't let partisan concerns stifle our voices when it comes to policy, legislation, and litigation on those issues," she said.

Her top passion is voter services, and she boasts of four absentee satellite voting centers opening in St. Louis County and another four in St. Louis City. Louise is also particularly proud of the League's work supporting Medicaid expansion, increasing the minimum wage, and redistricting. She currently serves on the Development Committee and the Get Out the Vote Committee of the Metro St. Louis League. She is also a forum moderator and Vice President of LWVMO.

Louise has been involved in numerous professional organizations outside of the League, including the National Urban League, NAACP, and many special education, mental health, environmental and conservation organizations. She is interested in politics and the rights of all to vote, advocating for social justice and championing the underdog. She also enjoys reading, traveling, bird watching, crafting, and music of all types.

Louise has received several awards and recognitions including the 1984 Director's Award given by Walter Kopp, the St. Louis Public Schools' Director of Special Education, the *St. Louis Sentinel* Newspaper's "Yes, I Can Award" in 1990, the *St. Louis American* Salute to Excellence Award in 1991, and a 2001 resolution from the Missouri House of Representatives in recognition of 35 years of service in public education.

NANCY J. MILLER

MAY 1947- PRESENT

Nancy Joanne Shepherd was born in Des Moines, Iowa, the second of four children. She has an older sister and two younger brothers, one of whom is deceased. Her older sister grew up to become an elementary teacher in Newton, Iowa, and was an active League member there before moving to St. Louis.

Showing an early talent for leadership, Nancy was elected to the YWCA Junior Council of Des Moines and served as president of that group during her freshman year of high school. She attributes many of her skills in running a meeting to that position. Nancy was also part of a group that toured Washington D.C. and the United Nations during her junior year.

Nancy married her childhood sweetheart, Bill, in 1968, just before their senior year of college. They met in fifth grade and began dating during their senior year of high school. They have two children, Kara (also a League member) and Cory. They also count two "adopted" children as their own: Hung Q Ly and Hung V Ly, brothers from Vietnam who came into the family when they were 15 and 17 and are today successful adults.

Nancy graduated from the University of Iowa in 1969 with a bachelors in World Literature and Education, which she put to good use as a reading specialist, English teacher and curriculum coordinator. In her first years after college, Nancy lived and taught in Cedar Rapids, Council Bluffs, and Des Moines, Iowa. In 1973, the family moved to Wyoming, where she taught in Thermopolis. She also worked as an education consultant for the Presbyterian Church in a five-state area surrounding Denver.

She and her family moved to St. Louis in 1978. Bill became a principal in Kirkwood, and Nancy worked for the Kirkwood School District as a substitute teacher and designing study packets for the BEST tests.

Nancy graduated from UMSL in 1981 with a master's degree in secondary education and a minor in remedial reading. From 1981-1985 she taught English/Reading at Fort Zumwalt High School. In 1985, Nancy opened a reading lab at Affton High School. In 1991, she added department chair, AP English and district reading coordinator to her job. Nancy completed her PhD in education administration, with a specialty in curriculum at Saint Louis University in 1996. In the later part of her career, she served as curriculum coordinator for the Affton School District.

Nancy joined the League in the fall of 2007, shortly after she retired. She had long been interested in the League and its mission. Since then, she has served as editor of the *In League Reporter*, Speakers Bureau Chair, Civility Committee Chair, and timer and moderator for candidate forums. In 2011, she was appointed as second vice president, a position she held until 2017.

Nancy served as co-president with Louise Wilkerson from 2017-2021. One of the main struggles of the first two years of her presidency was Photo ID court cases. She testified in front of the Senate Local Government & Elections Committee. In the last year of her presidency, she and Louise did their best to maintain the day-to-day operations of the League while dealing with the COVID-19 pandemic.

Nancy was also active in having the LWVMO and the LWVUS adopt a social justice platform. She provided direction to the Metro League's new Policing Committee that studied criminal justice issues. The LWVMO's new position, adopted on May 15, 2021, said, "We support a criminal justice system that is just, effective, equitable, transparent, and that fosters public trust at all stages, including policing practices, pre-trial procedures, sentencing, incarceration, and re-entry. In addition to her work with the League, Nancy taught tax law and completed tax forms for AARP Volunteer Tax Preparers for many years and is still active in her church. She is currently on sabbatical from the League but hopes "to return to a more active role. I have such fond memories of and loyalties to the League," she said.

CATHERINE STENGER
APRIL 1943-PRESENT

Catherine Metzger was born in St. Louis to Vincent and Dolores Metzger. She grew up in a loving home with four younger siblings: Joan, Vincent (now deceased), Elizabeth and Frances. Catherine attended Notre Dame High School and met her future husband, John, while working at summer camp. Catherine attended Harris Stowe University, where she graduated with a bachelor's degree in elementary education in 1965. (Fun fact: all of her siblings became teachers, too.)

Catherine and John married after college in 1966. She worked for a while as an elementary school teacher for the St. Louis Public Schools and the Waynesville/Ft. Leonard Wood Public Schools. Then she quit working to stay at home with her three children: Christine, John C., and Laura for 25 years. Once they were grown, Catherine attended nursing school at St. Louis Community College and worked as a geriatric nurse for 13 years at Delmar Gardens. She also served as a St. Louis Zoo docent for 10 years.

Catherine joined the League in 2011. Since then, she has served on the board as membership chair, co-chair of the voter registration committee and first vice president.[173]

Catherine's passion is voter registration. With help from grants from the National League, in 2018, Catherine reached out to all libraries in St. Louis County, St. Louis City and St. Charles County to be part of National Voter Registration Day. They agreed and she and over 100 other League volunteers registered more than 75 voters at over 55 library locations that September. Similarly, she created a program that enables newly registered voters to receive notices of upcoming elections and deadlines for absentee voting, either by email or text. She also helped distribute business cards with QR codes for the VOTE411.org voters guide and the Secretary of State's website. In 2019, a grant from the Roblee Foundation allowed the League to purchase iPads that League volunteers use for online voter registration. In 2021, Catherine was honored with the Missouri League's Lenore Loeb Sterling Achievement Award for doubling the St. Louis League's voter registration totals and the number of members who help youth and new citizens register to vote.[174]

Catherine still works in voter registration—she's celebrating nine years and counting as co-chairperson—and regularly volunteers at naturalization ceremonies to register new citizens. She also serves on the Missouri League and St. Louis League boards.

Main Sources Chapter 6 – The 2010s

Annual Reports of the President, League of Women Voters of St. Louis, 2012-2020

Minutes of the Meeting of the Board of Directors of LWVSTL, July 26, 2017

Books
- McMillen, Margot. *Virginia Minor: A Woman in the Hall of Famous Missourians.*
- Newsletters
- *In League Reporter* - Winter 2010-November 2020
- *Metro News*, Winter 2010-Spring 2015

League documents regarding
- Coal Ash
- League 100th Anniversary Events
- LWVMO Guide to State Action 2017-2019
- Motor Voter
- Redistricting

Periodicals
- *EducationWeek*
- *The Guardian*
- *Iowa City Press-Citizen*
- *The Missouri Times*
- *Missouri Voter*
- *News Tribune*
- *St. Louis Business Journal*
- *St. Louis Post-Dispatch*
- *West End Word and Webster-Kirkwood Times*

Websites
- Axios
- Ballotpedia
- Center for American Women in Politics at Rutgers University
- Concealedcarry.com

- Health and Human Services
- KBIA
- KY3
- LegiScan
- Missouri Senate
- Missouri Women
- MSNBC
- NPR in Kansas City
- Show Me Integrity
- St. Louis Public Radio
- U.S. Department of Justice
- U.S. Census Bureau
- YouTube

For a complete list of sources, please see the endnotes at https://my.lwv.org/missouri/metro-st-louis/about/our-history

2010s

Kathleen Farrell, Sydell Shayer, Becky Clausen, Catherine Stenger, LWVUS Executive Director Nancy Tate, Linda McDaniel and Judith Smart after the 2012 election.

Linda McDaniel and Kathleen Farrell downtown at the 2016 Celebrate the Vote Festival.

The Celebrate the Vote Festival marked the 100th Anniversary of the suffragists' Golden Lane demonstration at the 1916 Democratic Convention.

Leaguers Louise Wilkerson, Agnes Garino, and Terry and Angie Dunlap were among the many Leaguers at the Women's March in January 2018.

Minimum Wage Study Group in 2018 included Carolyn Wolff, Joan Hubbard, Karen Cloyd, Nancy J. Miller and Angie Dunlap.

Julie Behrens, Barbara Harris and Anne Sappington distribute Voters Guides in March 2018.

Mickey Croyle gives a presentation for the Environmental Quality Committee.

Leaguers marched with Girl Scouts in the Webster Groves Parade on July 4, 2019.

Nancy J. Miller, Jean Dugan, Denise Lieberman, Nancy Price, Gillian Wilcox, Evelyn Maddox and Sabrina Khan at an August 2019 photo ID trial.

Former League President Pat Rich at the Centennial Tea at the St. Louis Woman's Club in March 2019.

100th Anniversary program booklet for the gala held at the Sheldon Concert Hall. Early League meetings were held in what is now the Sheldon's Green Room.

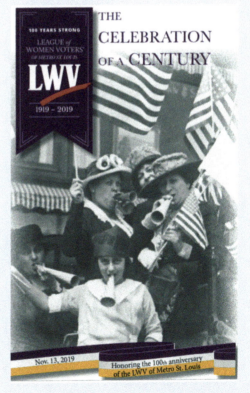

Nancy J. Miller and Louise Wilkerson enjoyed meeting Edna Gellhorn's granddaughter, Gay Gellhorn (center).

The gala honored past presidents Nancy J. Miller, Louise Wilkerson, Linda McDaniel, Debby Howard, Pat Rich, Agnes Garino, Judith Arnold, Mary K. Brown, Gail Heyne-Hafer (back row) Kathleen Farrell, Nancy Thompson, K Wentzien, Brenda Banjak, Ida West, Carol Portman and Sydell Shayer (front row). Not pictured is Nancy Bowser.

2020 and Beyond

PROTECTING VOTERS AND THEIR RIGHTS DURING THE COVID-19 PANDEMIC

THE COVID-19 PANDEMIC presented unprecedented voting challenges during one of the most important election cycles in U.S. history. The League, as part of the Missouri Voter Protection Coalition, was there to protect voter rights while enabling Missourians worried about the pandemic to vote safely.

When it became apparent that COVID-19 was not going to end before the April 2020 elections, Governor Parson moved the election to June 2. Unfortunately, he did not extend the March 11 registration deadline. The coalition wrote to him advising that because "Missouri law gives voters until the fourth Wednesday before the election to register…the deadline should be May 6."

The coalition also stressed that the state should "allow no-excuse absentee voting and waive the notary requirement for absentee ballots in the 2020 elections [because] Missouri statute 115.277 waives the notary requirement on absentee ballots for people confined at home due to illness." With pandemic closures, that is essentially what everyone was doing at the time. In addition, the letter recommended "expanding options for in-person absentee and early voting, allowing more citizens to vote over time rather than in a cluster on Election Day." It also called for implementing online voting and modifying polling places so that people could easily social distance.[1]

To help this along, the League, in partnership with the NAACP, filed a lawsuit in Cole County asking for a declaratory judgment that "physical distancing and fear of contracting COVID-19 are valid reasons to request an absentee ballot in Missouri," as well as "injunctive relief preventing local election officials from refusing such ballots or requiring them to be notarized." They argued that election authorities should be able to use the same methods to verify absentee ballots as they use to verify voter signatures in person at the polls, so they shouldn't need to be notarized.[2]

The judge in Cole County found against the League,[3] and so the coalition appealed to the Missouri Supreme Court.[4] The High Court unanimously voted to send the absentee ballot lawsuit back to the Circuit Court in Cole County.[5] The process was repeated with a disappointing result.[6]

COVID-19 did lead the General Assembly to loosen up voting procedures for 2020 elections. SB 631 allowed voters 65+ or with certain risk factors for COVID-19 "to request and return absentee ballots without a notary. Other voters were allowed to use a new 'mail-in ballot' that required a notarized signature and could only be returned by mail."[7] Republican Secretary of State Jay Ashcroft said he was confident Missouri's 2020 election was safe and secure, but the safe voting provisions expired on Dec. 31, 2020.[8]

VOTER SERVICES

The League's outreach to voters continued even amidst lockdowns and other pandemic concerns. Keeping everyone's health and safety in mind, efforts went virtual for a while, then came back in person as variants allowed.

VOTER REGISTRATION

Lockdowns hampered voter registration during the height of the pandemic, but by spring 2021, more than 250 League members were back out in the community, registering more than 1,020 new citizens and 500 youth to vote. They continued to help register voters at new citizen naturalization ceremonies, and parks, fairs and neighborhood events.[9] In addition, they worked with the Urban League and other groups to distribute hundreds of voter registration packets at food drives.

Toward the end of 2021, the League was awarded two grants for voter registration efforts in 2022: $1,500 from the LWVUS Education Fund for registering new citizens at naturalization ceremonies and $800 for registering students at area high schools, trade schools and colleges.[10]

VOTERS GUIDE

Even during the COVID-19 pandemic, the League continued to produce the Voters Guide. Volunteers worked remotely to gather information on candidates and ballot issues in St. Louis City and in St. Louis, St. Charles, Jefferson, Lincoln, Warren, and Franklin Counties. As part of a Making Democracy Work grant, the State League expanded coverage of the online guide at VOTE411.org and made it available statewide in 2020 and 2022.[11]

The Voters Guide included information on 232 candidates and 54 ballot issues, including six MSD propositions for the election on April 6, 2021. In both 2021 and 2022, the Voters Guide was printed in the *St. Louis Post-Dispatch,* and volunteers distributed thousands of copies to area libraries, nursing homes and other sites.[12]

CANDIDATE FORUMS

To keep voters safe, the League did not conduct in-person candidate forums in Spring 2021 but agreed to moderate three virtual candidate forums before the April 2021 municipal elections: candidates for St. Louis City mayor and comptroller, Rockwood Board of Education and Hazelwood School Board.[13]

Before the April 2022 municipal election, the League moderated 18 candidate forums. Almost all the forums were available virtually and recorded, resulting in a total audience of more than 12,000 voters.[14]

SPEAKERS BUREAU

The Speakers Bureau continued to give presentations as requested throughout the pandemic, using Zoom to present online when it was not safe to meet in person. From May 2021 to April 2022, Nancy Price and other volunteers gave 15 presentations on topics such as redistricting, voter suppression bills, the National Popular Vote, the For the People Act, the John Lewis Voting Rights Act, the filibuster, why voting is important, why America is so divided and what the League does about it, and miscellaneous ballot issues. They also made recordings of presentations available for those who couldn't make the originally scheduled date/time.[15]

VOTING LEGISLATION

FEDERAL ELECTION REFORM

In 2020, the Voting Rights Advancement Act, also known as the John R. Lewis Voting Rights Advancement Act, was introduced into Congress. Its aim was to "restore the full protections of the original, bipartisan Voting Rights Act of 1965." It was passed by the U.S. House,[16] but Senate Republicans voted to block debate and prevent the bill from receiving a floor vote.

On Feb. 23, 2021, the St. Louis League participated in a call-in day to Congress[17] and in the national John Lewis Voting Rights Day of Action on May 8 in support of this act and the For the People Act.[18] The House passed the For the People Act (HR1 and S1) in both 2021 and 2022, but Senate filibusters blocked action in that chamber, a move the League vocally protested.[19] Negotiations continue on revised proposals called the Freedom to Vote Act and the John R. Lewis Voting Rights Advancement Act.[20]

There was a bright spot in August 2021 when the 8th Circuit U.S. Court of Appeals affirmed a decision to award $1.1 million and $27,484 in expenses to the lawyers representing the Missouri League and the A. Philip Randolph Institute in a lawsuit to get the state to comply with the National Voter Registration Act of 1993. The 2019 suit stemmed from complaints that the Department of Revenue and license offices weren't updating voter addresses as required under law.[21]

Preserving Citizen Initiative Petitions

On April 28, 2021, League members from across the state joined with the cross-partisan group Show Me Integrity in Jefferson City for Lobby Day. This event was in protest of HJR 20 and HB 333, which would completely change the ballot initiative process and make it more difficult for citizen-initiated ballot measures to get in front of the people for a vote.[22] This is in opposition to a provision in Missouri's Constitution since 1908 (Article III, Section 50) that states, "The people reserve power to propose and enact or reject laws and amendments to the constitution by the initiative, independent of the General Assembly."[23]

Legislative bulletins and the *In League Reporter* alerted members that "more than 14 bills were introduced in the Missouri General Assembly in 2022 to make it more difficult for citizens to get an issue on the ballot and to win approval of a Constitutional amendment."[24] St. Louis League President Angie Dunlap, LWVMO President Marilyn McLeod and Denise Lieberman of the Missouri Voter Protection Coalition all submitted testimony against HJR 79. The proposed ballot measure would ask voters to require more signatures in eight Congressional districts (vs. six) for citizen-initiated ballot measures to get on the ballot and a 2/3 vote in favor (vs. a simple majority) for them to pass.

"Legislation that reduces the power of the voter is not in the interest of a democratic society," League President Angie Dunlap testified on February 1.

The *St. Louis Post-Dispatch* published a guest column by League Member Nancy Price on February 10 explaining why initiative petitions are crucial to giving voters a voice in government. She said, "Voters often feel the legislature is not addressing critical issues or has passed a law that needs to be stopped. The petition has allowed voter-initiated amendments (Medicaid and marijuana), the minimum wage statute, and repeal of the unwanted 'right to work' law. The proposed legislation would make it virtually impossible to pass anything. It would take away an important protection against legislators passing laws that could harm Missourians."

LWVMO President Marilyn McLeod shared the League's support for the citizen initiative petition at several public hearings. "The IP has worked for both conservative and liberal causes which shows that it is a valuable and valued part of our heritage and works for all Missourians of all different points of view," she said in April 13 testimony against HRJ 91.

More than a dozen members of the LWV of Metro St. Louis joined other League members from across the state in sharing their objections to HRJ 79 at a Voting Rights Lobby Day in Jefferson City on May 3, 2022. The Senate debated HJR79 the final week of session but adjourned on May 13 without taking action.

St. Louis City Unit/Reform St. Louis

In early 2021, the City Unit of the St. Louis League partnered with Show Me Integrity to set up Reform St. Louis, "a good government coalition"[25] dedicated to ending conflicts of interest among St. Louis alderpersons.[26] They took action by collecting 300,000[27] signatures for a St. Louis City charter amendment that "would require alderpersons to recuse themselves from voting where they have a financial or business conflict of interest and make their financial disclosure forms more publicly transparent" and "create an independent People's Commission to redistrict the wards of St. Louis City after every decennial census," instead of allowing the boundaries to be drawn by the Board of Aldermen as they were prior. In addition, passage of the amendment would "protect voter-chosen election methods, such as Prop D's approval voting, from being overturned by the Board of Aldermen without a confirmatory popular vote."[28]

Joan Hubbard, Anne Sappington, Kathleen Farrell and other City Unit members worked with 27 coalition partners to collect signatures for Prop R. By the beginning of June 2021, they had collected more than 2,500 signatures. This work continued over the next two months, during which time local League members joined Citizens for Fair Maps to advocate for a fair and transparent ward reduction process. City members went to 11 neighborhood association meetings across the city to educate the public about Prop R.[28] They testified at hearings, observed all redistricting Board of Alderman meetings, submitted letters to the editor, and spoke at press conferences and public forums on redistricting.

As 2022 dawned, the Prop R petitions were turned in to the Board of Election Commissioners (BOE). The League conducted spokesperson training and began presenting to city voters over the next four months. In total, the St. Louis City Unit's 58 volunteers spent more than 4,000 hours educating the public. By the time city voters went to the polls on April 5, they were well informed and approved Prop R by 13,293 (69.2% Yes) to 5,928 (30.8% No).

Advocacy for Prop R had an unintended, but positive, benefit: more than 160 people joined the League or were added to the mailing list. The League now boasts more young members, male members, and members of color.

Strict Photo ID

On Jan. 15, 2020, the Missouri Supreme Court ruled in *Priorities USA vs. Missouri* that the affidavit section of Missouri's Voter ID law was "misleading and contradictory," therefore, voters would no longer be required to present a photo ID in order to cast their ballots. A week later, the House Committee on Elections introduced HB1600, which rewrote the section in question and eliminated the requirement that voters be notified in advance about changes in the law. Voter Protection Coalition leader and League member Denise Lieberman testified against HB1600, calling it an attempt to reinstate a strict photo ID requirement.[29]

Legislators continued to try to limit the type of identification required to vote in Missouri in 2021 and 2022. HB2113, HB2140 and HB 334[30] would eliminate several forms of ID that voters have traditionally used, including a voter registration card from the election authority and a student ID from a Missouri college or university. The League opposes these restrictions, which were found unconstitutional by the Missouri Supreme Court.[31]

In February 2021, LWVMO Vice President Nancy Copenhaver submitted written testimony to the House Elections Committee saying HB334 "could disenfranchise thousands of voters and discourage voting by many people of color as well as older and disabled voters. Evidence shows that there is no voter impersonation fraud in Missouri; there is no need for this legislation."[32] Secretary of State Ashcroft testified against the bill, saying that it wasn't necessary. "I believe the elections were generally solid," Ashcroft said, adding that multiple post-election audits had not found any reason to think there was fraud. "I feel really good about the security we have at the state level."[33]

The General Assembly succeeded in passing legislation requiring an unexpired government-issued photo ID to vote in 2022. While the initial seven-page bill focused on voter ID, the Senate added many more anti-voter provisions. Despite strong coalition calls to reject HB1878, Governor Parson signed it into law in June to take effect on Aug. 28, 2022. The Missouri NAACP joined LWVMO in lawsuits challenging both its strict photo ID rules and its restrictions on soliciting voter registration and absentee ballot applications.

In a letter urging the governor to veto HB1878, LWVMO President Marilyn McLeod said it "provides unnecessary roadblocks to our most basic right, the right to vote." Her letter said,

> Among its many provisions, it requires an extremely limited form of ID to be able to vote which will disenfranchise thousands of citizens who are fully qualified to vote, including voters

whose driver's license recently expired.

New provisions in HB1878 would allow unnecessary voter purges, make it more difficult for people with disabilities to vote independently and prevent local election authorities from receiving grant funds to improve their outreach to the citizenry.

Limiting the right to vote for some citizens is a limit to the right to vote for all citizens.

As we understand it, this bill eliminates the requirement for the Secretary of State to inform the people of the change in requirements to be able to vote. Since the right to vote is the basis of all our rights, then properly informing the citizens could not be more critical.

The League is especially concerned about language that could limit our voter service activities. LWVMO has two part-time staff that help League members provide voter services, including mailing registration and absentee ballot request forms to voters upon request. League volunteers regularly register more than 10 new citizens at each naturalization ceremony in St. Louis.

The League was pleased to see safe voting provisions during the COVID-19 pandemic that were used in 2020 elections. There was no evidence of voter fraud with mail-in ballots that this legislation would ban.[34]

REDISTRICTING

On Jan. 14, 2020, the League defended Clean Missouri redistricting reforms at a Senate Rules Committee hearing on SJR 38, a Republican effort to have bipartisan commissions draw maps instead of an independent demographer. League member and LWVMO Secretary Louise Wilkerson said, "Instead of improving our redistricting process after the 2020 Census, SJR38 would give political parties more power and allow an unprecedented level of racial and political gerrymandering." LWVMO President Evelyn Maddox sent similar written testimony against HJR76 and HJR101, which are in the same vein.[35]

In February, the Senate approved SJR 38, much to the League's disappointment. Despite COVID-19 and stay-at-home orders, the House General Rules Committee held a public hearing on SJR38 on April 30 and then voted 9-4 along party lines to approve the resolution.[36] On May 13, the state House passed SJR 38 in a vote of 98-56.[37] It was then put on the November 3 ballot as Amendment 3. Voters approved it by 51%.[38]

In 2021, after the 2020 United States Census results were released, House and Senate Bipartisan Commissions met to create new maps. Since neither the House nor the Senate could agree on a map, both were drawn by commissions.

The League advocated hard for a fair and transparent process.[39] They partnered with Show Me Integrity to work on redistricting and ethics reform in the City of St. Louis through "a broad coalition, ensuring equitable racial, demographic and geographic representation as we develop and advocate for a ballot initiative mandating a more equitable and transparent method of ward reduction, and all future redistricting, for St. Louis City."[40]

The League position supports a fair and transparent process that keeps communities of interest together. A community of interest is "a group of people who share cultural or historic characteristics or economic interests; are contiguous on a map; and share a common bond linked to a set of public policy issues that would be affected by legislation." The members said keeping them together when drawing new maps encourages citizens to vote and lets them choose legislators that reflect their values. They also requested that maps be based on total population for representational equality and that when maps are drawn, citizens are given a chance to respond to them.[41]

The National League held a nationwide Redistricting Day of Action on April 29 to promote its People Powered Fair Maps initiative.[42] In Missouri, 18 League leaders from across the state gathered in Jefferson City on April 28 for a Protect the Ballot Initiative Rally and Advocacy Day. After an outdoor rally, League members met with individual legislators to make sure that access to the ballot for important popular reforms such as redistricting is preserved. The next day was the national kickoff, hosted by National League CEO Virginia Kase Solomon. In the afternoon, Leaguers learned from Fair Missouri and The Sierra Club about how to use map drawing software to map communities of interest. The day was capped off by a webinar by attorney Sharon Geuea Jones titled "Can Gerrymandering Be Stopped?"[43]

In July, the League found out they were recipients of $12,500 under a new Missouri Community Mapping Grant Project. President Angie Dunlap, Executive Director Jean Dugan, and Don Crozier from the St. Charles unit were among the members who drew 25 community of interest maps for redistricting in Senate Districts 2, 10, 15, 22 and 23. Experts at Tufts University used the maps "to develop sample legislative maps to share with the members of the House and Senate redistricting commissions."[44]

LWVSTL members Joan Hubbard, Nancy Price, Nancy Thompson, and Jean Kendall served on LWVMO's Fair Redistricting Committee in 2020-2022. They presented testimony at legislative commission hearings, attended most public meetings and submitted non-partisan maps developed by the Institute for Computational Redistricting (ICOR). Ahead of the commission's first meeting on Aug. 10, the Missouri League sent a letter to 350 community leaders across the state about the importance of avoiding gerrymandering and having a transparent redistricting process. They also educated advocates with chapters of both Delta Sigma Theta and Alpha Kappa Alpha sororities.[45]

Close to a dozen League members testified at October 16 and 21 commission hearings in St. Louis, while many others attended without speaking. Joan Hubbard represented LWVMO at the Senate Redistricting Commission hearing in St. Louis on October 21. She recognized the "once-a-decade impact that redistricting has on the power of voters and on the vitality of democracy in our state." She said, "In all 50 states, the League stresses that honorable redistricting requires fairness, accuracy, transparency and maximum public participation and input." Hubbard encouraged commissioners to keep communities of interest together, saying, "Maps should be drawn in a transparent way that allows ample time for experts to analyze, and testify and time for our committee members to respond."

On November 9, Nancy Price and Kathleen Farrell spoke to St. Louis City residents about redistricting of the city wards, the Missouri House and Senate, and U.S. Congressional districts.[46] St. Louis League President Angie Dunlap also testified before the St. Louis County Redistricting Commission in early November.[47]

The map of Missouri's 163 state House districts was finalized by the House Independent Bipartisan Redistricting Commission on January 19. It was the first redistricting cycle since 1991 that the map hadn't gone to a judicial panel.[48]

Unfortunately, the Senate Independent Bipartisan Redistricting Commission could not reach an agreement on a map for the state's 34 Senate districts. A panel of appellate court judges was appointed to finalize the Senate map, which they submitted to the Secretary of State on March 15. LWVMO President Marilyn McLeod said it was unfortunate that Missouri's Senate Redistricting Commission deadlocked. "The current system could and should be improved before the next U.S. Census," she said. "Redistricting should be done on a nonpartisan basis with the goal of fair maps that keep communities of interest together."

On Jan. 19, 2022, the House passed a "least change" Congressional map as HB2117 that would likely keep six Republican-leaning seats and two Democratic-leaning seats. Conservative Senators filibustered, promoting a 7-1 map. The House asked to go to conference after the Senate passed a revised version of the map on March 24, but the Senate didn't agree. The General Assembly finally approved a congressional district map on May 12 that will likely keep a 6-2 partisan split, with more Republican voters assigned to the 2nd and 3rd Districts. The Governor signed HB2909 on May 19.

The LWVMO Fair Redistricting Committee group asked the Institute for Computational Redistricting (ICOR), a research group at the University of Illinois at Urbana-Champaign, to conduct research and sample maps for LWVMO. Their report concluded that "compactness *and* good political fairness are achievable for Missouri." The League reached out to legislators before the 2022 session with research showing that 46.5 percent of Missouri voters supported Democrats in

2016, 2018 and 2020 elections for Governor, U.S. Senate, and President. Several legislators cited that research to support a 5-3 Republican-Democrat split and block conservative efforts to pass a 7-1 map. The bill signed by Governor Parson maintains a 6-2 split. The League is concerned that it splits 10 counties, and the 3rd District is not compact.

NATIONAL POPULAR VOTE

The League has long supported the National Popular Vote (NPV), the idea that the candidate with the highest number of votes from the people wins an election. This would be a major reform to the electoral college system in place today.

As early as 2018, the League advocated for Missouri's participation in the National Popular Vote Interstate Compact, with op-ed pieces in area newspapers and through voter education.[49] In the run-up to the 2020 presidential election, they supported HB 267, the National Popular Vote Interstate Compact Bill, filed by Rep. Peter Merideth (D-80) and sponsored by Democratic Reps. Tracy McCreery and Ian Mackey of St. Louis and James Barnes of the Kansas City area, but it was not assigned to committee. They also supported SB 292 filed by Senator Jill Schupp (D-24), which was assigned to the Local Government and Election Committee but did not get a hearing.[50]

The League also made a video explaining NPV (available online at lwvstl.org/issues) and created two subcommittees: one aimed at getting legislative support (chaired by Bob Allen) and one aimed at educating voters (chaired by Laurie Velasquez).

In 2021, the NPV committee held Zoom meetings to educate the public about the importance of this legislation,[51] and in November all unit meetings focused on the topic.[52] The League continues to support NPV efforts on a state and national level.

HEALTH CARE

Medicaid expansion was the main focus for the League's Healthcare Committee in the early 2020s. In August 2020, Missouri voters approved Medicaid expansion, and Governor Parson promised to proceed with implementation, even though he was concerned about the cost.[53] However, in spring 2021, the House Budget Committee voted along party lines, 21 to 9, not to fund Medicaid expansion.[54]

In response, Governor Parson withdrew the Medicaid application in May and a lawsuit quickly followed. Joel Ferber of Legal Services of Eastern Missouri filed on behalf of three women who won't be able to get needed medical care without Medicaid expansion. The trial began June 18 in Cole County[55] where Circuit Judge Jon Beetem later ruled that the ballot measure was unconstitutional.[56] The case moved to the Missouri Supreme Court on July 13. The Court ruled unanimously on July 22 that Medicaid expansion is constitutional.[57] Open enrollment for the 275,000 adults between ages 19 to 64 living below 138% of the federal poverty level took place from July 1 through November.

The League took the lead in educating the public by preparing flyers,[58] holding panel discussions and making videos for social media.[59] The State, however, was slow in processing claims, and citizens said the registration process was complex and time consuming.

On Jan. 13, 2022, a constitutional amendment (HJR 117) was referred to the House Budget Committee that all but repeals Medicaid expansion.[60] Missouri League President Marilyn McLeod submitted a powerful letter opposing the bill at a March 22 Senate Appropriations Committee hearing,[61] but the committee passed the bill anyway. The General Assembly did not pass HJR117 and ended up fully funding Medicaid expansion through June 2023.[62]

ENVIRONMENT

In a world where climate change is increasingly difficult to ignore, the League is keeping an eye on environmental issues in Missouri. Mickey Croyle, Environmental Quality Chair and League representative for the Missouri Coalition for Clean Energy, attended the second virtual Missouri Environmental Summit in December 2021. The focus was on upcoming legislation with environmental impact but also included sessions on how to improve the environment during the COVID-19 pandemic.[63]

COAL ASH

As mentioned in the previous chapter, in 2013, the League opposed Ameren's proposal to create two new landfills for coal ash, a toxic waste product resulting from burning coal. Although that proposal was withdrawn and the company later issued a "Committed to Clean" Integrated Resource Plan in September 2020, when the Sierra Club graded Ameren as part of their Beyond Coal Campaign in 2021, Ameren received a 'D.' According to the U. S. Energy Information Administration, coal "provided 70% of Missouri's electricity net generation in 2020, and more coal was consumed for this purpose in Missouri than in any other state except for Texas." Ameren only plans to retire 18% of its coal capacity by 2030, while other coal-burning energy companies have pledged to end use of coal plants completely as early as 2028, turning instead to clean energy.[64]

This is significant because coal ash has negative effects on air and water quality, as demonstrated in July 2021 when Ameren's Coal Ash plant at Labadie was found to be in noncompliance with the Clean Water Act of 1987. The League's Environmental Quality Committee testified at the public hearing on July 1, asking the Missouri Department of Natural Resources (DNR) to withdraw the draft permit and reissue a stronger one that meets the Clean Water Act.[65]

While the DNR did issue a new operating permit for the plant in December 2021, it had the opposite effect of what the League desired. According to NPR, the permit "specifically allow[s] pollutants from its coal ash basins to be released into groundwater...for the next five years." In addition to groundwater, experts say the Missouri River will be polluted as well, which is the main source of drinking water for St. Louis.[66]

METROPOLITAN SEWER DISTRICT

The League continues to partner with the Metropolitan Sewer District (MSD) on both wastewater and stormwater-related concerns. They supported an April 2021 wastewater bond issue and rate proposal measure that was on the ballot[67] as Propositions Y, 1, 2, 3, 4, and 5.[68] Voters overwhelmingly passed Proposition Y by 81.6%, preventing a large rate increase and allowing MSD to make needed upgrades. The other five measures passed as well, but those were more related to the way MSD does business than its direct effect on customers.[69]

In November, MSD held a series of virtual town hall meetings regarding stormwater issues within the St. Louis region. MSD has seen an increase in stormwater-related requests that are caused by an increase in major flooding and erosion due to climate change. The meetings were held to help educate the public on sewer and stormwater utilities and seek input on public willingness to support capital projects to address the flooding and erosion.[70]

EQUAL RIGHTS AMENDMENT RATIFICATION

First introduced by suffragist Alice Paul in 1923, Congress passed the ERA in 1972. Since then, Leagues in Missouri and across the country have worked to engage lawmakers and organize at the grassroots level to ensure equal rights for all, regardless of sex.

On Jan. 27, 2020, Virginia became the 38th state to ratify the Equal Rights Amendment. The text of the ERA is as follows: "Section 1. Equality of rights under the law shall not be denied or abridged by the United States or by any State on account of sex. Sec. 2. The Congress shall have the power to enforce, by appropriate legislation, the provisions of this article. Sec. 3. This amendment shall take effect two years after the date of ratification."[71]

Some advocates believe the National Archivist can now proceed with final certification of the amendment. Many League members believe Congress should vote to remove the deadline for ratification and eliminate any ambiguity before the ERA is certified as an official amendment to the U.S. Constitution.

On March 17, 2021, the House of Representatives passed a resolution 222-204 to remove the deadline to ratify the Equal Rights Amendment, despite a ruling by a federal judge a few weeks before that said time had already run out. President Joe Biden applauded the House's effort. "[I]t is long past time that we enshrine the principle of gender equality in our Constitution," Biden said, adding that "no one's rights should be denied on account of their sex."

A companion joint resolution in the Senate, which was introduced by Lisa Murkowski (R-Alaska) and Ben Cardin (D-Maryland), may be a more difficult victory. At least 10 Republicans will have to join all 50 Democrats for it to pass and the ERA to be added to the Constitution.

While women have made significant progress toward equality over the years, they continue to battle systematic discrimination in the form of unequal pay, workplace harassment, domestic violence, and more. The League believes the ERA will pave the way for further legislative progress towards gender equality and will allow the courts to closely scrutinize sex-based discrimination.

LEAGUE ACTIVITIES

Celebrating the Centennial

Aug. 26, 2020, was the 100th anniversary of the ratification of the 19th Amendment, which granted women the right to vote after a 70+ year struggle. As they had done the year before for the League's 100th birthday, the St. Louis Centennial Committee planned a year's worth of events to recognize the efforts of our foremothers during the 2020 centennial.

The League began celebrations with the Women's March in downtown St. Louis in January. In February, the Missouri League and all eight local Leagues in Missouri held special events to celebrate the Centennial of the National League of Women Voters and show how "Women Power the Vote" in 2020. The St. Louis League delivered cookies to election authorities, the *St. Louis Post-Dispatch*, and the *St. Louis American* on Valentine's Day and posted a "Historic Hometown Heroine" on Facebook each day that week. The special posts honored Victoria Woodhull, Virginia Minor, Edna Gellhorn, Beatrice Grady, Marian English and Marie Byrum.[72]

On March 8, the League hosted "suffragist cinema," showing the movie *Iron Jawed Angels: Lead, Follow, or Get out of the Way* about Alice Paul at the St. Louis County Library Headquarters. It was followed by a brief discussion of suffrage history and women's political power in the 100 years since the League of Women Voters was founded.[73]

Two weeks later, the COVID-19 pandemic began with lockdowns across the world. The St. Louis League was forced to cancel Trivia Night in March and re-schedule many events or move them online, including the Missouri and National League Conventions.

In lieu of its normal July 4 parade, Webster Groves held a "reverse parade," in which parade watchers drove through the streets to see decorated homes. The League decorated the yard of former president K Wentzien to spotlight suffrage and voting. Members also purchased suffragist yard signs from the Kirkwood-Webster Groves branch of the American Association of University Women (AAUW) saying, "Thank You, Suffragists! Celebrate Women's Right to Vote."

On August 22, the U.S. Postal Service released a limited-time Women's Suffrage stamp. Two days later, several members of the League's Centennial Committee attended a small, socially-distanced event at the Missouri Botanical Garden for the designation of the yellow Suffrage Rose in the Gladney Rose Garden.

August 26th was full of activities for the centennial date. In partnership with AAUW, the League received proclamations marking the centennial from St. Louis Mayor Lyda Krewson and St. Louis County Executive Dr. Sam Page. St. Louis League members dressed in suffrage colors of yellow, white and purple gathered on the steps of the Missouri History Museum to form a tableau and host a media event at which League co-president Louise Wilkerson and Katie Moon, exhibit manager for the History Museum's "Beyond the Ballot" suffrage exhibit spoke about the importance of the day. The Missouri League held a virtual celebration featuring a presentation on the history of women's suffrage in Missouri by St. Louis member Nicole Evelina. Several churches across the area rang their bells at noon. After dark, the Saint Louis Wheel at Union Station, the Old Courthouse, and streetlights on Market Street from Union Station to the riverfront were lit in purple and gold, the suffrage colors.

On September 13, members enjoyed a rescheduled virtual presentation from Dr. Carolyn Jefferson Jenkins, the first woman of color to serve as president of the National League and author of *The Untold Story of Women of Color in the League of Women Voters*, on the injustices faced by black suffragists.

In 2022, the National Votes for Women Trail added a roadside marker on Locust Street to recognize the 1916 Golden Lane demonstration where thousands of women dressed in white and gold lined Locust Street as Democratic Convention delegates walked to the Coliseum at Jefferson and Locust. The suffragists stood silent to signify that the absence of the right to vote silenced women's voices. Members of the League and AAUW helped unveil the marker at a July 3 event at the Schlafly Tap Room, 2100 Locust, one of the buildings where the women stood.

LEAGUE DIVERSITY, EQUITY AND INCLUSION POLICY

The League of Women Voters supports equal rights for all under state and federal law regardless of race, color, gender, religion, national origin, age, sexual orientation, or disability. The St. Louis League adopted a Diversity, Equity and Inclusion (DEI) policy in April 2021 that says:

> "LWV of Metro St. Louis is an organization fully committed to diversity, equity, and inclusion in principle and in practice. Diversity, equity, and

inclusion are central to the organization's current and future success in engaging all individuals, households, communities, and policy makers in creating a more perfect democracy.

"There shall be no barriers to full participation in this organization on the basis of gender, gender identity, ethnicity, race, native or indigenous origin, age, generation, sexual orientation, culture, religion, belief system, marital status, parental status, socioeconomic status, language, accent, ability status, mental health, educational level or background, geography, nationality, work style, work experience, job role function, thinking style, personality type, physical appearance, political perspective or affiliation and/or any other characteristic that can be identified as recognizing or illustrating diversity."

In keeping with this policy, the League began offering training and education in DEI in June 2021, beginning with self-directed modules comprised of videos, articles, PowerPoint presentations, quizzes, short writing exercises and other activities.[74] This was followed in August by a virtual discussion based on a video series called Uncomfortable Conversations with a Black Man, created by former professional football player and media personality Emmanuel Acho.[75]

The League further showed its commitment to diversity with members participating in the YWCA Stand Against Racism Challenge. This virtual learning was followed by a discussion group with the St. Louis League to share learnings and DEI book discussion group on the voting rights chapter "Never a Real

Democracy." LWVMO has a DEI book group that's discussed *The Sum of Us: What Racism Costs Everyone and How We Can Prosper Together* by Heather McGhee and *Dying of Whiteness: How the Politics of Racial Resentment Is Killing America's Heartland* by Jonathan M. Metzl.[76]

Continuing League Activities

Volunteers continue to be active in voter services, including registering voters at high schools and naturalization ceremonies, offering Speakers Bureau presentations on a variety of topics, observing government meetings, and preparing and distributing a print and online Voters Guide before each election.

Anne Sappington led the League's work to prepare the Voters Guide for the April 2022 municipal elections with summaries of 270 candidates and more than 80 local ballot issues. After the *St. Louis Post-Dispatch* published the guide on March 17, volunteers distributed 8,000 copies to more than 50 locations.

Nancy Price heads the Speakers Bureau, responding to dozens of requests for presentations each year. Volunteers develop PowerPoint presentations on a variety of topics, including the history of women's suffrage, redistricting, and voting rights. Most presentations switched from in-person to Zoom in 2020 due to COVID-19, which allowed them to be recorded and shared on the lwvstl.org website and on YouTube.

The Metro League has active committees working on Voter Access, Getting Out the Vote, and Diversity, Equity & Inclusion (DEI), as well as Development and Investments. Issue committees in 2022 include Education, Environmental Quality, Gun Safety, Health Care, National Popular Vote, Policing and Reproductive Rights.

LOOKING FORWARD

As the League looks forward in to the latter half of the 2020s and beyond, they are bolstered by the successes of their past and wiser for the challenges they have faced. While no one can know exactly what will come next, League members know they will get through it together, standing on the shoulders of all the women and men who have come before them.

"Making a success of American democracy is a never-ending commitment, requiring tenacity, patience and a sense of humor," Nancy M. Neuman wrote in the conclusion to her 1994 book, *The League of Women Voters: In Perspective 1920-1995*. A quarter century later, this sentiment remains truer than ever as we face obstacles no one could have ever foreseen. But as Nancy also wrote, we are well prepared for any kind of battle: "The League gives citizens the tools to make a difference. ... A key benefit of membership is the League's political clout: it magnifies the voice of the individual citizen in government and politics."[76]

And that has always been what the League is about. From educating the new female voter in the 1920s to taking up local issues in the 1930s and beyond, our purpose has always been to empower voters to make use of one of their most fundamental rights: the franchise; through it they can and do change the course of our communities, states, country and ultimately, our history. Protecting that precious right is protecting democracy itself, and after more than 100 years, the League isn't slowing down anytime soon.

Main Sources Conclusion – 2020 and Beyond

Annual Reports of the President, League of Women Voters of St. Louis, 2020-2022

In League Reporter – March 2020-August 2022

League documents regarding
- ERA
- League 100th Anniversary Events

Periodicals
- *Associated Press*
- *The Riverfront Times*
- *The New York Times*
- *St. Louis Post-Dispatch*

Websites
- Ballotpedia
- Missouri House of Representatives
- Missouri Voter Protection Coalition
- NPR Kansas City

For a complete list of sources, please see the endnotes at https://my.lwv.org/missouri/metro-st-louis/about/our-history.

2020s

Sarah Riss (top center) and Barbara Harris (center) with Kirkwood City Council candidates in a 2020 virtual forum.

Suffrage celebration at Missouri History Museum on August 26, 2020.

Agnes Garino and Jean Dugan with suffrage rose at Missouri Botanical Garden.

Reform St. Louis News Conference on Feb. 23, 2021.

LWV of Metro St. Louis board members in 2022: Gena McClendon, Stephanie Wiegers, Cheri Crockett, Victoria Turner, Joan Hubbard and Catherine Stenger (back row) and 2nd VP Nancy Price, President Angie Dunlap, Secretary Sarah Manuel, Treasurer Denise Herrington and 1st VP Nancy Thompson (front row).

Lifetime Members

Some of the Women Who Marked 50 Years as League Members

Barbara Adelman *
Joyce Armstrong
Jane Arrigo *
Marilyn Beabout
Janet Becker *
Ruth Bettman *
Garnet Blake *
Lois Bliss *
Helen Booth*
Joan Botwinick
Mrs. Ingram F. Boyd, Jr. *
Stefany Brot
Mary Ellen Brucker *
Louise Carr
Margaret Carr
Katherine Chambers
Emma Lee Chilton *
Lee Chubb *
Milly Cohn *
Esther Clark
Marjorie Courtney
Florence Craft *
Sharon Danziger
Beatrice Davis *

Jean Dean *
Sue Dellbringge
Selma Dennis *
Virginia Deutch *
Helen Drazen *
Irene L. Dulin *
Kay Dusenbery
Pauline Eades *
Naomi Edmonds
Shirley Eder *
Terry Fischer *
Suzanne Fischer
Doris Flowers *
Agnes Garino
Alice Gerdine *
Maxine Gilner
Lillian Goldman
Joy Guze *
Frances Hall *
Mickey Hall *
Rachel Haspiel *
Lillian Heifetz*
Helen Hilliker *
Rhoda Hochman

Virginia Horner
Debby Waite Howard
Ann Husch *
Elise Joerger
Anne Johnson
Robin Jones
Mrs. William B. Kountz *
Beatrice Kornblum *
Marguerite Kowert
Elizabeth Latzer
Lois Lindell *
Billie Linder
Yvonne Logan *
Mrs. Joseph Magidson *
Ernestine Magner *
Linda C. McDaniel
Cynthia Mitchell
Ann Moller
Dorothy Moore *
Esther Mueller *
Clara Mutshnick *
Barbara Nelson
Ann Niederlander *
Mrs. Edmond Noonan *
Mrs. Carl Otto *
Martha Panetti *
Marjorie Tooker Patton *
Susan Philpott
Carol Portman
Madelon Price
Babette Putzel *
Silvia Rava *
Marjorie Reinhart *
Ramona Rhoads

Patricia Rich
Shirley Richman *
Mary Jane Robbins
Claire Robertson
Mrs. George K. Robins *
Dorothy Roudebush *
Selma Schlafman *
Adelaide Schlalfly *
Jan Schoenfeld
Ellen Jane Schwartz
Elise R. Schweich
Sydell Shayer
Helen Shopmaker *
Carol Sipes
Ruth Siteman
Nancy Smith
Selma Soule
Eldora Spiegelberg *
Ellen Tenney *
Peggy Vickroy
Eleanor Smith Waite *
Lee Wallas *
Bertha Wallbrunn
Lolli Wehrli *
K Wentzien
Ida West *
Mrs. Norman Wolff *

(* deceased)

League of Women Voters Past Presidents

LWV of St. Louis

(In the early years, a Democrat, Republican and Independent often served together.)

Marian (Mrs. Fred) English (known later as Mrs. Chauncey Clarke), 1919
Mrs. E. T. Senseney (I), 1919-21
Mrs. C. B. Faris (D), 1920
Ethel (Mrs. Harry E.) Sprague (R), 1920
Emma (Mrs. E.M.) Grossman (D), 1921 Margaret (Mrs. Charles) Swingley (R), 1921
Pearl (Mrs. Fred) Reid (D), 1922 Mrs. C. V. Beck (R), 1922 Mrs. D. O. Ives (I), 1922
Frances (Mrs. Roscoe) Anderson (D), 1923-24
Elsie (Mrs. A.S.) Rauh (R), 1923
Helen (Mrs. Evarts) Graham (I), 1923-24
Florence Weigle (R), 1924
Mrs. Frank Crunden (D), 1925 Mrs. George Mangold (I), 1925
Edna Fischel (Mrs. George) Gellhorn (R), 1925

Josephine (Mrs. Harry) January, 1926-27
Estella (Mrs. Theodore) Kelsey (R), 1926 Tess (Mrs. Virgil) Loeb (I), 1926
Florence (Mrs. Donovan) Curran, 1928-29
Mrs. H. M. McClure Young, 1930-31
Marion (Mrs. Victor) Weir, 1932-33
Louise G. Smith, 1934
Delphine Smith (Mrs. J. Hardin Smith, Jr.), 1934-35
Mrs. Christensen Light, 1936
Jeanne Blythe, 1937-40
Dorothy (Mrs. George) Roudebush, 1941-42
Edna Fischel Gellhorn, 1943-44
Teresa Fischer, 1945–47
Margaret Steele (Mrs. L. Mathews) Werner, 1948
Margaret (Mrs. Conrad) Sommer, 1949-50
Delphine Smith, 1951-52
Avis (Mrs. Harry G.) Carlson, 1953-54
Roddy (Mrs. Gilbert) Harris, 1955-57
Laurene (Mrs. Walter) Strehlman, 1958-60
Margaret Lippman (Mrs. L. F.) Pinkus, 1961–64
Jeanne Blythe, 1965-66
Virginia Deutch, 1967–68
Elaine Levine (Mrs. Mitchell) Yanow, 1969–70
Frances Olenick, 1971
Betty Ann Gilbert, 1972-75

League of Women Voters Past Presidents

Mary Greensfelder, 1976-78
Debby Waite, 1979-80
Lucy Hale, 1981-1983
Debby Waite (Mrs. Jack Howard), 1983-1984
Ida West, 1984-1989
Cay Thompson, 1989-90
Zoe Shipman, 1991
Judith Arnold, 1992-94
Clarene Royston, 1995
Judith (Mrs. Richard) O'Briant, 1996
Donna Brooks, 1997
Marjorie Jokerst, 1998

Past Presidents of St. Louis County League and LWV of Metro St. Louis

Prior to the merger of the County Leagues in 1981, there were presidents of local Leagues, including Clayton, Kirkwood, University City, Webster Groves and County Area Leagues. (In 1999 the County League and City League merged. The current organization is the League of Women Voters of Metro St. Louis.)

Roseanne Newcomb, 1981-83	Nancy Ulman (now Thompson), 2002-03
Mary Kirkpatrick, 1983-85	Norma Jean Downey, 2003-04
K Wentzien, 1985-87	Nancy Bowser, 2004-05
Vivian G. Schmidt, 1987-89	Jeanne Morrel Franklin, 2005-07
Mary K. Brown, 1989-91	Doris Buzzell, 2007-09
Susan Trice, 1991-95	Becky Clausen and Linda McDaniel, 2009
Gail Heyne-Hafer, 1995-97	Linda McDaniel and Kathleen Farrell, 2010-17
Jean Dean, 1997-99	Louise Wilkerson and Nancy J. Miller, 2017-21
K Wentzien, 1999-2001	Angie Dunlap, 2021-present
Elise Joerger, 2001-02	

Presidents of LWV of Metropolitan St. Louis (ILO)

Ruth McCluer, 1966-69	Janet Becker, 1975-77
Libby Karlow, 1969-70	Pat Rich, 1977-81
Mickey Hall, 1970-71	Agnes Garino, 1981-85
Peggy Vickroy, 1971-73	
Ramona Culp, 1973-75	

Presidents of the LWV Information Service (previously CIRC)

Janet Becker, 1975-77	Sydell Shayer, 1985-86
Pat Rich, 1977-81	Barbara Shull, 1986-91
Agnes Garino, 1981-85	Debby Howard, 1991-92

Other League Presidents

BRENTWOOD

Mrs. Knowlton Caplan	Mrs. Norman Hill
Mrs. T.M. Elliott	Mrs. R.J.W. Koopman
Mrs. E.A. Hassebrock	

CENTRAL COUNTY

Mrs. James J. Harmon, Jr	Maxine Engel
Mrs. J.A. Singmaster	Pat Rich
Libby Karlow	Dolores Beiger
Mary Kirkpatrick	Carole Stevens
Ramona Culp	

CLAYTON

Ella Stinson	Mrs. L.S. Vagino
Mrs. Louis Shifrin	Mrs. Ray S. Moore
Mrs. Turner White, Jr.	Mrs. Thomas J. Cole
Mrs. Peter Wulfing	Mrs. Arthur Stockman
Mrs. John Wightman	Mrs. Archie D. Carr
Arlene Bishop	Marie Shanley

FERGUSON

Geneva Wooster	Alice Krueger
Dorothy Sproul	Elise Fiebert
Jean Dean	Gladys McCluer
Kate Allen	Bobbie McKibban
Marion St. Clair	Delores Bretch

League of Women Voters Past Presidents

FLORISSANT

Mrs. C.E. Tennant	Mrs. Ray Johnson
Mrs. V.A. Arensmeyer	Mrs. Ray A. Bliesner
Mrs. H.D. Pershing	Mrs. William Pfeffer

KIRKWOOD

Mrs. George Tittman	Mrs. T. Perry Smirl
Mrs. E.E. Williams	Mrs. Roland Read
Mrs. J.K. Broderick	Mrs. Samuel Johnson
Mrs. Tucker	Mrs. Hervey Roberts
Mrs. J.H. Herren	Mrs. Robert Humber
Mrs. E.W. Peabody	Mrs. Oliver Blase
Mrs. Frank Goodwin	Mrs. L.P. Whiting
Mrs. H.C. Walker	Esther Holsen
Mrs. H. Chadeayne	Esther Osborne
Mrs. J.C. Hoester	Ruth Hamilton
Mrs. E.E. Pickel	Mrs. M.T. Buhl
Mrs. Frank Tillman	Lucille Congdon
Mrs. Angus Moore	Ruth Phelan
Mrs. J.E. Donovan	Emily Brandhorst
Mrs. T.S. Carswell	Lois Bliss
Mrs. H. Jungmann	Alice Muckler
Mrs. W. Lampmann	Agnes Garino

Normandy

Mrs. Carroll Nelson	Mrs. W. Wunnenberg
Clarissa Heinz	

North County

Ann Jenner	Laurel Peek
Kathy Schroeder	Linda McDaniel
Deane Wagner	Mary Flesher
Joyce Berney	Rosemary Wynne
Arline Kiselewski	Elaine Blodgett
Pat Waters	

Southwest County

Brenda Banjak	Georgeanne Sears

University City

Annetta Fuchs	Lois Bowen
Dorothy Moore	Zelda Robbins
Mary Bryant	Louise Reals
Hazel Roos	Clarissa Heinz
Grace Treiman	Ronnie Blitz
Elizabeth Moore	Dorothy Friberg
Roslyn Moss	Elsie Plessner
Dorothy Roudebush	Rita Kaplan
Mildred Greeson	Becky Enoch
Dorothy Birk	Evelyn Schrieber
Marie Breslo	Elise Joerger
Gwen Hudson	Janet Becker
Eleanor Kaplow	Carol Portman
Nancy Bowser	Terri Berry

Webster Groves

Mrs. E. Cushing	Mrs. Raymond Cray
Mrs. James Cook	Mrs. Glenn Ogle
Mrs. J.J. Curtis	Mrs. L.F. Booth
Mrs. H.A. Gleick	Mrs. John Stockham
Mrs. Jasper Blackburn	Mrs. R.I. Brambaugh
Mrs. Elwood Street	Mrs. Ernest Bashford
Mrs. D.E. Horton	Mrs. James Forsyth
Mrs. R.K. Cross	Frances Olenick
Mrs. S.J. Ewald	Mary Taylor
Mrs. S.R. Irish	Ellen Walters
Mrs. Ross Moyer	Emma Lee Chilton
Mrs. Peter Kassius	Dorothy Drinkhouse
Mrs. S.C. Gribble	Marge Beyer
Mrs. A.J. Pastene	Ernestine Magner
Mrs. George Reddish	Penelope Gale
Mrs. F.K. Habenicht	Marjorie Reinhart
Mrs. Kennerly Woody	Georgeanne Sears
Mrs. Leslie Prichard	

Acknowledgements

Nicole Evelina would like to thank the following individuals and groups for help with this project:

- A.J. Medlock at the St. Louis Research Center of the State Historical Society of Missouri at UMSL for help in researching the League from 1960 to the early 1980s;
- Jean Dugan and Agnes Garino of the St. Louis Metro League of Women Voters for their guidance on this book and access to League files from the 1980s to today;
- Agnes Garino and Sydell Shayer for sharing their personal files and memories in support of this project;
- Anna Reynolds for conducting the oral histories that helped inform this book;
- Laurie Murphy for helping to organize the League files at the office;
- Kim Hallemann and other League members who caught errors while proofreading;
- Teresa Sauer for compiling the index, and
- League members who volunteered to be interviewed for oral histories in 2021, including: Joyce Armstrong; Brenda Banjak; Julie Behrens; Elaine Blodgett; Mary K. Brown; Stefany Brot; Marjorie Courtney; Mickey Croyle; Esther Clark; Naomi Edmonds; Sue Dellbringge; Kathleen Farrell; Agnes Garino; Maxine Gilner; Debby Howard; Linda McDaniel; Anna Mennerick; Nancy Miller; Cindy Mitchell; Claire Robertson; Madelon Price; Sydell Shayer; Carol Sipes; Judith Smart; Steve Smith; Nancy

Thompson; K Wentzien and Louise Wilkerson. This book wouldn't have nearly as much wisdom, insight, or personality without your memories.

And to all of the League members who contributed to, edited, or proofread this book in its many drafts. I couldn't have done it without you!

Index

A

Acho, Emmanuel–341
AFL-CIO–245
Albright, Madeleine–171
Alda, Alan -71
Allen, Bob–333
Allen, Catherine–294
Ameren UE–242, 286-287
American Assn. of University
  Women/AAUW–245, 247, 296,
  335, 339-340
Anniversaries of the League
  50th Anniversary–37
  60th Anniversary–101
  65th Anniversary–145, 169
  70th Anniversary–146, 254
  75th Anniversary–204
  90th Anniversary-292
  100th Anniversary – v, 294, 315
Army Corps of Engineers–98, 135-
  136, 142
Arnold, Judith–171, 173, 186, 213,
  317, 353
Ashcroft, Jay (Secretary of
  State)–320, 327
Ashcroft, John (Governor)–73, 122,
  177, 201-203
Apportionment–see Redistricting
Awards–155, 220, 249, 254, 295,
  304, 320
  Harriett Woods Award–155,
    213, 254
  Lenore Loeb Award–223, 305

B

Banjak, Brenda–115, 130, 160,
  167, 259, 297, 317, 358, 360
Banks, Jet (State Senator)–184
Barker, Amy–102
Barnes, Eleanor–259
Barnes, James (State Rep.)–333
Becker, Janet–55, 102-104, 113,
  248, 349, 355, 358
Beetem, Jon E. (Judge)–269, 334
Behrens, Julie–115, 297, 311, 360
Benson, Lucy Wilson (LWVUS
  President)–41, 65-66
Bergen, Polly–74
Biden, Joe (President)–283, 285,
  337
Big Vote–118-121, 167
Blackwell, Earl (State Senator)–89
Bland, Mary Groves (State Rep.)–
  245-246
Bliss, Lois–130, 251-253, 259,
  349, 357
Blodgett, Elaine–191, 261, 358,
  360
Blue Cross Blue Shield–172, 182-
  185
  Missouri Dept. of
    Insurance–183
  Missouri Foundation for
    Health–185, 281
  RightChoice Managed Care–
    183-185
Blunt, Matt (Governor)–228
Blunt, Roy (Governor, U.S.
  Senator)–270

Blythe, Jeanne–40, 352
Board of Alderpersons, St. Louis City–18, 32, 83, 232, 275-276, 299, 325-326
Bollinger, Claralyn–249
Bombeck, Erma–74
Bond, Christopher (Governor)–59, 65, 69-70, 144, 154, 199, 228
Bond Issues–8-9, 16, 36-37, 80, 85, 88, 137, 241, 336
Bonner, Dennis (State Rep.)–246
Bosley, Freeman, Jr. (Mayor)–186
Bosley, Irma–94
Bowser, Nancy–210-211, 218, 239-240, 261, 317, 354, 358
Brady, Jim & Sarah–202
Brooks, Donna–171, 353
Brooks, Mary–190
Brown, Mary K.–116, 171, 175, 297, 317, 354, 360
Bruce, Betsey–254, 295
Burns, Ann–74
Burns, Mrs. W. Parker–32
Bush, George H.W. (President)–120, 192
Bush, George W. (President)–xi, 223-224, 227
Busing (see Desegregation)
Buzzell, Doris–218, 237, 250, 354
Byrum, Marie–338

C

Calloway, DeVerne (State Rep.)–65
Campaign Finance Reform (see Elections)
Candidate Forums 118-119, 249, 266-268, 322
Cardin, Ben (U.S. Senator)–337
Carlson, Avis–i, iiv, 23, 26, 49, 51, 167, 352
Carnahan, Jean (U.S. Senator)–217
Carnahan, Mel (Governor)–179, 184, 190, 199, 245
Carnahan, Robin (Secretary of State)–209, 229
Centennial of 19th Amendment–338
Charters–25-28, 82-84, 230-231
    Creve Coeur–82
    Kirkwood–159, 231, 252
    Olivette–82
    St. Louis City–26, 127, 161, 232, 325
    St. Louis County–82, 158, 169, 210, 231
    Webster Groves–231
Chatfield, Gail (State Rep.)–198
Chilton, Emma Lee & Steve -100
China–ii, 41, 156
Citizens Information/Resource Center (see League of Women Voters Information Service)
Citizenship Education Clearinghouse–46, 174
    Kids Voting–127, 163, 193
City Redevelopment–31-37, 42, 74
Clark, Carolyn–167
Clark, Esther & Jim–93-94, 100, 259, 349, 360
Clausen, Becky–264, 291, 309, 354
Clay, Bill (U.S. Rep.)–118, 124-126, 139
Clean Missouri–264, 272-274, 329
Climate Change–ii, 218, 242-244, 335-336
    Pew Center on Global Climate Change–218, 243
    U.S. Mayors' Climate Protection Agreement–243
Clinton, Bill (President)–176
Clinton, Hillary (U.S. Senator)–199, 263

Coalitions
- Missouri Clean Energy coalitions–242
- Missouri Coalition for the Environment–135, 288
- Missouri Sunshine Coalition–218
- Missouri Voter Protection Coalition–269, 319, 324, 326
- Reform St. Louis–325, 347
- Show Me Integrity–274-276, 323, 325, 329

Cloyd, Karen–311
Clusen, Ruth (LWVUS President)–69
Cofer-Wildsmith, Marina–192
Cohn, Milly–101, 349
Constitutional Convention–19, 23, 89
Conway, Jim (Mayor)–113
Cook, Marlow W. (U.S. Senator) –66
Cooperman, Jeanette–77
Copenhaver, Nancy–327
Couzins, Phoebe Wilson–295
Courts / Lawsuits
- Cole County Circuit Court–228, 274, 320
- Eighth District Court of Appeals–323
- Lawsuits–89, 124, 133, 136, 176, 182-184, 208-209, 271, 320, 323, 327
- Missouri Court of Appeals–19, 84, 185
- Missouri Supreme Court–62, 84, 177, 185, 193-194, 228, 269, 277, 326-327, 334
- St. Louis Circuit Court–84, 129, 135, 185, 194
- U.S. Supreme Court -7-8, 29, 53, 57, 128, 182, 188, 224, 269, 281
- Western District Court of Appeals–185, 274

COVID-19–152, 319-320
Crockett, Cheri–347
Croyle, Mickey–221-222, 255-256, 286, 313, 335
Crozier, Don–330
Curls, Phil (State Senator)–190

D

Deakin, James–4
Dean, Jean–171, 349, 354
Death Penalty–157, 233-234, 283-285
Deeken, Bill (State Rep.)–284
Deland, Michael–191
Desegregation–7-12, 54, 88-90, 129-131, 159, 185-188, 234-235, 277
Deutch, Virginia–29-30, 38, 40, 47-50, 169, 349, 352
Dirck, Edwin (State Senator)–126
Discrimination–7, 10, 25, 63-66, 76-78, 132-134, 201, 270, 338
Diversity, Equity and Inclusion Policy (DEI)–340-342
Dodd, Christopher (U.S. Senator)–226
Doll, Dotty (State Rep.)–69
Dowden-White, Dr. Priscilla–213
Downey, Norma Jean–218, 354
Drey, Kay–288
Driskill, Joe (State Rep.)–200
Dugan, Jean–297, 313, 330, 345, 360
Dunlap, Angie–311, 324, 330-331, 347, 354
Dunlap, Terry–311
Durbin, Richard (U.S. Senator)–199

E

Eagleton, Thomas (U.S. Senator)–76, 146, 154
Earnhardt, Oscar–46
East-West Gateway Coordinating Council–18, 77, 79-80, 91, 143, 192, 285
Education–7, 85, 129, 185, 234, 277
    Busing–7-12, 88-90, 130-131, 185-187, 234-236, 277-278
    Charter Schools–234-236, 278-279
    Community College/Junior College–12-13, 42, 46, 85
    Dept. of Health, Education and Welfare–8
    Funding—236-238, 279-280
    Liddell vs. Board of Education–89-90, 129
    Missouri Dept. of Elementary and Secondary Education (DESE)–186, 238
    No Child Left Behind Act–237-238
    Special School District–13-14, 87
    State Board of Education–11, 277
    Vocational–12-14, 87
    Voluntary Interdistrict Choice Corp (VICC)–12, 130, 186-188, 235, 277-278
Elbrecht, Barbara–115
Elections–55
    Campaign Finance–iii, 56-57, 84-87, 102, 116, 118-119, 125, 128-132, 172, 178-181, 209, 224

    Election Reforms–59-60, 118, 223
    Motor Voter–175, 271
    Presidential Debates–iiii, 54, 119
    Primaries–61, 121
    Show Me Integrity–(see Coalitions)
    St. Louis Board of Elections–54, 61, 224, 326
    St. Louis County Board of Elections–221
    Voter Access–224
    Voter ID Laws– 6, 123, 227, 268, 326
    Voter Registration–6, 59, 172
    Voting Rights Act–xi, 58, 269, 322
    Voting Machines–54, 59, 220, 266
Energy–98, 140, 242, 286
    Ameren UE–242, 286, 335
Environment
    Air Pollution/Quality–17, 93, 138, 192, 286
    Coal Ash–286, 335
    Hazardous Waste–140
    Solid Waste–95, 141
    Water Pollution/Quality–15-16, 90, 137, 192
Equal Pay Act–1, 63, 132
Equal Rights Amendment (ERA)–62-74, 147, 244-247, 337-338
Eveloff, Vivian–292

F

Farrell, Kathleen–209, 263, 271, 293, 298-299, 309, 317, 325, 331
Ferber, Joel–334
Ferraro, Geraldine (VP Candidate)–115
Fischer, Teresa–12, 44-46, 352
Fitch, Rachel Farr–183-184

Focus St. Louis–187, 219, 249, 253
Ford, Gerald (President)–58
Foreman, Mary–99
Franklin, Jeanne Morell–218, 354
Fraser, Barbara (State Rep.)–148, 280
Freeholders Plan (see Govt. Reorganization)
Freeman, Frankie–38, 65
Friedan, Betty–1
Friedman, Gerry–102
Fundraising (see League Financing)

G

Gant, Mary (State Senator)–72
Garino, Agnes–100, 102, 115, 130, 157-160, 169, 213, 259, 297, 311, 317, 345, 349, 355, 357, 360
Garland, Merritt (U.S. Atty. General)–285
Gellhorn, Edna–iv, 38, 295, 338, 351-352
Gellhorn, Gay–v, 295, 317
Gephardt, Dick (U.S. Rep.)–118, 126, 139, 199
Gerrymandering (see Redistricting)
Gibbons, Mike (State Senator)–280
Gilbert, Betty Ann–298
Gilkey, Bertha–191
Gilner, Frank–101
Gilner, Maxine–101, 259, 349
Golden Lane–249-250, 263, 297, 309, 340
Goldstein, Merle–80
Goode, Wayne (State Senator)–96, 178
Goodman, Ellen–245
Gore, Al (Vice President)–223-224
Government Reorganization efforts
    Board of Electors–128
    Board of Freeholders–15, 19-20, 127-128,

    Borough Plan–18-22
    St. Louis County Boundary Commission–159
Graham, John D. (State Rep.) –29
Granny D. (See Haddock)
Grants–ix, 56, 76, 118, 174, 264, 270, 321, 330
    Danforth Foundation–56
    Deer Creek Foundation–174
    Roblee Foundation–265, 305
Grassley, Charles (U.S. Senator)–xi
Green, LaDonna–34
Greensfelder, Mary–64, 113, 169, 353
Griffin, Bob (State Rep.)–198
Griffins, Martha (U.S. Rep.)–63
Guard, Joyce–225, 297
Gun Safety/Gun Control–125, 146-152, 211-212

H

Haddock, Doris (Granny D.)–181
Hadley, Della (State Rep.)–69
Hale, Julie–113
Hale, Lucy–116, 353
Hall, Loretta–191
Hall, Mickey–101, 297, 349, 355
Hall of Famous Missourians–295
Halleman, Kim–360
Hamilton, Jean (Judge)–219
Hancock Amendment–193, 228
Hancock, Mel (State Senator)–162
Hardy, Eleanor–38
Harmon, Clarence (Chief of Police/Mayor)–201, 234
Harper, Roy W. (Judge)–218
Harris, Barbara–311, 345
Harris, Rodney–24
Harrison, Dorothy–6
Hartzler, Vicky (U.S. Rep.)–245
Hastert, Dennis (U.S. Rep.)–180
Hawley, Josh (U.S. Senator)–270

Health Care–196, 280, 334
   Affordable Care Act (ACA)–281
   American Rescue Plan–283
   Medicaid–183, 198, 281-283, 334
   Mental Health–24, 280
   Missouri Foundation for Health–185, 281
Heaney, Gerald W.–11
Herrington, Denise–347
Heyne-Hafer, Gail–213, 215, 317
Hoffsten, Chantal–297
Holden, Bob (Governor)–190, 236, 280
Housing–8, 31-36, 74-76, 188-190, 269
Howard, Debby Waite–116, 145, 149, 160-163, 317, 350, 353
Howard, Raymond (State Senator)–64
Hubbard, Joan–299, 311, 325, 331, 347
Human Development Corp. (HDC)–5
Hungate, William (Judge)–130

I

Initiative Petitions–272, 323-325, 330, 334
In League Reporter (see Publications)
International Institute–219

J

Jefferson-Jenkins, Dr. Carolyn (LWVUS President)–227, 250
Jewish Community Relations Council–157
Joerger, Elise–115, 218, 350, 354, 358
Johnson, Lyndon B. (President)–38, 120
Jokerst, Marjorie–171, 203, 353
Jones, Emil (IL State Senator)–246-247
Jones, Herb (Kirkwood Mayor)–159
Jones, Kay–66
Jones, Sharon Geuea–330
Jones, Tim (State Rep.)–295-296
Jones, Tishaura (Mayor)–275
Joyce, Pat (Judge)–274

K

Keaveny, Joseph (State Senator)–284
Kelly, Kathleen–249
Kendall, Jean–331
Kennedy, John F. (President)–1
KETC-TV, Channel 9–118
Khan, Sabrina–313
Kilpatrick, Katherine–280
Kimmey, Dr. James–199
King, Dr. Martin Luther, Jr.–1-2, 206
Kirkpatrick, James (Sec. of State)–59, 62
Kirkpatrick, Mary and Suzanne–116, 249, 356
Kirkwood–v, 86, 89, 158-160, 207, 231, 252, 295
KMOX-TV, Channel 4–199
Knox, William (Judge)–271
Krewson, Lyda (Mayor)–339
KSD Radio–76, 118
KSDK-TV, Channel 5–267

L

Land Use–97
   Riverport Dome–134-136, 205
Lead Poisoning–244
League of Women Voters Information Service–55, 102-104, 108, 113, 117, 150-151, 162, 248, 250-254, 265, 355

League of Women Voters in Perspective 1920-95–Epigraph, 343
League of Women Voters in St. Louis: The First 40 Years–i, vii, 51
League of Women Voters of Missouri–iv-ix, 66, 96, 125, 139, 158, 197-198, 233, 268, 271-272, 275, 297, 321, 324, 327, 329-332, 342
League of Women Voters of the United States –iii, viii, xi, 41, 65, 69, 97, 148, 200, 224, 226, 229-230, 250, 289, 292
League Financing–37, 53, 71-74, 151-152
    League in the Loop–115
    Metropolitan Finance Campaign–53-54
    Theatre Parties–151-152
    Trivia Night–294, 339
League Metropolitan Council–39-40, 87
League Office and Staff–xii, 297
League Restructuring/Mergers–viii-x, 203-204, 150, 291, 354
Lieberman, Denise–269, 313, 324, 326
Lifetime Members (50+ years)–349-350
Local Leagues/Units–x, 115, 149
    City of St. Louis–x, 29, 32, 129, 173, 186, 190, 325
Lumpe, Sheila (State Rep.)–132

M

Mackey, Ian (State Rep.)–333
MacNamara, Elisabeth (LWVUS President)–292
Maddox, Evelyn (LWVMO President)–271, 313, 329, 321
Making Democracy Work–ix, 276,
Mandela, Nelson–171
Mannies, Jo–292
Manuel, Sarah–347
Marches
    Celebrate the Vote–249-250, 309
    March for Women's Lives–249
    Shoulder to Shoulder–205
    Women's March–293, 311
Maxwell, Kay (LWVUS President)–249, 259
McCandless, Dr. Karl–20-22
McCaskill, Claire (Auditor/U.S. Senator)–155, 217
McClendon, Gena–347
McConnell, Mitch (U.S. Senator)–226, 271
McCoy, Sherman–199
McCreery, Tracy (State Rep.)–333
McDaniel, Linda–179, 183, 199, 208-210, 213, 271-272, 291, 293, 309, 317, 354
McLeod, Marilyn (LWVMO President)–324, 327-328, 332, 334
McNary, Gene (County Executive)–75-76, 135, 142-143
McReynolds, Amber–275
Medlock, A.J.–360
Meredith, James (Judge)–90, 130
Meridith, Peter (State Rep.)–275, 333
Merit System–23-27
Merritt, Mary–254
Metro News (see Publications)
Metropolitan St. Louis Sewer District (MSD)–15, 90, 137, 139, 240, 288, 336
    Bond Issues–241, 288, 321, 336
    Finances–240
    Rate Commission–193

Meyer, Walter L. (State Rep.)–7
Mikulski, Barbara (U.S. Senator)–73
Miller, Nancy J.–269-273, 300, 301-303, 317, 354
Milligan-Ciha, Chris–174
Minimum Wage–290-291, 311, 324
Minogue, Becky–213
Minor, Virginia–295-296, 363
Mission Statement–248
Missouri Botanical Garden–107, 116, 144, 339, 345
Missouri Constitution–18, 23, 85, 128, 162
Missouri Dept. of Natural Resources (DNR)–141, 241, 287, 336
Missouri Historical Society/History Museum–48, 144, 223, 339, 345
Missouri Human Rights Commission–78, 133, 245
Missouri Women's Network–247, 296
Mitchell, Cindy–249
Modrell, Dianne–249, 282
Mondale, Walter (Vice President)–iii, 120, 159
Moon, Katie–339, 345
Moore, Dorothy–169, 350, 358
Moore, Ruth–33
Monsey, Janet–xi
Murkowski, Lisa (U.S. Senator)–337
Murphy, Laurie–360

N
Nat'l. Assoc. for the Advancement of Colored People (NAACP)–9, 90, 125, 269, 320, 327
National Organization of Women (NOW) –53, 63, 73
National Popular Vote (NPV)– 229, 333
National Women's Political Caucus–53, 64, 146, 154
Naturalization Ceremonies (see Voter Registration)
Nelson, Kathryn–213
Neuman, Nancy (LWVUS President)–Epigraph, iii
Newcomb, Roseanne–150, 354
Nickels, Arlene–218
Nixon, Jay (Governor, Atty. General) –134, 190, 268, 278, 290
Nixon, Richard (President)–90
Non-Partisan Court Plan–84-85
Now, Rebecca–294

O
Obama, Barack (President)–134, 217
O'Briant, Judith–171, 353
Olenick, Frances–24, 352
O'Rourke, Fr. Kevin–199
Osborne, Esther–38, 357

P
Page, Sam (County Executive)–339
Parson, Mike (Governor)–280, 282, 319, 327, 333-334
Past League Presidents–351-359
Patterson, Deborah–113
Paul, Alice–62, 337-338
Pay Equity–1, 63, 131-134, 338
Pelosi, Nancy (Speaker of the House)–155, 217
Pharis, Marjorie–35
Philpott, Susie–35, 350
Photo ID (see Elections)
Poelker, John (Mayor)–59
Polk, Charles–240
Pollution (see Environment)
Portman, Carol, Darwin & Family–215, 218, 249, 253-255,

369

317, 350, 358
Powell, John–125
Presidential Debates (see Elections)
Price, Nancy–123, 313, 322, 324, 331, 342, 347
Publications–110, 326
Pulitzer, Joseph (State Rep.)–25

Q
Quinn, Doris (State Rep.)–69, 72
Quinn, Robert Jr.–128

R
Rauh, Elsie–38
Reagan, Ronald (President)–iii, xi, 74, 120, 159, 202,
Redistricting–28-30, 123, 177, 272, 325, 328-333
Redlining (see also Housing)–74-79
Reno, Janet (US Atty. General)–176
Reproductive Rights–39, 125
Reynolds, Anna–xii, 360
Reynolds, Mary Beth–223
Rice, Condoleezza (U.S. Sec. of State)–217
Rich, Pat–106-107, 315, 317, 355
Ridings, Dorothy (LWVUS President) –148
Riss, Sarah–345
Roos, Lawrence (County Executive/ Charter Chair)–38, 83
Roosevelt, Eleanor (First Lady)–xi
Ross, John–201
Royston, Clarene–171, 191, 353
Russell, Robert G. (Judge)–185

S
Sappington, Anne–311, 325, 342
Sayman, Helene–136
Sayman, Luella–38,
Schark, Patricia–259
Scheve, May (State Rep.)–178

Schlafly, Phyllis–64, 66, 69, 133, 245
Schmidt, Vivian–116
Schoemehl, Vince (Mayor)–136
School Districts
  Clayton–86, 130
  Kirkwood–130
  Ladue–86, 188
  Mehlville–10
  Normandy–277
  Pattonville–130
  Ritenour–130, 188
  Riverview Gardens–277
  Rockwood - 86
  St. Louis City–86, 89, 187-188, 222, 277
  University City–15, 130
  Webster Groves–15
Schrieber, Evelyn–169, 358
Schroeder, Patricia (U.S. Rep.)–204
Schupp, Jill (State Senator)–333
Schwartz, Virginia (LWVUS Board)–169
Seddon, SaLees–32
Shayer, Sydell–v, 41, 125, 151, 155-157, 163, 167, 177, 208, 232-233, 259, 285, 309, 311, 317, 350, 355, 360
Shear, Sue (State Rep.)–xi, 64, 111, 146-148, 201
Sheldon Concert Hall–v, 315
Shewmaker, Richard D.–20
Shipman, Zoe–171
Shipton, Janet–104-105, 111, 132
Shull, Barbara–102, 135, 162-163, 169, 213, 355
Sierra Club– 243, 286, 288, 330, 335
Simpson, Alan (U.S. Senator)–176
Simpson, Joanne–280
Simpson, Peter L. (St. Louis Alderman)–18

Sipes, Carol–259, 350
Slay, Francis (Mayor)–235
Smart, Judith–309
Solomon, Virginia Kase–330
Soraghan, Pat–259
Speakers Bureau (see Voter Services)
Special School District (see Education)
Spradling, Al. Jr. (State Rep.)–24
Spurgeon, Dr. Oral–14
Stanton, Elizabeth Cady–295
Stenger, Catherine–304-305, 309, 347
Stinson, Ella–38, 169, 356
Stix, Erma–38
St. Louis Board of Aldermen (See Board of Alderpersons)
St. Louis County Park System–36
St. Louis Post-Dispatch–v, 4, 21, 132, 138, 176, 183, 203, 209, 232, 238, 266, 292, 321, 342
Sue Shear Institute–147, 292

T
Tate, Nancy–309
Teasdale, Joe (Governor)–101
Term Limits–181-182
Thompson, Cay–116, 175, 353
Thompson, Nancy (Ulman)–239, 240, 317, 331, 347, 354
Topham, Suzanne–102
Transit–79, 142, 195
Trice, Susan–171, 202, 354
Tucker, Raymond (Mayor)–38
Turner, Dr. Deborah (LWVUS President)– Epigraph, xi
Turner, Victoria–347

U
Uchitelle, Dr. Susan–11

V
Vedder, Adolph–38
Velasquez, Laurie–333
Vickroy, Peggy–xi, 297, 350, 355
Voter Registration–i, ii, 4-6, 59, 172-177, 218, 264, 271, 304, 321-328
  Naturalization Ceremonies–218-220, 249, 264, 321, 328
Voter Services–117-121, 265-266
  Big Vote–118-119, 121, 167
  Cable TV Programs–174, 205, 265-266
  Candidate Forums–118, 266-268, 322
  CIRC–x, 55, 150, 248, 355
  LWVSTL website–296, 342
  Smart Voter website–221-222
  Speakers Bureau–322, 342
  Your Voice Is Your Vote program–265
  Voters Guide–266, 311, 321, 342
  VOTE411.org–222, 265, 321
  Voter Hotline–55, 116, 248, 266
Voting Legislation–175, 322-323

W
Waite, Debby (see Howard)
Waite, Eleanor–169
Walters, Ellen–169, 359
Wamser, Jerry–43
Washington University–20, 282, 295
Webster Groves–x, 92, 295, 313, 339, 359
Webster University–152, 205
Wehling, Beth–223
Welfare–81
Wentzien, K–128, 135, 148, 171,

204, 206-208, 213, 225, 317, 339, 350, 354
West, Ida Perkins Johnson–42-44, 113, 169, 225, 249, 317, 350, 353
Westfall, George (County Executive)–240
White, Lexi–295
White, Ronnie (State Rep.)–201
Wiegers, Stephanie–347
Wilcox, Gillian–313
Williams, Deleta (State Rep.)–245
Wilkerson, Louise–299-301, 311, 317, 329, 339, 354
Wilson, Betty–90, 96, 169
Wilson, Joanne and Raleigh–249
Wilson, Mary G. (LWVUS President)–229, 250
Wilson, Vicky Riback (State Rep.)–246
Wimes, Brian (Judge)–271
Wolff, Carolyn–311
Women's Voices Raised for Social Justice–243, 270
Woods, Harriett (State Senator/Lt. Governor)–xi, 72, 74, 118, 132, 153-155, 205, 213

Y
Young, Esther–204

Z
Zoo-Museum District–iii, 107, 116, 144, 159

About the Author

Nicole Evelina has been a member of the League of Women Voters of Metro St. Louis since 2018. She volunteered for the Centennial Committee, helping plan events celebrating the St. Louis League's 100th anniversary in 2019 and the Centennial of the 19th Amendment in 2000. She is currently serving on a committee to help memorialize St. Louis suffragists, including Virginia Minor and Edna Gellhorn.

Nicole is also a *USA Today* bestselling author and biographer who writes historical fiction, non-fiction, and women's fiction. Her books have won more than 40 awards, including four Book of the Year designations. Nicole was named Missouri's Top Independent Author by Library Journal and Biblioboard as the winner of the Missouri Indie Author Project in 2018 and has been awarded the North Street Book Prize and the Sarton Women's Book Award. One of her novels, *Madame Presidentess*, was previously optioned for film.

Nicole's biography of St. Louis suffragist couple Virginia and Francis Minor, *America's Forgotten Suffragists*, will be published on March 1, 2023, by Globe Pequot. She is represented by Amy Collins of Talcott Notch Literary. You can find her online at http://nicoleevelina.com/.

League of Women Voters of Metro St. Louis
8706 Manchester Rd., Suite 104
St. Louis, MO 63144
314-961-6869
league@lwvstl.org

For complete endnotes, go to lwvstl.org

Printed in the USA
CPSIA information can be obtained
at www.ICGtesting.com
LVHW071119101023
760689LV00024B/352